Dr. B.R. Ambedkar's Ideas and Thoughts

About the Editors

Prof. Xavier P. Mao did his M.A. from North-Eastern Hill University (NEHU), M.Phil. from Delhi University, M.Litt. from Sydney, Australia, Ph.D. from NEHU. He started teaching at the post-graduate-level in North-Eastern Hill University since 1988. He was a part-time teacher at Sydney University, Australia during the year 1996-97. He has published more than 20 edited books. He has number of papers in half a dozen Journals of National and International repute. From time to time he contributed articles to the newspapers and used to give Radio talks. Currently, he is the President of North-East Central Universities Teachers' Association since 2013. At present he is serving as Professor and Head of Department of Philosophy, North-Eastern Hill University, which is a Central University and as per the National Assessment and Accreditation Council 2005, NEHU University is rated as 15th position among top 10 Universities in India. He is currently national member of the Indian Council of Philosophical Research (ICPR), New Delhi. The book entitled as "*Virtue and Morality*" published in 2011 is used as reference book in some universities and colleges.

Dr. Subhash C. Arya is currently Associate Professor, Electronics and Communication Engineering Department, School of Technology, NEHU, Shillong. Before joining NEHU, he was Assistant Professor from January 2007 to February 2010 at E & I Department, Indian School of Mine, Dhanbad. He worked as a Research Scholar on Modelling and Design of EDFA for WDM and DWDM Optical Fiber Communication System during 2004-2008 in E & I Department, ISM, Dhanbad. Dr. Arya has also worked in Aditya Institute of Technology, Delhi as a lecturer from September 2003 to March 2004. He received Ph.D. (Electronics Engg.), B.Tech. and Diploma in Electronics & Communication Engineering from ISM Dhanbad, G.G.S. Indraprastha University, Delhi and BTE Delhi, in the year 2009, 2003 and 2000, respectively. He has about 24 publications in International Journals, National Journals and International/National Conferences.

Dr. B.R. Ambedkar's Ideas and Thoughts

Editors
Xavier P. Mao
Subhash C. Arya

CONCEPT PUBLISHING COMPANY PVT. LTD.
NEW DELHI-110059

ISBN-13: 978-93-5125-281-8

First Published 2021

Published and Printed by

Concept Since 1974

Concept Publishing Company Pvt. Ltd.
A/15-16, Commercial Block, Mohan Garden
New Delhi-110059 (India)
T: +91-11-41101460
E: publishing@conceptpub.com, W: www.conceptpub.com

Cataloging in Publication Data--Courtesy: D.K. Agencies (P) Ltd. <docinfo@dkagencies.com>

National Seminar on "Dr. B.R. Ambedkar's Ideas and Thoughts" (2013 : Shillong, India)
Dr. B.R. Ambedkar's ideas and thoughts / editors, Xavier P. Mao, Subhash C. Arya.
pages cm
"A National Seminar on "Dr. B.R. Ambedkar's Ideas and Thoughts" was organized during (March 11 & 12, 2013) in the Permanent Campus of North-Eastern Hill University, Shillong"--Page 112.
Includes bibliographical references and index.
ISBN 9789351252818

1. Ambedkar, B. R. (Bhimrao Ramji), 1891-1956--Political and social views--Congresses. 2. Dalits--India--Congresses. 3. Human rights--India--Congresses. 4. Women's rights--India--Congresses. 5. Sex discrimination against women--India--Congresses. 6. India--Social conditions--20th century--Congresses. I. Mao, Xavier Pfokrehe, 1962- editor. II. Arya, Subhash C., editor. III. North Eastern Hill University, organizer. IV. Title.

LCC DS481.A43N38 2013 | DDC 305.51220954 23

Preface

At the outset we are extremely grateful to the Indian Council of Philosophical Research (ICPR), New Delhi-110062 for their valuable suggestion to organize national seminar on "Dr. Ambedkar's Thoughts and Ideas" along with the generous fund provided for the purpose. The various contributors to this book have dwelt on different aspects on Dr. Ambedkar's thoughts and convictions. Dr. Ambedkar was strongly of the view that Indian society would not advance very far as long as *Chaturvarna* and caste system exist. Annihilation of caste in India is imperative for the building of modern advanced Indian nation/state. The important ideals of equality, liberty and fraternity cannot be built on the foundation of fixed, rigid and graded inequality embedded in caste system. According to him, the caste system is exclusive and inward looking. That is how inter-dining and inter-marrying among the different castes are rigidly observed. The present-day phenomenon of honour killing is the direct result of emphasis on adhering strictly within the boundaries of the different castes. Anybody who transgresses the caste boundary is done to death in the name of the so-called "honour of the family and caste". It logically follows from this argument that encouragement and active promotion of inter-marriage and inter-dining can effectively annihilate caste system in India. To effectively establish inter-caste marriage and inter-caste dining the root cause for preventing such happening is because of the blind belief in the various *Shastras* of the Hindu religion, consequently he is of the strong view that the *Shastras* should be rejected out rightly. For nearly four thousand years the caste system has strong grip on the minds of the Indians because of the fear of questioning and rejecting the *Shastras* as if they are ordained and fixed by God. True to his conviction of the root cause of rigid caste system deriving from *Shastras*, he has abandoned the *Shastras*, thereby Hindu religion and embraced Buddhism as his new religion along with his about 8 lakh followers as the panacea for the perennial disease of caste-ridden Indian society. To prevent imitation of caste system in Hinduism, in Buddhist religion he has prescribed 22 vows to his followers as preemptive measures so that they can be true adherents of Buddhist principles of life based on open mind and logical reasoning. Part of his holistic vision of freedom and emancipation of all sections of the society including women, Dr. Ambedkar specifically promulgated Hindu Code Bill on 5th February, 1951, however, his proposal for equal rights for women could not be passed in the Parliament due to the various reactionary forces and conservative traditionalists and as a result he had resigned from Nehru's Cabinet from portfolio of the Law Ministry as Cabinet Minister. This clearly shows he was far ahead of his time. He had emerged as a doctor with his excellent diagnosis of the fatal diseases of the Hindu community, however, the Brahmins opposed tooth and nail to his emancipator medicine of liberation of the oppressed sections of the Hindus, i.e. women and Scheduled Caste. Further, Dr. Ambedkar wanted to reinvigorate and revitalize the democratic ideals into the polity and various institutions of the Indian society. He also played instrumental role in creating the Multi-Purpose River Valley Projects and Large Dam Technologies in India such as the Damodar Valley Project 1944 on the lines of Tennessee Valley Authority, Bhakra-Nangal Dam, the Sone River Valley projects and Hirakud Dam. Besides all these important ideas and projects as a true revolutionary, he has introduced many other innovative ideas and schemes which are welfare oriented in India based on enlightened liberal democratic ideas.

Xavier P. Mao
Subhash C. Arya

Acknowledgements

We would like to express our deep appreciation and gratitude to the Indian Council of Philosophical Research (ICPR), New Delhi, for the generous financial grant and the valuable suggestion provided us to organize national seminar on the life and thoughts of Dr. B.R. Ambedkar at NEHU, Shillong. We are also greatly indebted to the prestigious Concept Publishing Company (P) Ltd., New Delhi for its thorough and meticulous proof reading carried out by their expert academic committee. We do extend our thanks and appreciation to the North-Eastern Hill University, for providing supplementary financial assistant. We also thank to paper contributors for their timely completion of full papers and having complied with our request. We thank the research scholars of the Department of the Philosophy, NEHU, Shillong, for rendering their valuable services and time. We express our deep appreciation to the media for widely covering the two days national seminar in different media, both print and electronic. Lastly, but not the least we are indebted to the other individual who have in one way or the other contributed to the overall success of the seminar.

NEHU, Shillong-22
24th April, 2018

Xavier P. Mao
Subhash C. Arya

Contents

List of Contributors

Dr. Ashraful Islam Ahmed, Department of History and Culture, Jamia Millia Islamia, New Delhi.
E-mail: *ashraful940@gmail.com*

Dr. Binod Kumar Agarwala, North-Eastern Hill University, Shillong (Meghalaya).

Chintamani Rout, Department of Law, North-Eastern Hill University, Shillong (Meghalaya).

Dr. Dipanjali Das, Department of Philosophy, North-Eastern Hill University, Shillong (Meghalaya).
E-mail: *dipanjali2012@gmail.com*

Kakali Bezbaruah, North-Eastern Hill University, Shillong (Meghalaya).
E-mail: *kbezbaruah0@gmail.com*

Dr. Lamsing M.Umlong, Assistant Professor, Department of Philosophy, Sankardev College, Shillong (Meghalaya).

Md. Shah Noorur Rahman, Department of History, NEHU, Shillong (Meghalaya).

Nagesh Chaudhary, Bahujan Sangharsh (*Marathi Fortnightly*) Raahate Colony, Wardha Road, Nagpur (Maharashtra).
E-mail: *chaudhari.nagesh@yahoo.co.in*

Praveen Mishra, P.G. Department of Law, Tripura University, Agartala, Tripura.
E-mail: *praveen mishra.law@gmail.com*

Dr. Preeti Hazarika, Department of Commerce, Dibrugarh University, Dibrugarh (Assam).
E-mail: *prityhazarika1997@gmail.com*

Dr. Subhash C. Arya, Associate Professor, Electronics and Communication Engineering Department, School of Technology, NEHU, Shillong (Meghalaya).

Dr. Surender Dagar, Department of Education, Central University of Haryana (Haryana).

Prof. Xavier P. Mao, Professor and Head of Department, Department of Philosophy, NEHU, Shillong (Meghalaya).

Important Life Events of Dr. Babasaheb Ambedkar

1891	April 14	Born at Mhow in Madhya Pradesh as fourteenth child of Subedar Ramji Maloji Sakpal and Mrs. Bhimabai Ambedkar.
1896		Death of the mother, Mrs. Bhimabai Ambedkar.
1900	Nov.	Entered the Government High School at Satara.
1904		Entered the Elphinstone High School at Bombay.
1906		Married Ramabai, daughter of Mr. Bhiku Walangkar, one of the relations of Gopal Baba Walangkar.
1907		Passed Matriculation Examination, secured 382 marks out of 750.
1908	Jan.	Honoured in a meeting presisded over by Shri S.K. Bole, Shri K.A. (Dada) Keluskar Guruji presented a book on the life of Gautam Buddha written by him. Entered the Elphinstone College, Bombay.
1912	Dec.	Birth of the Son Yeshwant.
1913		Passed B.A. Examination with Persian and English from University of Bombay, secured 449 marks out of 1000.
1913	Feb.	Death of father Subedar Ramji Maloji Sakpal Ambedkar at Bombay.

1913	July	Gaikwar's Scholar in the Columbia University, New York, reading in the Faculty of Political Science.
1915	June 5	Passed M.A. Examination majoring in Economics and with Sociology, History, Philosophy, Anthropology and Politics as the other subjects of study.
1916	May	Read a paper on 'The Castes in India' before Prof. Goldernweiser's Anthropology Seminar. The paper was later published in *The Indian Antiquary* in May 1917. It was also republished in the form of a brochure, the first published work of Dr. Ambedkar. Wrote a Thesis entitled "The National Dividend of India—A History and Analytical Study" for the Ph.D. Degree.
1916	June	Left Columbia University after completing work for the Ph.D. to join the London School of Economics and Political Science, London as a Graduate student.
1917		Columbia University conferred a Degree of Ph.D.
1917	June	Return to India after spending a year in London working on the thesis for the M.Sc. (Econ.) Degree. The return before completion of the work was necessitated by the termination the scholarship granted by the Baroda State.
1917	July	Appointed as Military Secretary to H.H. the Maharaja Gaikwar of Baroda with a view as Finance Minister. But left shortly due to illness. Treatment meted out to him because of his lowly caste.
1918		Published "Small Holdings in India and Their Remedies".
		Gave evidence before the Southborough Commission on Franchise. Attended the

		Conference of the Depressed Classes held at Nagpur.
1918	Nov.	Professor of Political Economy in the Sydenham College of Commerce and Economics, Bombay.
1920	Jan. 31	Started a Marathi Weekly paper *Mooknayak* to champion the causes of the depressed classes. Shri Nandram Bhatkar was the editor, late Shri Dyander Gholap was the editor.
1920	Mar. 21	Attended depressed classes Conference held under the Presidency of Chhatrpati Sahu Maharaj at Kolhapur.
1920	Mar.	Resigned Professorship at Sydenham College to resume his studies in London.
1920	May	Memorable speech in Nagpur criticized Karmaveer Shinde and Depressed Classes Mission.
1920	Sept.	Rejoined the London School of Economics. Also entered Gray's Inn to read for the Bar.
1921	June	The thesis "Provincial Decentralization of Imperial Finance in British India" was accepted for M.Sc. (Econ.) Degree by the London University.
1922-23		Spent some time in reading Economics in the University of Bonn in Germany.
1923	Mar.	The Thesis "The Problem of the Rupee –Its origin and its solution" was accepted for the degree of D.Sc. (Econ.). The thesis was published in December 1923 by P.S. King and Company, London. Reissued by Thacker and Company, Bombay in May 1947 under the title "History of Indian Currency and Banking," Vol. 1.
1923		Called to the Bar.
1923	Apr.	Returned to India.
1924	June	Started practice in the Bombay High Court.

1924	July 20	Founded the "Bahishkrit Hitkarini Sabha" for the uplift of the depressed classes. The aims of the Sabha were—educate, agitate, and organize.
1925		Published "The Evolution of Provincial Finance in British India"—dissertation on the provincial decentralization of "Imperial Finance in India".
1926		Opened a hostel for Untouchable students at Barshi.
		Gave evidence before the Royal Commission on Indian Currency (Hilton Young Commission). Nominated Member of the Bombay Legislative Council.
1927	Mar. 20	Started *Satyagraha* at Mahad (Dist. Kolaba) to secure to the untouchables the Right of Access to the Chavdar Tank.
1927	Apr. 3	Started a fortnightly Marathi paper *Bahishkrit Bharat.* Dr. Ambedkar himself was the editor.
1927	Sept.	Established "Samaj Samata Sangh".
1927	Dec.	Second Conference in Mahad.
1928	Mar.	Introduced the "Vatan Bill" in the Bombay Legislative Council.
1928	May	Gave evidence before the Indian Statutory Committee (Simon Commission).
1928	June	Professor, Government Law College, Bombay. Principal, Government Law College, Bombay.
1928-29		Member Bombay Presidency Committee of the Simon Committee.
1930	Mar.	*Satyagraha* at Kalaram Temple, Nasik to secure for the Untouchables the right of entry into the temple.
1930-32		Delegate, Round Table Conference representing Untouchables of India.
1932	Sept.	Signed with Mr. M.K. Gandhi the Poona Pact giving up to save Gandhi's life

		electorate granted to the Depressed Classes by Ramsay MacDonald's Communal Award and accepting, instead representation through joint electorates.
1932-34		Member, Joint Parliamentary Committee on the Indian Constitutional Reform.
1934		Left Parel, Damodar Hall and came to stay in 'Rajagriha' Dadar (Bombay). This was done in order to get more accommodation for his library which was increasing day by day.
1935	May 26	Death of wife Mrs. Ramabai Ambedkar.
1935	June	Dr. Ambedkar was appointed as Principal of Government Law College, Bombay. He was also appointed Perry Professor of Jurisprudence.
	Oct. 13	Historical Yeola Conversion Conference held under the Presidentship of Dr. Ambedkar at Yeola District, Nasik. He exhorted the Depressed Classes to leave Hinduism and embrace another religion. He declared: "I was born as a Hindu, but I will not die as a Hindu". He also advised his followers to abandon the Kalaram Mandir entry *Satyagraha*, Nasik.
	Dec.	Dr. Ambedkar was invited by the Jat Pat Todak Mandal of Lahore to preside over the Conference. Dr. Ambedkar prepared his historical speech "The Annihilation of Caste". The Conference was cancelled by the Mandal on the ground that Dr. Ambedkar's thoughts were revolutionary. Finally, Dr. Ambedkar refused to preside and published his speech in book form in 1937.
1936	Jan. 12-13	The Depressed Classes Conference was held at Pune, Dr. Ambedkar reiterated his resolve of the Yeola Conference to leave

		Hinduism. The Conference was presided over by Rav Bahadur N. Shina Raj.
	Feb. 29	Dr. Ambedkar's Conversion Revolution was supported by the *Chamars* (Cobblers) of East Khandesh.
	May 30	Bombay Presidency Conversion Conference (Mumbai Elaka Mahar Parishad) of Mahar was held at Naigum (Dadar) to sound their opinion on the issue of Conversion. Mr. Subha Rao, popularly known as Hydrabadi Ambedkar, presided over the Converence. In the morning Ascentics shaved their beards, moustaches and destroyed their symbols of Hinduism in an Ascetic's Conference.
	June 15	Conference of Devadasis was held in Bombay to support Dr. Ambedkar's Resolution of Conversion.
	June 18	Dr. Ambedkar-Dr. Moonje talks on Conversion. Pro-Sikkhism.
	June 23	Matang Parishad in support of Conversion.
	Aug.	Dr. Ambedkar founded the Independent Labour Party, a strong opposition party in Bombay's Legislative Council.
	Sept. 18	Dr. Ambedkar sent a delegation of 13 members to the Golden Temple, Amritsar to study Sikkhism.
	Nov. 11	Dr. Ambedkar left for Geneva and London.
1937		Dr. Ambedkar organized the "Municipal Workers' Union", Bombay in 1937.
	Jan. 14	Dr. Ambedkar returned to Bombay.
	Feb. 17	The First General Elections were held under the Government of India Act of 1935. Dr. Ambedkar was elected Member of Bombay Legislative Assembly (Total Seats 175. Reserved Seats 15. Dr. Ambedkar's Independent Labour Party won 17 seats).

	Mar. 17	The Mahad Chowdar Tank case was decided in favour of D.C. by which they got a legal right to use the public wells and tanks.
	July 31	Dr. Ambedkar received a grand reception at Chalisgaon Railway Station.
	Sept. 17	Dr. Ambedkar introduced his Bill to abolish the Mahar Watan in the Assembly.
	Dec. 31	Reception at Pandharpur on the way to Sholapur, where he was going to preside over the Sholapur District D.C. Conference.
1938	Jan. 4	Reception given by the Sholapur Municipal Council.
1938	Jan.	The Congress Party introduced a Bill making a change in the name of Untouchables, i.e. they would be called *Harijans* meaning sons of God. Dr. Ambedkar criticized the Bill, as in his opinion the change of name would make no real change in their conditions. Dr. Ambedkar and Bhaurav Gaikwar protested against the use of the term *Harijans* in legal matters. When the ruling party by sheer force of numbers defeated the I.L.P., the Labour party group walked out of the Assembly in protest under the leadership of Dr. Ambedkar. He organized peasant's march to Bombay Assembly. The peasants demanded the passing of Dr. Ambedkar's Bill for abolition of the *Khoti* system.
1938	Jan. 23	Dr. Ambedkar addressed a Peasants's Conference at Ahmedabad.
1938	Feb. 12-13	Dr. Ambedkar addressed historical Conference of Railway workers at Manmad (District Nasik).
1938	Apr.	Dr. Ambedkar opposed creation of a separate Karnataka State in the national interest.

1938	May	Dr. Ambedkar resigned from the Principalship of the Government Law College, Bombay.
1938	May 13-21	Dr. Ambedkar went on tour to Konkan Region. He also went to Nagpur in connection with a court case.
1938	Aug.	A meeting was held at R.M. Bhat High School, Bombay, for exposing Gandhiji's attitude in disallowing a D.C. man being taken into the Central Ministry.
1938	Sept.	Dr. Ambedkar spoke on the Industrial Disputes Bill in the Bombay Assembly. He bitterly opposed it for its attempt to outlaw the right of workers to strike. He said: If Congressmen believe that *Swaraj* is their birthright, then the right to strike is the birth-right of workers.
1938	Oct. 1	Dr. Ambedkar addressed a large gathering at Bawala, near Ahmedabad. On return he addressed another meeting at Premabhai Hall, Ahmedabad.
1938	Nov. 6	The Industrial Workers strike. The procession (under the leadership of Dr. Ambedkar, Nirankar, Dang, Pasulkar etc.) was organised from Kamgar Maidan to Jambori Maidan, Worli.
1938	Nov. 10	Dr. Ambedkar moved a Resolution for adoption of the methods for birth-control in the Bombay Assembly.
1938	Dec.	Dr. Ambedkar addressed the first D.C. Coference in Nizam's dominion at Mahad.
1939	Jan. 18	Dr. Ambedkar addressed a large gathering at Rajkot.
	Jan. 19	Ambedkar-Gandhi talks.
	Jan. 29	Kale Memorial Lecture of Gorkhale School of Politics and Economics, Poona reviewing critically the All India Federation Scheme set out in the

		Government of India Act of 1935. The speech was issued in March 1939 as a tract for the times under the title "Federation *vs.* Freedom".
	July	Dr. Ambedkar addressed a meeting organised for Rohidas Vidya Committee.
	Oct.	Dr. Ambedkar-Nehru first meeting.
	Dec.	The Conference at Haregaon was held under the Presidentship of Dr. Ambedkar to voice the grievances of Mahar and Mahar Watandars.
1940	May	Dr. Ambedkar founded the "Mahar Panchayat".
1940	July 22	Netaji Subhas Chandra Bose met Dr. Ambedkar in Bombay.
1940	Dec.	Dr. Ambedkar published his *Thoughts on Pakistan.* The second edition with the title *Pakistan or Partition of India* was issued in February 1945. A third impression of the book was published in 1946 under the title *India's Political What's What: Pakistan or Partition of India.*
1941	Jan.	Dr. Ambedkar pursued the issue of recruitment of Mahars in the Army. In result the Mahars Battalion was formed.
1941	May 25	Mahar Dynast Panchayat Samiti was formed by Dr. Ambedkar.
1941	July	Dr. Ambedkar was appointed to sit on the Defence Advisory Committee.
1941	Aug.	The Conference was held at Sinnar in protest of tax on Mahar Watans. Dr. Ambedkar launched a no-tax campaign. He saw the Governor. Finally, the tax was abolished. The Mumbai Elaka Conference of Mahars, Mangs and Devdasis were organised under the Chairmanship of Dr. Ambedkar.

1942	Apr.	Dr. Ambedkar founded the All-India Scheduled Castes Federation in Nagpur.
1942	July 18	Dr. Ambedkar addressed All-India D.C. Conference at Nagpur.
1942	July 20	Dr. Ambedkar joined the Viceroy's Executive Council as a Labour Member.
1942	Dec.	Dr. Ambedkar submitted a paper on "The Problems of the Untouchables in India" to the Institute of Pacific Relations at its Conference held in Canada. The paper is presented in the proceedings of the Conference. The paper was subsequently published in December 1943 in the book form under the title *Mr. Gandhi and Emancipation of the Untouchables.*
1943	Jan. 19	Dr. Ambedkar delivered a Presidential address on the occasion of the 101st Birth Anniversary of Justice Mahadev Govind Ranade. It is published in book form in April 1943 under the title *Ranade, Gandhi and Jinnah.*
1944		Dr. Ambedkar founded "The Building Trust and the Scheduled Caste Improvement Trust".
1944	May 6	Dr. Ambedkar addressed the Annual Conference of the All-India S.C. Federation at Parel (Bombay). The speech was later published under the title "The Communal Deadlock and a way to solve it."
1944	June	Dr. Ambedkar published his book *What Congress and Gandhi have done to the Untouchables*––a complete compendium of information regarding the movement of the Untouchables for political safeguards. Dr. Ambedkar attended the Simla Conference.

1944	July	Dr. Ambedkar founded "People's Education Society" in Bombay.
1946		Dr. Ambedkar gave evidence before the British delegation.
1946	Apr.	Opening of Siddharth College of Arts and Science in Bombay.
1946	May	The Bharat Bhushan Printing Press (founded by Dr. Ambedkar) was burnt down in the clashes between D.C. and the Caste Hindus.
1946	June 20	Siddharth College started.
	Sept.	Dr. Ambedkar went to London to urge before the British Government and the Opposition Party the need to provide safeguards for the D.C., on grant of Independence to India and thus to rectify the wrongs done to the D.C. by the Cabinet Mission.
	Oct. 13	Dr. Ambedkar published his book *Who were Shudras?* An enquiry into how the *Shudras* came to be the fourth *Varna* in the Indo-Aryan Society.
		Dr. Ambedkar was elected Member of the Constitution Assembly of India.
	Nov.	Dr. Ambedkar's First speech in the Constituent Assembly. He called for a "Strong and United India".
1947	Mar.	Published "States and Minorities". A memorandum of Fundamental Rights, Minority Rights, safeguards for the D.C. and on the problems of Indian states.
1947	Apr. 29	Sardar Vallabhbhai Patel in the Constituent Assembly moved Article 17 of the Constitution of India for the abolition of Untouchability and it was passed.
1947	Aug. 15	India obtained her Independence. The Bombay Legislature Congress Party elected Dr. Ambedkar to the Constituent

		Assembly. Dr. Ambedkar joined Nehru's Cabinet. He became the First Law Minister of Independent India. The Constituent Assembly appointed him to the Drafting Committee, which elected him as a Chairman on 29th August, 1947.
1948	Feb.	Dr. Ambedkar completed the Draft Constitution of Indian Republic.
1948	Apr. 15	Second marriage—Dr. Ambedkar married Dr. Sharda Kabir in Delhi.
1948	Oct.	Published his book *The Untouchables.* A thesis on the origin of Untouchability. Dr. Ambedkar submitted his Memorandum, "Maharashtra as a Linguistic Province" to the Dhar Commission. The Linguistic Provinces Commission.
1948	Oct. 4	Dr. Ambedkar presented the Draft Constitution to Constituent Assembly.
1948	Nov. 20	The Constituent Assembly adopted Article 17 of the Constitution for the abolition of Untouchability.
1949	Jan.	Dr. Ambedkar Law Minister of India visited Hyderabad (Deccan).
1949	Jan. 15	His admirers presented Dr. Ambedkar with a Purse at Manmad. He addressed a large gathering.
1949	Jan. 21	He stayed at Aurangabad in connection with his opening proposed College. During the stay he visited Ajanta-Ellora Caves.
1949	Mar./May	Dr. Ambedkar visited Bombay in connection with College work and for a medical check-up.
1949	Sept.	Meeting between Dr. Ambedkar and Madhavrao Golwalkar, Chief of RRS at the residence of Dr. Ambedkar at Delhi.
1949	Nov.	Dr. Ambedkar came to Bombay for college work meeting and medical check-up.

1949	Nov.	Dr. Ambedkar addressed the Constituent Assembly.
1949	Nov. 26	Constituent Assembly adopted the Constitution. Dr. Ambedkar came to Bombay for check-up.
1950	Jan. 11	Dr. Ambedkar addressed the Siddharth College Parliament on the Hindu Code Bill. In the evening he was presented with silver casket containing a copy of the Indian Constitution at Nare Park Maidan, Bombay.
	May	Dr. Ambedkar's article "The Buddha and the Future of His Religion" was published in the journal of Mahabodhi Society, Calcutta. Dr. Ambedkar addressed the Young Men's Buddhist Association on "The Rise and Fall of Hindu Women". Dr. Ambedkar spoke on the "Merits of Buddhism" at the meeting arranged on the occasion of Buddha Jayanti in Delhi.
1950	Sept. 1	Dr. Rajendra Prasad, the First President of the Indian Republic laid the foundation stone of Milind Mahavidyalaya, Aurangabad. Dr. Ambedkar delivered a speech on the occasion (The printed speech is available with Mr. Surwade).
1950	Dec.	Dr. Ambedkar went to Colombo as a Delegate to the World Buddhist Conference.
1951	Feb. 5	Dr. Ambedkar, Law Minister introduced his "Hindu Code Bill" in the Parliament.
1951	Apr. 15	Dr. Ambedkar laid the foundation stone of "Dr. Ambedkar Bhavan" at Delhi.
1951	July	Dr. Ambedkar founded "The Bhartiya Buddha Jansangh".
1951	Sept.	Dr. Ambedkar compiled a Buddhist prayer book *Buddha Upasana Patha.*

1951	Sept. 9	Dr. Ambedkar resigned from the Nehru Cabinet because, among other reasons, the withdrawal of Cabinet support to the Hindu Code Bill in spite of the earlier declaration in the Parliament by the Prime Minister Pt. Jawaharlal Nehru, that his Government would stand or fall with the Hindu Code Bill. Dr. Ambedkar published his speech in book form under the title *The Rise and Fall of Hindu Women.*
1951	Sept. 19	The Marriage and Divorce Bill was discussed in the Parliament.
1951	Oct. 11	Dr. Ambedkar left the Cabinet.
1952	Jan.	Dr. Ambedkar was defeated in the First Lok Sabha elections held under the Constitution of Indian Republic. Congress candidate N.S. Kajrolkar defeated Dr. Ambedkar.
1952	Mar.	Dr. Ambedkar was introduced into Parliament as a Member of the Council (Rajya Sabha) of States, representing Bombay.
1952	June 1	Dr. Ambedkar left for New York from Bombay.
1952	June 15	Columbia University (USA) conferred the Honorary Degree of LL.D., in its Bi-Centennial Celebrations Special Convocation held in New York.
1952	June 16	Dr. Ambedkar returned to Bombay.
1952	Dec. 16	Dr. Ambedkar addressed Annual Social Gathering of Elphinstone College, Bombay.
1952	Dec. 22	Dr. Ambedkar delivered a talk on "Conditions Precedent to the Successful Working of Democracy" at the Bar Council, Pune.

1953	Jan. 12	The Osmania University conferred the honorary Degree of LL.D. on Dr. Ambedkar.
1953	Mar.	The Untouchability (Offences) Bill was introduced in the Parliament by the Nehru Government.
1953	Apr.	Dr. Ambedkar contested the By-election for Lok Sabha from Bhandara Constituency of Vidarbha Region, but was defeated by Congress Candidate Mr. Borkar.
1953	May	Opening of Siddharth College of Commerce and Economics in Bombay.
1953	Dec.	Dr. Ambedkar inaugurated the All-India Conference of Sai devotees at the St. X'avier's Maidan, Parel, Bombay (His inaugural speech is available with Mr. Surwade.
1954	May	Dr. Ambedkar visited Rangoon to attend the function arranged on the occasion of Buddha Jayanti.
1954	June	The Maharaja of Mysore donated 5 acres of land for Dr. Ambedkar's proposed Buddhist Seminary to be started at Bangalore.
1954	Sept. 16	Dr. Ambedkar spoke on the Untouchability (Offences) Bill in the Rajya Sabha.
1954	Oct. 3	Dr. Ambedkar broadcasts his talk "My Personal Philosophy".
1954	Oct. 29	Shri R.D. Bhandare, President of Bombay Pradesh S.C. Federation presented a purse of Rs. 1,18,000 on behalf of S.C.F. to Dr. Ambedkar at Purandare Stadium, Naigaum (Bombay).
1954	Dec.	Dr. Ambedkar participated as delegate to the 3rd World Buddhist Conference at Rangoon.

1955	April 3	Delivered a speech "Why Religion is Necessary".
1955	May	Dr. Ambedkar established Bharatiya Bauddha Mahasabha (The Buddhist Society of India).
1955	Aug.	Founded Mumbai Rajya Kanishtha Garkamgari Association.
1955	Dec.	Published his opinions on linguistic states in book form under the title *Thoughts on Linguistic States*.
1955	Dec.	Dr. Ambedkar Installed an image of Buddha at Dehu Road (near Pune).
1955	Dec. 27	Dr. Ambedkar spoke against reservation of seats in the Central and State Legislatures.
1956	Feb.	Dr. Ambedkar completed his *The Buddha and His Dhamma, Revolution and Counter-revolution in Ancient India.*
1956	Mar. 15	Dr. Ambedkar wrote and dictated the Preface of *The Buddha and His Dhamma*.
1956	May 1	Dr. Ambedkar spoke on Linguistic States in the Council of States. Dr. Ambedkar spoke on BBC London on "Why I like Buddhism". Also, he spoke for Voice of America on "The Future of Indian Democracy".
1956	May 24	Dr. Ambedkar attended a meeting at Nare Park organised on the eve of Buddha Jayanti, Shri B.G. Kher, Chief Minister of Bombay was Chief Guest. This meeting was the last meeting of Dr. Ambedkar in Bombay.
1956	June	Opening of Siddharth College of Law in Bombay.
1956	Oct. 14	Dr. Ambedkar embraced Buddhism at an historic ceremony at Diksha Bhoomi, Nagpur with his millions of followers. Announced to desolve S.C.F. and establish Republican Party.

1956	Nov. 20	Delegate, 4th World Buddhist Conference, Khalinandu, where he delivered his famous speech "Buddha of Karl Marx".
1956	Dec. 6	*Maha Nirvana* at his residence, 26 Alipore Road, New Delhi.
1956	Dec. 7	Cremation at Dadar Chawpatti—Now, known as Chaitya Bhoomi, Dadar (Bombay).

1
Editors Note

Xavier P. Mao
Subhash C. Arya

Perhaps it may not be an exaggeration to say that Dr. B.R. Ambedkar was one of the great men of modern time in India. He shaped the destiny of the scheduled castes and tribes of India. B.R. Ambedkar was soaked in the liberal political and social ideas on the contemporary period. He being a *Dalit* suffered so much the brunt of rotten caste system. A highly educated man who studied in some of the best universities in the West was put to humiliation by many. Even his own peon would not give him a glass of water to drink on the ground that he was an untouchable. Rightly B.R. Ambedkar has been regarded as one of the important architects of the Constitution of India.

It is true that M.K. Gandhi, the father of the Indian nation vehemently spoke against the practices of Untouchability in India. Gandhi could not see the drafting of the Constitution of India and the practice of untouchability as a cognizable offence. It was only through the intense effort of Ambedkar that the practice of untouchability in any form was treated as a cognizable offence. Seen in this light, Ambedkar can be regarded as one of the greatest men of contemporary India. Whatever may be the basis or origin of caste system in due course of time caste system was regarded as a very powerful weapon of discrimination and exploitation. The Hindu scriptures particularly *Bhagavad Gita* treats caste system as a kind of division of labour. According to the author of *Bhagavad Gita*, it is the competence or capacity of a person that should constitute the fountainhead of caste system. *Guna* (competence) and *karma* (action) constitute the twin pillars of caste system. But, it may be pointed out in this connection that the author of *Bhagavad Gita* fails to distinguish fact and value relating to caste system. It is necessary that ordering of society should be based on competence and capacity of an individual. But historically speaking, the basis of ideal ordering degenerated into an ordering of society based on birth. Somebody is Brahmin only if he is born of Brahmin parents. This shift from competence to birth not only degenerated caste system based on division of labour to hierarchical ordering of society based on birth. It is necessary to mention in this connection that nowhere in the world operates in such very rigid system except in India. It is very interesting to note that Ambedkar was not in favour of reservations of jobs for SC and ST for indefinite period of time. As a matter of fact he suggested that such a reservation should be there for an initial fixed period of 10 years only. Accordingly 10 years limit was inscribed in the Constitution for such type of reservation. But now things are different. After Constitutional Amendment for jobs and employment for SC and ST the reservation policy is for all practical purposes extended for indefinite period of time. The benefits of reservations given to SC and ST have inspired other caste groups to demand for the same. The Mandal Commission report and its aftermath are glaring testimony to the above point. Even in Tamil Nadu Brahmins are demanding some kind of reservation for them because they are in minority. This situation brings into focus that the policy of reservation is not an effective method of fighting age old social injustice. The confusion gets worst confounded when demand is made to create clear cut reservation quota even in multi-speciality hospital. To demand reservation in certain kinds of jobs and in certain institutions is intelligible, but to demand reservation in multi-speciality hospitals is absolutely unintelligible and meaningless. Reservation policy has exhibited the inner contradiction and absurdity. The contradiction is bound to be inherent in the reservation policy itself if it is beyond certain limits. Had B.R. Ambedkar been alive today he would have looked against at the policy of reservation followed at present in India. By this we do not mean to argue that reservation is an absurd idea instead we would suggest that equal opportunity should be extended to all irrespective of caste, sex, creed and religion. An effective and meaningful way to fight out and eliminate the age old tyranny of exploitation and oppression in the name of caste, creed, sex, religion etc. legislation should be made in Parliament. The policy of reservation may be a stop gap measure, but it cannot be treated as a permanent panacea for centuries old exploitation, oppression and discrimination. It is a fact that even after scientific and technological revolution oppression, exploitation and discrimination continue to be there throughout the world in some form or the other. In Indian context after Independence, wealth has increased multifold to use or borrow a jargon from economics. GDP (Gross Domestic Product) is on the increase. But, it is surprising that poverty and misery are on the increase. Some people wallow in a castle of luxury of wealth and property while a large number of populace get impoverished day by day. There is no need to collect any data or statistics to prove this point; one has to simply go to a crowded railway station in cities and towns to see through this point. Slums grow day by day and children of this slum keep on moving and loafing in the streets is a clear-cut signal to our failure to eradicate poverty, illiteracy and misery from Indian society. What is wrong? Where does the shoe pinch? The answer to these questions we wish to give the naked truth that in India some privileged sections of the society have created socio-economic order where money and wealth get accumulated in the hands of few. And this major excessive money is used at the time of election and these people are in turn protected for all their ill gotten money by the elected politicians. This is how the vicious circle continues. Unless and until we check and change the process of wealth getting accumulated in the hands of few, we cannot eliminate poverty and misery. Perhaps the idea of partyless democracy suggested by late Jaya Prakash Narain in late sixties is partly the solution. Further, austere life in the higher echelons of society is bound to percolate to the masses. Instead our day-to-day life clearly shows that privileges, benefits and other perks are added to the pay package of persons belonging to the higher status of the Government. Unless and until this practice comes to a stop, poverty and misery from the Indian soil cannot be eliminated. It is a fact that caste in due course of time has done some damage in different forms to the Indian psyche. Perhaps because of this reason caste was not taken into account at a particular stage in census enumeration. Surprisingly, Government of India has taken a decision to reintroduce caste in the last census operation. It may be suggested that in this connection that while taking important decision for a large number of people for long-term measures utmost care must be taken. The reason being in the social ordering of human society, there is no one absolute and eternal method. Laws and rules are necessary for managing and running a state, but what is most necessary and primary is the change in psychic condition of humankind. It may not be out of place and exaggeration to say that Constitution of India is one of the best constitutions in the world. Further, the legal provisions in this country are superb, but at the same time it is true that Indians are most degenerate. Rape, theft, murder and embezzlement of public fund are day-to-day affairs in India. Crimes of all types are on the increase day by day. Historically speaking, any great people including saints and prophets are born in India. But, when we look at concrete facts of life, one gets tremendous shock. Perhaps, it appears more than true that our religion and culture have no impact on our life. In fact, the gap between text and context is yawning very wide. What should be done to save the situation? It is necessary to make comprehensive and effective laws. But what is most necessary is to bring about changes in psychic spheres. It is one thing to frame laws and rules and another thing to implement it or put it into practice. We have succeeded in framing good and effective laws, but miserably fail in putting it into practice. This is the lacuna in the Indian state as it has been suggested earlier. All out efforts should be made to save the situation, more so people at the helm of affairs should take a vow to lead an austere and moral life. Discrimination primarily is a psychic origin, so discrimination, exploitation and oppression can be eliminated only through a thorough psychic change revolution. B.R. Ambedkar was aware of it, he took bold initiative in this direction. Perhaps, he was aware of what is going to happen in India in succeeding years. Abolition of discrimination, exploitation and oppression resulting in caste system is the begin-all and not the end-all. Today in India to prevent rape cases there is suggestion that there is nothing short of hanging and death sentence that be awarded to rapist. But no step has been taken to change the existing social and economic order and other conditions that in a way inspire and induce not to commit rape. To conclude, human and social problems are very complex and complicated and this type of problem requires comprehensive method and technique. To do this, we should offer right type of ovation or respect to our founding fathers of our Constitution particularly the chief architect Dr. B.R. Ambedkar.

2

Dr. B.R. Ambedkar's Ideas and Thoughts

Brief Proceedings

Xavier P. Mao
Subhash C. Arya

The first ever national seminar in NEHU, Shillong on 'Dr. B.R. Ambedkar's Ideas and Thoughts' was organized by Department of Philosophy, School of Humanities, North-Eastern Hill University, Shillong on March 11-12, 2013 under the directorship of Dr. X.P. Mao, Associate Professor in Department of Philosophy. The main theme of seminar was "Caste Discrimination in Higher Education System in India", in view of about 20 suicide cases of SC/ST meritorious students in important institutes of national repute like IITs, IISc Bangalore, AIIMS etc. Papers were received from different parts of India and were divided among different categories according to theme and sub-themes of the seminar.

As per programme schedule, inaugural session of one hour duration started by 10.30 AM under the able chairmanship of Prof. B.K. Agarwala, the Head of the Philosophy Department. On the call of chairman, Dr. X.P. Mao gave welcome address to the congregation during the opening ceremony. In his welcome address Dr. X.P. Mao stated that Dr. B.R. Ambedkar along with M.K. Gandhi and Subhas Chandra Bose was one of the chief architects of modern India. Further, he said that Article 311 and reservation policy or positive discrimination for the Scheduled

Castes and the Scheduled Tribes enshrined in the Constitution were significant contribution of Dr. B.R. Ambedkar for the protection of employees from the arbitrary will of the employer which was known as pleasure principle during the British Rule and special positive measures for the oppressed and the isolated tribes to bring them on par with the other advanced sections of the society. Prof. B. Myrboh (Pro-VC, NEHU) was the Chief Guest. The Chief Guest said that being Professor of Chemistry, he could not study much about Dr. Ambedkar's contribution to the nation and society. However, being ST he is very much aware of the reservation policy and other benefits about whom Dr. Ambedkar fought in his entire life for the betterment of depressed class people such as SC and ST in India. He further elaborated that when Ms. Mayawati became Chief Minister of Uttar Pradesh, Dr. Ambedkar's name started figuring more frequently in the media and Dr. Ambedkar becomes issue of debate, study and research and more importantly potent guide and inspirational source for *Dalits* and Tribes in India. In fact, in recent time a survey was done by TV channel IBN was Live there in a debate on "Ambedkar's legacy lasts more than Gandhi's?" to emphasize the contribution of Dr. Ambedkar in reforming a caste-ridden Indian society. The Guest of Honour, Prof. Sujata Miri in her address reiterated the yeomen contribution made by Dr. Ambedkar in the writing of the Constitution of India. She argued that the need for representation of the marginalized people and tribes in every walk of life opens up the possibility of reinterpretation of the whole of Indian tradition. She strongly argued that division in the name of mainstream and margin is not conducive for reception of ideas of Ambedkar.

The Key Note address was delivered by Mr. Anoop Kumar, Director, Insight Foundation, New Delhi, who presented his keynote address on the Caste Discrimination in the Higher Education System in India. Firstly, he showed a documentary prepared by him as a part of his activity and research, titled, "Death of Merit" of about 20 minutes.There he interviewed one of the victims of caste discriminated family. This documentary (in two parts) was based on the testimonies of parents and other relatives of Balmukund Bharti, a final year MBBS student at All

India Institute of Medical Sciences (AIIMS), New Delhi, who committed suicide on 3rd March, 2010. Here, the documentary movie describes how Balmukund, a very bright *Dalit* student, was forced to commit suicide due to the casteist prejudices of the faculty members of country's premier educational institution.This documentary is not just about Balmukund, but is an effort to sensitize concerned people about what happens with *Dalit* students, the kind of harassment they have to suffer, in such elite educational institutions because of their caste backgrounds. Through this self-prepared documentary movie, Mr. Anoop tried to show the live evidences of caste discrimination in Higher Education system even today. According to Mr. Anoop, in eyes of law, every citizen is equal, however, at the ground level, Manu's law of inequality still exists in contemporary India. The people of India is united by the Constitution of India, but we cannot find the unity literally in true sense as the caste system still prevails in India and specially in our education system. India is still today far behind Ambedkar's vision of casteless society. Questioning the notion of merit, often bandied about in bastions of higher education, Anoop Kumar pointed to the sheer inability of varsities to handle student diversity.

Mentioning the large number of student suicide cases in IIT, Kanpur, he coined the serious question "How can an institution not be able to deal with a situation where a student is failing in all the subjects? That means there is a crisis. A student is failing, not attending class and nobody is bothered. There have been around nine suicides at IIT Kanpur in the past four years—seven SC/ST and two General students. The administration's response has been that the student was not able to deal with the rigour of academics. In a tragedy too, institutions talk of 'merit'. This is a perverted claim of merit." The system, he felt, was "brutal" not just to *Dalit* students alone, but to all students. There was, therefore, a need to challenge the idea of merit itself. "The claim of merit depends on the difference of some six percentage points. Places like the IITs are where the upper castes derive their claims of merit."

After hearing Mr. Anoop, audiences were very much shocked and amazed. Many questions, doubts, clarifications were asked to Mr. Anoop. He effectively gave answers with concrete instances and statistics. There were very heated debate and discussion as well as criticism against his presentation. It shows that his presentation was highly effective and provocative. At the end, he was presented a memento by the organizing committee as a token of gratitude.

First Session: The First Session Started at 1:00 P.M.

The session was chaired by Prof. Sujata Miri for the theme of "Caste, Religion and Gender Discrimination and Caste Annihilation in India". In that session, total eight papers were received out of that three authors were physically available to present their papers. Mr. Ashraful Islam Ahmed from Jamia Millia Islamia, New Delhi, Mrs. Vijaya Maitraiya from Nagpur University, Nagpur and Mr. Surender Dagar from Central Univeristy, Haryana. Firstly, Prof. Sujata Miri introduced all authors to audiences and then explained about the theme of the session. On the call of Chair, Mr. Ashraful has presented his paper on, "Dr. B.R. Ambedkar and His Perception of Gender Equality: Some Explorations and Conjectures." In his paper, Mr. Ashraful highlighted the operation of gender inequality both at the systemic level and at the functioning of patriarchy has made Ambedkar's views on women's oppression and Hindu social order significant to modern Indian feminist thinking. He further emphasized that Indian women's movement; Ambedkar provides the powerful source of inspiration to formulate a feminist political agenda which simultaneously addresses the issues of caste, class and gender.

Mr. Surendar Dagar in his paper entitled, "Dr. Ambedkar: Women Liberation and Empowerment", emphasizes Dr. Ambedkar's contribution to the Constitution of India like Hindu Code Bill, protection of women's right in the form of fundamental rights and directive principles of state policy and fundamental duties. His approach of social reform was at two levels—on the one hand Hindu family and the other level at Hindu society. The Hindu family level problems were like child marriage, widow marriage prohibition, *Sati* etc. and at the Hindu society level, the abolition of untouchability, caste system and change of law on adoption, marriage and succession. The Hindu Code Bill is an excellent example of Dr. Ambedkar's commitment for the cause of women because this Bill enabled women on par with men in matters of property, adoption and marriages. He also highlighted Ambedkar's contribution towards the equal status of women with men by empowering women with economic independence.

After the three papers were presented the Chairperson Prof. Sujata Miri opened the session for discussion, questions, comments and suggestions. This session has generated very interesting and heated debate and discussion. After threadbare discussion on the questions and criticism, the session was closed for lunch break at 1.30 to 2:30 P.M.

Second Session: The Second Session was Started from 2:30 P.M.

The Theme: "Life, Mission and Philosophy of Dr. Ambedkar". Second Session started at 2:30 P.M. in the Chairmanship of Prof. Raghunath Ghosh from North Bengal University, West Bengal. In his key note address entitled, "Ambedkar on Neo-Buddhism", Prof. Raghunath Ghosh pointed out that Ambedkar's views differ from classical Buddhism and Navayana Buddhism is cogent, practical and sociologically important.

Then the first paper for the second session was presented by Ms. Dipanjali Das (Research Scholar from NEHU). Her paper was on Dr. Ambedkar's Contribution for the Untouchables' Right and the Concept of Justice, Equality, Right, Liberty etc. She also highlighted the struggle of Dr. Ambedkar for the lower caste people and to give them equality among the other Indians. How Dr. Ambekar fought for the development, right and liberty during his time is pointed out.

Day Two, March 12, 2013

The introductory speech was given by Dr. Xavier P. Mao.

First Session of day two: started at 10.30 A.M.

The theme was Human Rights and Constitutional Reforms with special reference to Dr. Ambedkar.

The key note address was given by Prof. Jagat Pal on "Social Thoughts of Baba Saheb B.R. Ambedkar".

Prof. Jagat Pal has brought out the three values of Baba Saheb Ambedkar which are Equality, Liberty and Fraternity. Dr. Ambedker's idea of social justice is based on the Concept of Man and Betterment of Humanity. To his understanding man was conceived as body, mind, intellect, ideas, concept and inspiration. The idea and concept of man was understood in Biological and Ideological forms.

The first paper was presented by Dr. C. Rout on "Human Rights and Constitutional Reforms with Special Reference to Abolition of Untouchability and Role of Dr. Ambedkar". Here he points out on the law in the Constitution of India and how they were formed for the *dalits*. Besides having the law there is no awareness among the people due to the lack of proper education and because of the oppression and subjugation of the upper caste people.

The second presenter was Ms. Kakali Bezbaruah. Her paper was on "Dr. B.R. Ambedkar on Human Rights and Constitutional Reforms." In her paper, she tried to explore Ambedkar's contribution towards Human Rights and Constitutional Reforms and examined his philosophy to reconstruct India.

At the end of first session of second day, house was open to discussion. There, participants have taken keen interest in Constitutional Reforms. Lot of questions were asked from the audience to Prof. Chintamani Rout and being an expert in Law, he was able to satisfy most of the questions.

At the end of first session of second day, organizing committee has presented a momento to the Chairperson of the session Prof. Jagat Pal, Dean of School of Humanities, NEHU, Shillong, then session was closed for the lunch from 12:30 to 1:30 P.M.

Second Session of day two: Started at 1:30 P.M.

Key Note Address was given by Prof. B.K. Agarwala entitled, "*Varṇa, Svabhāva* and *Dharma*: Theory of Revision of Institution in *Bhagavad Gītā*". Prof. B.K. Agarwala said that the most important legacy of Dr. Ambedkar is drafting the Constitution of India and it was not just filling with paper and pen, but it has to do with the challenge he faced to bring-up his people to give them equality in the Constitution. But the caste system which has been practiced from thousands of generations has to be understood in a philosophical view and form. There are different *varṇas* in the Hindu system and these *varṇas* have their work appointed and it has been followed. He brings the quote of Lord Krishna and Arjuna during the battle of *Mahābhārata*.

In order to preserve the purity of blood, social interaction was prohibited with the members of the vanquished group. Those who did not follow the rule or violate it were forced to live away from the dominating group. Such people became outcastes and later untouchables and his struggle was against it. He also highlighted his efforts to do something for the emancipation of the depressed classes, its result and finally, the limitations of Ambedkar.

The first paper in the second session was presented by Dr. Md. Shah Noorur Rahman entitled, "Ambedkar's Struggle against Untouchability". According to him Dr. Ambedkar left the mark as to how one could attain the highest glory through self-help and self-respect. He also presented Ambedkar's struggle against social discrimination throughout his life and against the system of *Caturvarṇa*—categorization of Hindu Society into four *varṇas* and the Hindu caste system.

The last paper was presented by Mr. Lamsing M. Umlong entitled, "The Principles of Liberty, Equality and Fraternity: The Trinity of Ambedkar's Social Thoughts". The ideal to be realized is one man or woman, one value in walks of life whether political economic or social. This idea of one value is to be achieved by stopping religious, social and economic exploitation of man or woman by man or woman. The absence of exploitation in any form is the essence of socialism.

After the presentation of all papers, the session was open for discussion. This session has also drawn a lot of appreciation and certain new questions were raised particularly with regard to other religions in respect of caste system.

The session was closed for tea break at 3:30 P.M. to 4:00 P.M.

Valedictory Function: It was started at 4 P.M. under the chairmanship of Prof. Jagat Pal, Dean of School of Humanities. Dr. Xavier P. Mao delivered the welcome address and rapporteur report on the entire proceedings of the seminar was read out to the audience. The valedictory address was delivered by Prof. Sujata. All the paper presenters were given the certificate by Prof. Sujata Miri. At the end concluding remarks were given by Prof. Jagat Pal about the successful and satisfactory completion of seminar. Most of the participants have given positive feedback and appreciated efforts done by organizing committee. They also praised about the hospitality provided by organizing committee members specially Deputy Director Dr. Subhash C. Arya, Associate Professor, Department of Electronics and Communication Engineering, NEHU, Shillong. The participants and organizing committee expressed their deep gratitude and thanks to the Indian Council of Philosophical Research, New Delhi (ICPR) and North Eastern Hill University, Shillong for providing necessary fund, logistics support for the successful conduct of the national seminar.

3
Dr. Ambedkar's Contribution for the Untouchables' Rights and the Concepts of Justice, Equality, Liberty etc. in this Context

Dipanjali Das

Introduction

Human beings are social beings. They cannot survive without a society. A society always carries some social values. To lead a systematic life in a moral society we have to always go through some terms like 'Right', 'Duty', 'Law', and 'Equality'. All these terms generally come under a term called 'Justice'. Let us see a brief exploration of the concept of Justice.

Justice is a kind of "ultimate value or concept" which harmonizes all other values like liberty, equality, fraternity, law, welfare etc. In the ancient Indian literature justice has been considered as equivalent to *Dharma*. The works of Manu, Yājñavalkya and Bṛhaspati which deal with the institutions of marriage, remarriage, inter-caste marriage etc. In other words, justice is nothing except that various sections of society should do the work for which they are best suited and should indulge in undue interference in others affairs.

It is not easy to explain what justice means, because justice is related both to law and morality. Moreover, justice denotes our duties as well as rights. According to some writers, justice means nothing but Equality. Some others are of the view that justice lays emphasis on freedom, the rights of individuals.

According to D.D. Raphael, "Justice protects the rights of the individual as well as the other of the Society." Society comprises various sections such as students, teachers, workers, farmers, rulers, women, men etc. The doctrine of justice asserts that there should be conciliation between the claims of all of these various sections of society.

Benn and Peters say, "To act justly, then, is to treat all men alike except where there are relevant differences between them."

Nature and Attributes of Justice

While explaining the nature and attributes of justice, the scholars have brought to light some points, some of them have been entered which is related with our theme as follows:

1. *The criterion of impartiality*: Impartiality is significantly important in the scheme of justice. It means that nobody shall be discriminated against on grounds of religion, descent, caste, sex or place of birth. Nobody shall be deprived of facilities and rights only on these grounds or any of them. "Equality before the law" is an important aspect of justice.
2. *Relevant differences for treating man differently*: In the context of justice it has been stated earlier that nobody should be subject to discrimination. But, it does not imply that no discrimination can be made even on just and proper grounds. An employment programme named '*Antyodaya*' was launched in India with the objective that those who are very poor should be given financial assistance to enable them to take up self-employment in different vocations. This programme will be considered just and proper. There are reasons why a large section of society is destitute and is exploited even now. It cannot be made prosperous overnight, but their sufferings can be mitigated to some extent. Arthur Okun says, "Society cannot stop rain, but it does manufacture umbrellas.

Similarly, when the question of fulfilling duties arises, some concessions and immunities are granted to those who are handicapped or blind.

3. *Individual freedom as well as larger good to society*: The concept of justice lays an emphasis on "the dignity of an individual". Citizens are being provided various kinds of freedom for the sake of safeguarding their respect and dignity. For example, the freedom of expression and speech, the freedom of practice and propagate any religion and the domestic freedom which can help an individual to attain self-fulfilment.

Let us Come to Social Justice

Social justice is a comprehensive concept. It includes along with it the principle of social welfare, the ideas of economic and political justice as well. Moreover, the concepts of liberty, equality of opportunity and the ideal of fraternity are also part of social justice.

Hobhouse has in his famous work "The elements of social justice" dealt with various factors related to this concept, such as rights, duties, liberty, criminal procedure, distribution of wealth, inherited wealth and social and unsocial wealth etc. Here, let us discuss some of the important elements of social justice:

1. *Revision of the social order*: Our views regarding proper and improper are subject to constant change. It, therefore, becomes necessary that the society is modified in accordance with the changing conditions. Evil and very contemptible practices like 'Untouchability' have been prevalent in the Indian society. The calling of Social Justice demands that there should not be any discrimination between man and man and all should be provided with adequate opportunities for self-development. The Constitution of India has specially made this provision. Articles 14,15,16,17 of the Constitution provide that "The State shall not deny to any person equality before the law. For example, the

Article 15 commands that "The State shall not discriminate against any citizen on grounds only of religion, caste, sex, place of birth etc. or any of them." No citizen shall on these grounds be subject to any restriction with regard to access to shops, public restaurants, hotels and places of public entertainment. Nor shall a citizen be subject to any disability with regard to the use of wells, tanks etc.

2. *Protection of the interests of minorities*: Protection of the interests of minorities is an essential aspect of Social Justice. The minorities should possess the right to preserve their language, script and culture. According to the Constitution of India, the minorities have a right to establish educational Institutions for the purpose of safeguarding their culture and language. The State, while giving financial aid, shall not discriminate against such minority institutions.

Dr. Ambedkar was a victim of cast discrimination. He was born on 14 April, 1891 in Madhya Pradesh. His father was a Subedar in the Indian Army and posted in Mhow Cantonment, Madhya Pradesh. His parents belonged to Hindu *Mahar* caste which was considered as "untouchable" by the so-called upper caste society in that era. He was discriminated and humiliated by every side of the society. Ambedkar was often asked by the teachers in his school to sit outside the class. Even he could not select his favourite subject (Sanskrit) for study. Discrimination followed wherever he went, he could not drink water directly from the well even if he was very much thirsty.

After completing his higher study from the USA, Ambedkar was appointed as the Defence Secretary to the King of Baroda. But there also he had to face the humiliation for being an "Untouchable".

In 1990, Ambedkar was honoured with the "Bharat Ratna", India's highest civilian award, given for the highest degree of national service. As a leading *Dalit* Scholar, Ambedkar had been invited to testify before the Southborough Committee, which was preparing the Government of India Act of 1919. On hearing this

Ambedkar argued for creating separate electorates and reservations for *Dalits* and other religious communities. In 1920, he published the weekly "*Mooknayak*" (leader of the silent) in Bombay. Ambedkar introduced this journal to criticize the orthodox Hindu politicians and the Indian political community to fight against caste discrimination.

In 1926, he became a nominated member of the legislative council. By 1927, Dr. Ambedkar decided to launch active movements against "untouchability". In 1928, he was appointed to the Bombay Presidency Committee to work with the all European Simon Commission. This Commission had sparked great protest across India, and while its report was ignored by most of the Indians. Ambedkar himself wrote a separate recommendation for future constitutional reforms. In 1929, he ended his second journal "*Bahiskrit Bharat*" (Excluded India).

Despite his increasing unpopularity, controversial views and intense criticism of Gandhi and the Congress, Ambedkar was by reputation and exemplary jurist and scholar. In 1947, the new Congress-led government invited Ambedkar to serve as the nation's first Law Minister. On August 29, 1947, Ambedkar was appointed as the chairman of Constitution Drafting Committee, charged by the Assembly to write free India's new Constitution.

The text prepared by Ambedkar provided Constitutional guarantee and protections for a wide range of civil liberties for individual citizens including freedom of religion, the abolition of "untouchability" and the outlawing of all forms of discrimination. Ambedkar emphatically argued for extensive economic and social rights for women and also won the Assembly's support for introducing a system of reservation of jobs in the civil services, schools and colleges for members of Scheduled Castes and Scheduled Tribes, a system similar to affirmative action.

Moreover, this great architect of Constitution of India hoped to eradicate the socio-economic inequalities and lack of opportunities for India's deprived classes through this contribution which have been clicked our India. Speaking after the completion of his work, Ambedkar said, "I feel that the Constitution is workable; it is flexible and it is strong enough to hold the country together both in peace time and in war time. Indeed, if I may say so, if things go wrong under the new Constitution the reason will not be that we had a bad Constitution. What we will have to say is that Man was vile."

Constitutional safeguard for the development of Scheduled Castes and Tribes:

1. Untouchability has been abolished and cannot be practiced in any form whatsoever. No person can be deprived of the use of shops, hotels, places of public entertainment, ponds and wells on grounds only of religion, caste, creed and place of birth or any one of them.
2. The religious institutions of the Hindus have been thrown open to all sections of the Hindu society. Under the Hindu institutions the Sikh, Jain and Buddhist institutions are also included.
3. There will be no bar for admission into government aided educational institutions on grounds of religion, caste, creed or language. In order to safeguard the educational interests of these people, some special provisions have been made.

Conclusion

These are the great reforms which can give at least a better life to the victims. In this way Ambedkar showed the great respect to the discriminated community in India. Most of the people can only show their empathy to the victims, but there are only less than a few people who can reform the bad traditions and give justice to the innocents.

Thanks to Dr. Ambedkar who has contributed the important portion of his life for the upliftment of the *Dalits* and other victims like this and has given a life worth living.

4
The Principles of Liberty, Equality and Fraternity
The Trinity of Ambedkar's Social Thought

Lamsing M. Umlong

The political and social ideals which developed into actions as propounded by Bhimrao Ambedkar were influenced by his own caste status and the Maharashtrian world around him. His social movement aimed at the eradication of the social evils like Untouchability, caste rigidity, social inequality, widow burning female infanticide, social inequality based upon caste and community, discrimination against women and various ill treatments based upon cultural and religious traditions. In his endeavour he was joined by various distinguished personalities of his day. Ambedkar extensively studied the great works of Buddha, Kabir and Phule, who preached the cardinal value of social equality and the abolition of rigid caste system. Like the social religious reformers, Ambedkar believed that political reform should be preceded by social reform. No progress can be achieved in the society without social equality. Political democracy would be meaningless in the absence of social democracy. While the philosophy of Buddha taught him the doctrine of love for all, Phule inspired Ambedkar to strive to establish a society based upon liberty, equality and fraternity—the quintessence of a real democratic society.

Ambedkar's legacy as a socio-political reformer had a deep effect on modern India. In post-Independence India his social political thought has acquired respect across the political spectrum.[1] Dr. Ambedkar's very name became a sign of victory of the downtrodden and long exploited.[2] Every great person has a vision that impels all her/his works. Its discernibility may vary from case to case generally being the function of the degree of turbulence around her/him, his/her position with the power structure in the given environment, her/his own equipment and conception of self-role.[3] It is a moot point as to what extend a great person, who is essentially anchored in his/her space and time, could transcend these barriers and be equally effective in a different situation. A great person basically is the product of prevailing social relations. It is a particular moment in history that reflects an acute demand for such a person.[4] Generally the classes that share the vision and ideology of such persons tend to iconize them with specific attributes of their class choice, in an attempt to institutionalize the latter with this scenario in view, the trend of ionization of such a great person as Ambedkar, the attempt to institutionalize this idea is a gauge to assess the forces of *status quo* in society.[5]

Babasaheb Ambedkar envisioned his idea in the famous three principles: liberty, equality and fraternity. They were the basis for the ideal society of his conception.[6] For Ambedkar's conception of these three principles has been derived from the teachings of Buddha. Therefore, his ideas of liberty, equality and even fraternity are different from the French Revolution, familiar to Marx, there is *prima facie* scope to argue that Marx's ridicule on these principles does not apply to him.[7] Ambedkar insists that the conception of the ideal society ought to have all the three together. Absence of any would not be acceptable to him. The society of his dream could only be seen within a kind of spiritual frame. In Ambedkar's case a society without these principles is not a perfect/ideal society. It is his vision and inevitably, he had to attribute the origin of them to some spiritual source.

According to Ambedkar there are three factors required for the uplift of an individual. They are sympathy, equality and liberty. He strongly believes in the importance of the individual to the extent that, for him, any religion which does not recognize individual freedom is not acceptable. An individual is a part of society but religion must not concentrate only for social welfare by neglecting the individual development.[8] Ambedkar addresses these three issues of sympathy, equality and liberty by pointing a finger towards the Hindu social status and the treatment they give to others. So far as sympathy is concerned, it is nil. The sense of brotherhood and oneness in Hinduism is out of question. The relations of the neighbouring Hindus and untouchables of the village, no one can say that they are brothers. They can rather be called two opposite armies in warring camps.[9] The point to drive home here is to relate to the principle of fraternity as described by Ambedkar which refers more to the sense of belonging to one community even though one belongs to the different section in the context of Hindu traditions. There must be a sympathetic consideration towards his fellow beings. Every sort of dreadful effect must be prevented and hatred must be stopped from entering the mind. The Hindus of his days lacks this kind of treatment towards others. About equality, Ambedkar stresses that the kind of inequality that is prevalent in our country will not be found anywhere in the world.[10] Nowhere in the history on mankind can be seen inequality more intense than Untouchability.

As he believes in spiritual source of these principles, inequality springs from religion as different from that of cultural traditions, legal bases or even from constitutional authority. In other words inequality here is attached to religious dogmas where one who belongs to the so-called high caste treats others at par with animals. The view that some groups are unequal to another exists among Hindus themselves and not with the way the Hindus are looking at those who embrace other religious segment, for instance the Muslims or the Christians. Thus it proves that if there is any reason for your being treated as Untouchables and unequals, it is your relation with the Hindu religion. In such a state of inequality and injustice some Hindus try to soothe the untouchables. They say, "Get educated yourselves, be clean and then we will touch you, we will treat you on par."[11] Thus social equality for Ambedkar can be built only when the kind of religion we adhere to, should also be practiced in the day-to-day life among those who claim to follow it.

Regarding freedom, he says, you may have freedom guaranteed by law, or personal freedom for example to possess and enjoy your property or to own money but it should be in the real sense of the term. The real freedom is guaranteed by real rights and the real rights are the rights to be exercised by those who fall or are subjects to the authority which frames these rights. In short, that which is permitted by the society to be exercised can alone be called right. A right which is guaranteed by law but is opposed by the society is of no use at all.[12] The untouchables are in need of social liberty more than that which is guaranteed by law. So long as you do not achieve social liberty, whatever freedom is provided by law to you is of no avail. Freedom is not restricted to physical freedom alone. Man has a body as well as a mind. Thus, he needs physical as well as mental freedom. In fact freedom of the mind is of prime importance. The principle is, he should be free to act according to his free will and he should be able to make the maximum use of the abilities he possesses. The freedom of the mind is the real freedom.[13] In the context of Hindu religion man cannot have real freedom. This is because of the dictation of the instructions sought from the scripture. There is no room for reason and thus the mind is still in bondage and mental slavery is the worst form of slavery and that is why we need to break this bondage for progress from all sides.

To conclude I would like to address a few vows out of the 22 famous vows prescribed by Ambedkar to his followers during the historic religious conversion to Buddhism on 15 October, 1956 at Deeksha Bhoomi, Nagpur in India. It is interesting to note that these oaths or vows reflect the principles of his socio-democratic ideas in which the ingredients of liberty, equality and fraternity are present. According to him, any democratic society in lieu of these components cannot be called so. Some of these vows are:

(i) I do not believe in the incarnation of God.
(ii) I shall not act in manner violating the principles and teachings of the Buddha.
(iii) I shall believe in the equality of man.
(iv) I shall endeavour to establish equality.
(v) I shall have compassion and loving kindness for all living beings and protect them.

(vi) I shall not take intoxicants like liquor, drugs, etc. (i) and (ii) refer to liberty, (iii) and (iv) refer to equality and (v) and (vi) refer to fraternity or fellow feeling.

Notes

1. Gupta Shyam Shanker Prasad, *Life and Works of Ambedkar,* Centrum Press, New Delhi, 2011, p. 11.
2. *Ibid.*, p. 12.
3. *Ibid.*, p. 13.
4. *Ibid.*, p. 14.
5. *Ibid.*, p. 15.
6. *Ibid.*, pp. 62-63.
7. *Ibid.*
8. Singh Ravindra Prasad, *Ambedkar and Indian Caste System*, ABD Publishers, 2010, p. 34.
9. *Ibid.*, p. 34.
10. *Ibid.*, p. 35.
11. *Ibid.*
12. *Ibid.*, p. 38.

References

Agarawal, S., *Dr. Ambedkar: The Man and His Message: A Commemorative Volume,* Prentice-Hall of India, New Delhi, 1991.

Ambedkar, B.R., *Annihilation of Caste: An Undelivered Speech*, Arnold Publishers, New Delhi, 1990.

Barill, C., *Social and Political Ideas of B.R. Ambedkar*, Aalekh Publishers, Jaipur, 1977.

Das Hari Hara, *Indian Political Thought*, National Publishing House, Jaipur, 2005.

Jadhav, N., *Dr. Ambedkar's Economic Thought and Philosophy*, Popular Prakashan, Bombay, 1993.

Jatav, D.R., *Dr. Ambedkar's Role in National Movement*, Boudha Sahitya Sammelan, New Delhi, 1979.

Kadam, K.N., *Dr. Ambedkar: The Emancipator of the Oppressed*, B.R. Publishing, Delhi, 1994.

Narain, A.K. and Ahir, D.C., *Dr. Ambedkar, Buddhism and Social Change*, B.R. Publishing, Delhi, 1993.

Nim, H.L., *Thoughts on Dr. Ambedkar*, Siddhartha Educational and Cultural Society, Agra, 1969.

Zelliot, Eleanor, *From Untouchable to Dalit: Essays on the Ambedkar Movement,* Manohar Publishers, New Delhi, 1992.

5

Dr. B.R. Ambedkar

Women Liberation and Empowerment

Surender Dagar

> *"We shall see better days soon and our progress will be greatly accelerated if male education is persuaded side-by-side with female education..." are the words of Young Ambedkar.*[1]

Introduction

What is a woman? Is she a womb? Is she a commodity or a living being like rest of us? Why is she identified with reference to him always (like we always use Mrs. 'X' or Mrs. 'Y' in order to identify a married woman? Does 'he' ever link himself to 'her' like this? These are the questions which really need to be contemplated.

"Women constitute half the world's population, perform nearly two-thirds of its work hours, receive one-tenth of the world's income, and less than one-hundredth of the world's property."[2]

God has gifted women with compassion, tender-heartedness, caring nature, concern for others. These are very positive signs which imply that women can be leaders. In order to help women to be in limelight, they need to be empowered. Therefore, empowerment of women is the prerequisite to transform a developing country into a developed country. In India the problem of low status of women is very deep rooted. Discrimination against a girl starts from the mother's womb and continues into infancy, childhood and adulthood. The family system in India creates a superior status to the husband and subordinate and submissive status to the wives. It has been strongly highlighted in the Fourth World Conference on Women that across cultures throughout the world there has been traditionally strong discrimination overt and covert against women, biases and prejudices which today prevent their effective participation in public activities. Several reformers brought influences at various times to put an end to the oppression of women in India. Among them it was Dr. Ambedkar who had been successful to come to the rescue of which Indian women should always be grateful.

The role played by Dr. Babasaheb Ambedkar, as chairperson of the Drafting Committee of the Constitution, has left imprint on the social tapestry of the country after Independence, and shaped the socio-political fabric of India today. The vision of Dr. Ambedkar about women is explicitly depicted in Constitution of India. Right from our Constitutional objectives as inserted in the very Preamble of our Constitution, i.e. to secure Equality of Status and opportunity and to promote Fraternity, assuring the dignity of each individual, a number of other Constitutional protections have been given for protecting the interest of women.

The Constitution of India provides for women equality before law for all persons[3], prohibition of discrimination on grounds of religion, race, caste, sex or place of birth.[4] However, special provisions may be made by the state in favour of women and children[5], equality of opportunity for all citizens relating to employment or appointment to any office under the state[6], state policy to be directed to securing for men and women equally the right to an adequate means of livelihood[7], equal pay for equal work for both men and women[8], provisions to be made by the state for securing just and humane conditions of work and maternity relief[9], promotion of harmony by every citizen of India and renouncement of such practices which are derogatory to the dignity of women[10] and reservation of not less than one-third of total seats for women in direct election to local bodies, viz. Panchayats and Municipalities.[11]

In his chapter on "Castes in India: their mechanism, genesis and development", Dr. Ambedkar described how women were treated cruelly by way of *sati*, enforced widowhood and girl marriages just to maintain strict endogamy in a caste.[12] The social evils regarding women in Hindu religion as well as in Muslim society were highlighted by him. As a researcher, Dr. Ambedkar extensively studied the position of women in both the religions and thrown light on denial of rights to her and ultimately the status of individual. He stated that the consequences of *purdah* system on Muslim women were that it deprives her of mental and moral nourishment.

Role of Dr. Ambedkar in Women Liberation

Right from the beginning of his struggle for the eradication of caste prejudices, he started involving women in the struggle. He realised that the real progress of the *mulnivasi* could not be achieved without liberating the women themselves. He started motivating the women. His first demand of adult franchise, which was met in the early 1920s after resistance from the Brahmins, gave voting rights to untouchables as well as to women. That was the beginning of an era of liberation for women.

Dr. Ambedkar thought for social reform at two levels, one at the Hindu family and second at Hindu society. The problems related to Hindu family were child marriage, widow marriage and *sati* etc. the abolition of untouchability, the caste system and change of laws on adoption, marriage and succession relate to the problems of Hindu society. Dr. Ambedkar's education in Western countries and seeing the status of women in those countries made him to be committed towards the downtrodden women and women in general. As per Ambedkar, Manu propounded the theory of perpetual slavery for women. Women were not allowed to be free in any respect. Women were treated as the property and objects of pleasure. According to Ambedkar Manu is responsible for the degradation of women in India.

Dr. Ambedkar and the Uniform Civil Code

Dr. Ambedkar was a brilliant lawyer who played a big role in putting together the Constitution. He supported the idea of a Uniform Civil Code, which meant that the laws would be the same for all Indians. He fought all his life for equal rights for everyone. He urged the members of Constituent Assembly to have a common code which would replace the Hindu law regarding seven important matters that are the right to property of deceased Hindu to both male and female, the order of succession among different heirs, the law of maintenance, marriage, divorce, adoption and minority and guardianship. Since 1950, no successful effort made to implement the Constitutional Mandate under Article 44. In a historic judgement, the Court directed the Union Government through the Secretary to Ministry of Law and Justice to file an affidavit by August 1995 indicating the steps taken and efforts made by the Government towards securing a Uniform Civil Code for the citizens of India.[13]

Dr. Ambedkar and Hindu Code Bill

Hindu Code Bill is a glorious example of Dr. Ambedkar's commitment to the cause of the women, but sad history of crusade. This Bill places the women on par with the men in matters of property, adoption and marriages. The Bill was a mixture of old and new. The Bill received criticism inside and outside the Parliament and resulted in breaking up the Bill into two parts. The marriage and divorce part could not be completed. Dr. Ambedkar felt it as it was killed and buried, unwept and unsung after four clauses were passed. Ambedkar accepted the amendments as a compromise and decided to have some rather than none. Justice Gajendra Gadkar had a high appreciation to Ambedkar for the Bill. He aptly says, "I for one who would hail it at times sweet revenge on the Hindu society as a whole. If Dr. Ambedkar gives us Hindu Code his achievement would go down in history as a very eloquent piece of poetic justice indeed."

Dr. Ambedkar—Economic Protection to the Women

There is no doubt in fact that most of the suppression and exploitation the women face is due to the economic dependency. With the recognition of women's right over her *Stridhana* as absolute, she is now regarded as competent to sell and dispose of her property. The daughter is assured of right in the property. Dr. Ambedkar is responsible for the equal status and empowering her with economical independency.

Dr. Ambedkar—A Modern Manu

The man who razed a copy of *Manusmriti* in 1927 into ashes gave Indians the largest and ever most elaborate Constitution in the human history and became the chief instrument in giving the Hindu community another *Smriti* of Law became the modern Manu in providing the laws that suit for the women of today.

Apart from these, Dr. Ambedkar then brought women, the *mulnivasi* women in particular into the struggle. In December 1927 during the Mahad Tank struggle, on the first day when the procession was taken out, women marched in the procession along with men. Second day, Dr. Ambedkar exclusively addressed women. He told them to participate in the struggle against the tyranny of caste system. He emphasized to them that men alone cannot fight this menace. The main theme of his speech was "Importance of participation of women in the struggle of depressed." He also wanted to prepare the women for a cultural change. He told them to change their style of dressing, to do away with unwanted ornaments, which they used to wear all the time and told them to send their girls to school, keep cleanliness etc. His speech was so effective that women dropped the unwanted ornaments in that meeting. Next day the women could be seen with their style of dressing changed completely. Thus, Dr. Ambedkar brought about a revolutionary change in the attitude of *mulnivasi* women. That gave an extra boost to his movement.

Dr. Ambedkar was an ardent supporter of family planning. He emphasized the need of family planning way back in 1938. At that time nobody even dreamt of it. He even criticized his own parents in public speeches because he himself was the 14th child in the family. This showed his concern for the well being of the women.

Dr. Ambedkar's Vision and Today's Reality

Dr. Ambedkar is an architect of Constitution of India. He provided strong Constitutional safeguards to women. Dr. Ambedkar's vision towards women can be seen in the form of various empowerments under various laws and policies. The Special Marriage Act sets four essential conditions for a valid marriage, i.e. monogamy, sound mind, marriageable age and the parties should not be too closely related. There are some grounds available to the wife only, both in Hindu and the Civil marriages provided to the women. Violent and forceful abortions and abortions without consent of women are crime under section 313.

The Hindu Succession Act gives male and female heirs almost equal rights to inheritance. Section 14 says that any property possessed by a female Hindu shall be held by her as full owner and not a limited owner. In 2005, Amendment in Hindu Succession Act, 1956 seems to be of great worth; whereby a daughter of a coparcener herself and all the rights related to ancestral property has been given to the women on equal footing with the male counterpart. Furthermore, the enactment of Protection of Women from Domestic Violence Act, 2005 is a welcome step in order to protect the interest of women in particular. Dr. Ambedkar introduced Hindu Code Bill in 1948 which was revolutionary in confinement of proprietary rights to women, but when not accepted by the Parliament, he resigned from the Ministerial post from the Cabinet in 1951. Apart from all such Constitutional and legal guarantees, there are certain laws and policies to empower women such as Equal Remuneration Act, 1976, The Maternity Benefit Act, 1961, Protection of Women from Domestic Violence Act, 2005, Dowry Prohibition Act, 1961, The Pre-Conception and Pre-Natal Diagnostic Techniques (Prohibition of Sex Selection) Act, 1994, The Prohibition of Child Marriage Act, 2006, Section 498A, IPC cruelty by husband or a relative of husband etc.

By inserting the various legal provisions we have probably won the battle, but, still we need to fight the war against gender discrimination in our day-to-day life. In any patriarchal society, women are second class citizens and widows third class. She has equal rights but, still unawareness, customary practices and other social construction prevent their full expression. Very often daughters are persuaded by the family and by the mother herself to relinquish her share so that she can continue her association with the natal home. The arguments given are that the natal family had acquired huge expense at the time of the marriage in solemnizing the same or on dowry. Further the day-to-day expenses on customary practices like *Bhaat, Teez, Bhaidooz* etc. after the marriage are to be borne by the parental family. Most of the women do require the emotional support from the parental family. But this support comes *in lieu* of willing away her property right. Ironically, by making the legal provisions, like amendments in the Hindu Succession Act, 1956, which have created the legal rights as far as ownership of property is concerned, the existing social constructions, prevailing customary practices have hijacked these rights and left this segment of the society in a situation of helplessness.

The shocking fact, that has come to light in a survey by the Mathura District Legal Services Authority (MDLSA) on the "Plight of Forsaken/Forlorn Women—Old and Widows Living in the religious place like Vrindavan in the State of Uttar Pradesh"[14], which highlighted that the bodies of widows who die in government-run shelter homes in Vrindavan are taken away by sweepers at night, cut into pieces, put into jute bags and disposed of as the institutions do not have any provision for a decent funeral. This, too, is done only after the inmates give money to the sweeper! This kind of sorry state makes us realize about the pathetic conditions of a single woman particularly after the death of her husband.

Taking cognizance of a report published in *The Hindu* on August 11, 2011 on the plight of the widows living in Vrindavan in Mathura district of Uttar Pradesh, Justice Altamash Kabir, Executive Chairperson of the National Legal Services Authority, had asked the U.P. State Legal Services Authority to survey the conditions of the women. In that survey it was found that in most cases widows are denied remarriage even after the death of their husband in childhood or young age. While some are forced to leave the marital home and native place by the family members just to division of share in the family property or to avoid maintenance in old age and bearing the burden of a non-productive family member, many others leave their homes due to physical and mental torture.

At the same time 73rd and 74th Amendments of our Constitution have inserted the provisions regarding the participatory role of the women in the Panchayati Raj Institutions at the grassroots level, but the ground reality whereby they are being governed by their counterpart is not hidden to anyone in the present society.

Further, the Protection of Women from Domestic Violence Act, 2005 is also seems to be a paper tiger in reality. As per the 5th monitoring report of the PWDWA brought out by the Lawyer's Collective and International Centre for Research on Women, the Protection officers are discouraging women from seeking justice and are pushing them into "settlement". On the question raised by this body while survey that is Domestic Violence a family affair?, 57.1 per cent of Delhi's protection officers said 'yes', which indicates that they still do not see it as a social problem.[15]

So, there is no dearth, as such, of the Legal provisions as far as the protection of the interest of women are concerned but the evil resides in the way of proper implementation of the statutory laws. We are best in making the law, but worst in implementing the same.

Skills development, employment, health, say in decision-making and other social issues including a basic transformation in archaic mind set about the attitude to women. The areas of concern from the viewpoint of women empowerment in India include, adverse female child sex-ratio which results in the phenomenon of missing girls before birth, higher death rate of female child, higher maternal death rate, higher rate of female illiteracy, lower rates of wages for women employees, high incidence of underweight women suffering from malnutrition and high incidence of heinous crimes against women such as, dowry deaths, rape, molestation and immoral trafficking.

Conclusion

Women should be given all-round development importantly social education, their well-being and socio-cultural right. Each and every section of Indian women be given their due share and it is a must to maintain and protect dignity and modesty of women. It is the need of the hour to give due share to each and every section of the Indian women and without removing social-stigma, no progress or development can be achieved. Everyone should understand the principles and ideologies of Dr. Ambedkar and try to follow them. It is high time to have such social movement, whereby we can deconstruct all our social constructs of gender discrimination and to achieve in particular the shorter mission in the form of faster, sustainable and inclusive growth and in general the Constitutional goals of justice, liberty, equality and fraternity by awareness, sensitization, imparting skills and building capacities within this vulnerable segment of the society.

Notes

1. Ratnesh Katulkar, "*Dr. Ambedkar on Women Liberation*", Available at *www.countercurrents.org/katulkar310808.html*
2. United Nations Report, 1980, *Programme of Action for the Second Half of the UN Decade for Women.*
3. Article 14 of the Constitution of India.
4. Article 15(1) of the Constitution of India.
5. Article 15(3) of the Constitution of India.
6. Article 16 of the Constitution of India.
7. Article 39(a) of the Constitution of India.
8. Article 39(d) of the Constitution of India.
9. Article 42 of the Constitution of India.
10. Article 51A(e) of the Constitution of India.
11. Articles 343(d) and 343(T) of the Constitution of India.
12. Ms. Vaishali Dhanvijay, 'Dr. Babasaheb Ambedkar's Efforts for Women Empowerment and Present Status of Women in Society' available at *eiirj1.weebly.com/uploads/1/0/8/0/10800505/vd16.pdf*
13. Sarla Mudgal *v.* Union of India, 1995 AIR 1531.

14. *The Hindu*, "Dignity Denied even in Death for Vrindavan Widows", 8-1-2012.
15. *The Tribune*, "Protection Officers Hardly of any help to Victims: Survey", 31-01-2012.

References

Castes in India: Their Mechanism, Genesis and Development, *http://en.wikipedia.org/wiki/Castes in India: Their Mechanism Genesis and Development.*

Prof. G Manoher Rao, *Dr. Ambedkar and the Constitution of India.*

J.N. Pandey, *The Constitutional Law of India.*

Pardeep Singh, *Women and Agenda of Inclusive Growth: Legal Prospective.*

Ratnesh Katulkar, *Dr. Ambedkar on Women Liberation.*

6

Dr. B.R. Ambedkar and His Perception of Gender Equality

Some Explorations and Conjectures

Ashraful Islam Ahmed

Introduction

Dr. Bhimrao Ramji Ambedkar (1891-1956), "a symbol of revolt" as mentioned by Pandit Jawaharlal Nehru, the first Prime Minister of Independent India, was one of the front-ranking nation-builders of modern India. He is popularly known as the 'pioneer' who initiated the 'liberation movement' of roughly sixty-five million untouchables of India. Dr. Ambedkar, notwithstanding all handicaps of birth, has made, by pursuit of knowledge in the humanities, social sciences, politics and law, an indelible imprint on the body politics of the country. Dr. Bhimrao Ramji Ambedkar's vision and life truly stands at the junction of the old and the new. He was indeed a man marking the beginning of a new era. It would have been a different India without him and, in a probability, a much more inequitable and unjust one. A glance of his copious writings would evidently show that despite his pre-occupations with the problems of the *dalits* (Untouchables), Ambedkar has in his own way, made significant contributions to the contemporary social and political ideas.

He avouched the mission of his life by proclaiming that "For the protection of human rights, several great men have immolated themselves at the altar of duty. Better to die in the prime of youth for a great cause than to live like an oak and do nothing." Dr. Ambedkar embodied a peerless personage among all the national leaders who only had the moral propriety to assert that "I am a man of character." He waged a valiant struggle against the diabolical contrivance to suppress and enslave humanity—the Brahmanical system to make the sub-human and servile majority regain their human personality through social, economic, political and cultural emancipation. He declared that "Our battle is for freedom. Our battle is not for few economic and political gains. Our battle is for the reclamation of Human Personality which was suppressed and mutilated...." Ambedkar did not lose sight of social problems of his day; he not only analysed and came up with the solutions of the problems, but strived hard to put them in action. The greatness of Ambedkar lies not just in espousing the foundations of a suffering society and providing a way out but by carrying out the mission of emancipation himself. He operationalized his ideas into action for reconstituting society as pragmatic philosopher. In fact, he has heralded a social and psychological battle against the system causing dehumanization, exploitation, coercion and suffering.

Dr. Ambedkar in his grand scheme of eliminating gender discrimination, fought for the rights of representation of women as democratic rights. Basing on the *prorata* of population, he reasoned that all sections of the society including women should get rights of representation in the spheres of education, employment, agriculture, industry, bureaucracy and governance of this country. Babasaheb Ambedkar debunked all those reforms that questioned only the traditions, but never intended to debase the ideological foundations of those customs. It was during the *Mahad Satyagraha* in 1927 that the aim of the movement was proclaimed by Dr. Ambedkar as, "not only removing our own disabilities, but also at bringing about a social revolution that will remove all man-made barriers of caste by providing equal opportunities to all to rise to the highest position and making no distinction between man and woman so far as civic rights are concerned." Education was assigned a revolutionary role in Ambedkar's conception of social progress and in his vision of a just and equal society. It was identified as a key instrument of liberation from oppressive structures of Hindu caste—patriarchy as well as of reconstruction of a new social order based on gender equality. Women were integral to this visionary egalitarianism and were consciously mobilised as political actors in the *dalit* liberation movement led by Ambedkar in the early decades of the twentieth century. An emancipatory discourse on gender was an important component of Ambedkar's philosophy of social democratic liberalism and permitted women an authentic identification with its underlying principles with a view to achieving a full and enlightened citizenship.

Dr. Ambedkar argued for extensive economic and social rights for women. He stated that women should be given all-round development importantly social, education and socio-cultural right. He emphasized that each and every section of Indian women be given their due share and it is a must to maintain and protect dignity and modesty of women. His Western education and deep understanding of the Western philosophies helped him to evolve as a visionary who had developed clear ideas for the emancipation of the *dalits* and women in India. He could translate many of his ideas and visions into specific policies and institutions during his stint as the architect of Constitution of India and as the Law Minister of India.

From time immemorial, the women in this land of ours were treated as a sort of thing. Her placing in the society was not at par with other human being. She had no rights. She could not move nor do anything at her will. In Hindu *Shastras,* she has been branded just like animals. From the verses of the *Ramcharitmanas* as written by Tulsi Das, "*Dhol, ganwar, shudra, pashu, naari; Ye sab tadan ke adhikari.*" One may easily draw inferences as to what status has been granted to our mothers. In *Manusmriti* the ancient Hindu Code-book, the status granted to women is quite visible and she was put to the lowest rung of humanity as she was treated at par with the animals and slaves by the proprietors of *Hindu Dharma.* Such was the placement earmarked to our mothers, sisters and even great grandmothers that the heads of humanity bend upon down with shame. Since, Ambedkar himself was a victim of oppression and discrimination in all its severity, his views about women's oppression and equal rights are more useful than anybody else's theory to strengthen the strategy for approaching the systemic challenges and contradictions in a more pragmatic way to bring women to the mainstream.

Dr. Ambedkar was of the firm opinion that until or unless, by applying dynamite, the Hindu *Dharma Shastras* are not blown-up, nothing is going to happen. In his treatises, "*The Riddle of the Woman*", "*The Woman and the Counter Revolution*", "*The Rise and Fall of Hindu Women*", "*Castes in India: Their Mechanism, Genesis and Development*" and through the issues of his journals "*Mooknayak*" (1920) and "*Bahishkrit Bharat*" (1927). Ambedkar tries to show how the gender relations and differences are constructed by Hindu Brahminical order which conditions women to conform a stereotype feminine behaviour, requiring them to be passive and submissive, suited only to a life of domestic and family responsibilities. In this direction, Dr. B.R. Ambedkar has tried to break down the barriers in the way of advancement of women in India. He laid down the foundation of concrete and sincere efforts by codifying the common Civil Code for the Hindus. Prior to these efforts of Dr. Ambedkar, the destiny of the Indian women depended upon the wrong notions and perceptions chalked out by the proprietors of orthodoxy. The writings and speeches of Ambedkar show what values India should develop and how it should modernize its social and political institutions. Ambedkar saw women as the victims of the oppressive, caste-based and rigid hierarchical social system. He believed that socio-cultural forces artificially construct gender relations, especially by *Manusmriti* and Hindu religion. As Simone De Beauvoir observed, "Women are made, they are not born".

In the "*Women and Counter Revolution*" and "*The Riddle of Women*", Ambedkar portrays the way in which Manu treated women. He points out that the laws of Manu on the status of women are very important in moulding the Hindu attitude and perspective towards women, perpetuated and maintained through

Hindu personal laws based on *shastras,* caste and endogamy, i.e. the base of Indian patriarchy. He attacks *Manusmriti* as a major source which legitimizes the denial of freedom, self-respect, right to education, property, divorce etc. He also suggests strategies for emancipation from oppression. He found their emancipation in Buddhist values which promotes equality, self-respect and education. Ambedkar believes that Buddha treated women with respect and love and never tried to degrade them like Manu did. He taught women *Buddha Dharma* and religious philosophy. Ambedkar cites women like Vishakha, Amrapali of Vaisali, Gautami, Rani Mallika, queen of Prasenjit who approached Buddha, as evidences of Buddha's treatment of women as equals.

According to Ambedkar, the society must be based on reason and not on atrocious traditions of caste system. Therefore, in "The Annihilation of Caste", he suggests as a means the annihilation of caste *"Make every man and woman free from the thraldom of the Shastras, cleanse their minds of the pernicious notions founded on the Shastras."* He found education, intercaste marriage and interdine as methods, which may eliminate castes and patriarchy. In Ambedkar's movement launched from 1920 onwards, women actively participated and acquired the confidence to voice their issues on various platforms. Venubai Bhatkar and Renubai Shambharakar are worth mentioning. In 1924, Bahishkrit Hitakarni Sabha was formed to work for the socio-political equality of depressed people and promoting their economic interests. Women started participating in *Satyagrahas* and also launched women's associations for untouchable women for spreading education and awareness among them. In the *Mahad Satyagraha* for temple entry in 1927, even caste Hindus participated. Shandabai Shinde was one such participant. In the *Satyagraha,* it was decided to burn the *Manusmriti* which humiliated women and *Shudras.* In the demonstration after the bonfire of the *Manusmriti,* more than fifty women participated.

In January 1928, a women's association was founded in Bombay with Ramabai, Ambedkar's wife, as its President. Along with the Depressed Classes Conference in Nagpur in 1930, women also had their separate conference. In the Kalaram Temple Entry *Satyagraha* at Nasik in 1930, five hundred women participated and many of them were arrested along with men and ill-treated in jails. To face tortures along with their men, women also organized their *Samata Sainik Dal.* When Ambedkar returned to India after attending the Round Table Conference in 1932, hundreds of women were present for the committee meetings. At various places depressed class women's conferences were held and they began to present their demands assertively. The encouragement of Ambedkar empowered women to speak out their feelings boldly. As Radhabai Vadale said in a press conference in 1931, "We should get the right to enter the Hindu temples, to fill water at their water resources. We call these social rights. We should also get the political right to rule, sitting near the seat of the Viceroy. We do not care even if we are given a severe sentence. We will fill all the jails in the country. Why should we be scared of lathi-charge or firing? On the battlefield does a warrior care for his life? It is better to die a hundred times than to live a life full of humiliation. We will sacrifice our lives but we will win our rights." The credit for this self-respect and firm determination of women goes to Ambedkar.

On 20th July, 1942, the All India Dalit Mahila Conference was organized and 25,000 women attended. Ambedkar was highly pleased with the awakening and activities of women. On 13th August, he wrote to one of his friends, Meshram about this. On 6th January, 1945, the All India Untouchable Women's Conference was held in Bombay (now Mumbai). Running newspapers, women's hostels, boarding schools, participating in *Satyagrahas* were some of the activities of women for acquiring the personality development to secure efficient administrative and leadership capacity as men have. Gaining inspiration and encouragement from Ambedkar, many women wrote on topics like Planning, Buddhist philosophy and such other topics. Women also wrote plays, autobiographies and participated in *Satyagrahas.* Tulsabai Bansode started a newspaper *Chokhamela.* This showed how Ambedkar created awareness among poor, illiterate women and inspired them to fight against the unjust social practices like child marriages and *devdasi* system. So far as social movement is concerned, his strategy was similar to Gandhian method though he had disagreements on many things with Gandhi. To him the emphasis was on reconstruction of the Hindu society on the basis of equality rather than the social reforms initiated by Brahmo Samaj or Arya Samaj because their attempts were limited only to the upper strata of the society. His in-depth study of *Smritis* and *Shastras* and his experience from the response of upper castes during his temple entry movement crystallized his conclusions on Hindu philosophy and society.

The role played by Dr. Babasaheb Ambedkar as chairperson of the Drafting Committee of the Constitution has left imprint on the social tapestry of the country after Independence and shaped the socio-political fabric of India today. The vision of Dr. Ambedkar about women is explicitly depicted in the Constitution of India. Equality of sexes is strongly backed by the Constitution through Articles 14, 15 and 16. The principle of gender equality is enshrined in the Constitution of India in its Preamble, Fundamental Rights, Fundamental Duties and Directive Principles. He laid down the foundation of social justice and according to him, there can be no social justice without gender equality. Since, Ambedkar was well convinced about the status of women, as the Chairman of the Drafting Committee, he tried an adequate inclusion of women's rights in the political vocabulary and Constitution of India. Therefore, by considering women's equality both in formal and substantial senses he included special provisions for women. Hence, there are Articles like 15(3), 51(A)(c), 16 and so on. His key work in the preparation of Constitution of India made it to be known as a New Charter of Human Rights. He looked upon law as the instrument of creating a sense of social order in which the development of individual should be in harmony with the growth of society. He incorporated the values of liberty, equality and fraternity in the Constitution of India.

Based on the belief that any scheme of franchise and constituency that fails to bring about representation of opinions as well as representation of persons falls short of creating a popular government, he submitted the Constitution with a warning. He said in his speech delivered in the Constituent Assembly on 25th November, 1949, "Political democracy cannot last unless there lies at the base of it social democracy." By social democracy he means a way of life, which recognizes liberty, equality and fraternity as principles of life. He further said: "On 26th January, 1950, we are going to enter into a life of contradictions. In politics we will have equality and in social and economic life we will have inequality. In politics we will be recognizing the principle of one man one vote and one vote one value. In our social and economic life, we shall, by reason of our social and economic structure, continue to deny the principle of one man one value. How long shall we continue this life of contradictions? How long shall we continue to deny equality in our social and economic life? If we continue to deny it for long, we will do so only by putting our political democracy in peril. We must remove this contradiction at the earliest possible moment or else those who suffer from inequality will blow-up the structure of political democracy which this Assembly has so laboriously built-up."

Ambedkar's defence for women as the Law Minister of free India appeared in the form of the Hindu Code Bill in Parliament on 11th April, 1947. The Bill provided for several basic rights to women. It sought to abolish different marriage systems prevalent among Hindus and to establish monogamy as the only legal system. It aimed at conferment of right to property and adoption of women. It provided for restitution of conjugal rights and judicial separation. It attempted to unify the Hindu Code in tune with progressive and modern thought. In 1948 when the Hindu Code Bill was introduced in Parliament and debated on the floor of the House, the opposition was strongly against the Bill. Ambedkar tried his level best to defend the Bill by pointing out the drawbacks of Indian society and arguing that the ideals in the Bill are based on the Constitutional principles of equality, liberty and fraternity and that in the Indian society characterised by the caste system and the oppression of women. Since, women are deprived of equality, a legal framework is necessary for a social change in which women have equal rights with men. He also pointed out that the aim of the Bill was *"to codify the rules of Hindu Law which are scattered in innumerable decisions of High Courts and of the Privy Council which form bewildering motley to the common man."* However, the Bill could not withstand the opposition from the Hindu orthodoxy. Therefore, on the eve of the first elections in 1951 Prime Minister Jawaharlal Nehru dropped the Bill by saying that there was too much opposition. On this issue, the then Law Minister Dr. Ambedkar resigned. Later, the original Bill was split into four different Bills with slight changes. Those were passed as the Hindu Marriage Act, 1955; The Hindu Succession Act, 1956; the Hindu Minority and Guardianship Act, 1956; and the Hindu Adoption and Maintenance Act, 1956. However, the Hindu Code Bill helped the resurgence of feminist movement in India. This crusade of Ambedkar to emancipate women from injustice inspired the women leaders in Parliament to keep the issue alive until its enactment. This was the starting point for women to recognize their position and pursue rights movement by acquiring strength from 'second wave feminism' started in the early 1960s. Women are still fighting issues such as rape, dowry death, communalism, fundamentalism, sexual harassment, violence—domestic, social, poverty and so on.

Conclusion

To conclude, we can say that the range of Ambedkar's struggle for securing human dignity is very vast. The underlying causes of gender inequality are related to social and economic structure and practices. Consequently, the access of women particularly those belonging to weaker sections like Scheduled Castes/Tribes, Other Backward Classes, Minorities etc. to education, health, and productive resources, among others are inadequate. Therefore, they remain largely marginalized, poor and socially excluded. At this moment, we must concentrate on imparting social education before giving any concrete shape to the political empowerment to the women. It is the need of the hour to give due share to each and every section of the Indian women. So, Ambedkar wanted to create an environment through positive economic and social policies for full development of women to enable them to realize their full potential, equal access to participation and decision-making in social, political and economic life of the nation. He developed a socio-ethical philosophy and steadfastly stood for human dignity and freedom, socio-economic justice, material prosperity and spiritual discipline. His name will glitter for ever in the firmament of world history not only as a great social philosopher, but also as a great revolutionary who dedicated his entire life for the amelioration of the teeming millions of the underdogs. However, his dream of society based on gender equality is yet to be realized and therefore, his thoughts are important for the social reconstruction that favours women's empowerment.

References

Ahir, D.C., 1990, *The Legacy of Ambedkar*, Delhi.

Ambedkar, B.R., 1987, "Women and Counter Revolution", "Riddles of Hindu Women", in *Dr. Baba Saheb Àmbedkar: Writings and Speeches*, Vol. 3, Department of Education, Government of Maharashtra, Bombay.

_____, 1979, "Castes in India: Their Mechanism, Genesis and Development", "Castes in India" in *Dr. Baba Saheb Ambedkar: Speeches and Writings*, Vol. 1, Education Department, Government of Maharashtra, Bombay.

______, 1950, "The Rise and Fall of the Hindu Women", *The Mahabodhi* (Calcutta), 59.5-6. 137-151.

Arya, Sudha, 2000, *Women, Gender Equality and the State*, Deep & Deep Publications, New Delhi.

Chirakarode, Paul, 1993, *Ambedkar: Boudhika Vikshobhathinte Agnijwala*, Dalit Books, Thiruvalla.

Heywood, Andrew, 1998, *Political Ideologies: An Introduction*, MacMillan Press, London.

Limaye, Champa, 1999, *Women: Power and Progress*, B.R. Publishing Corporation, New Delhi.

Mathew, Thomas, 1991, *Ambedkar: Reform or Revolution*, Segment Books, New Delhi.

Shabbir, Mohammad, (Ed.) 2008, *Ambedkar on Law, Constitution and Social Justice*, Rawat Publications, Jaipur.

Sharma, Sheetal, 2006, "Educated Women Empowered Women", *Yojana*, October, Vol. 50.

Thorat, Sukhdeo and Aryama, 2007, *Ambedkar in Retrospect: Essay on Economics, Politics and Society*, Rawat Publications, Jaipur.

7

Dr. B.R. Ambedkar in Elimination of Caste, Religion and Gender Discrimination in India

Preeti Hazarika

Introduction

In India so many social reformers emerged to fight against injustice in favour of *dalit* communities, however, a few leaders successfully communicated their own ideas to societies towards the welfare of depressed society. Particularly, Dr. Ambedkar worked for the *Dalit* rights, women rights, backward castes, minorities and working class people and struggled all his life for the minimum dignity of all human-beings irrespective of caste or class. He analyses that there is no society at all. We have multitudes of societies based on caste. People are not born as humans. They are born into castes and imbibe such notions of mind which do not allow humane interaction among them. "The first and foremost thing that must be recognized is that Hindu Society is a myth.... In every Hindu the consciousness that exists is the consciousness of caste. That is the reason why the Hindus cannot be said to form a society or a nation. He squarely blames "Brahmanism in instituting caste system has put the greatest impediment against the growth of nationalism." "Unless the social order is changed, no progress could be achieved. The community cannot be mobilized either for defence or for offence. Nothing can be built on the foundation of caste. No nation, no morality."

Ambedkar's Actions for Social Transformation

Dr. Ambedkar in his grand scheme of reconstruction of Indian society, fought for rights of representation as democratic rights. Basing on the prorata of population, he reasoned that all sections of the society including women should get rights of representation spheres of education, employment, agriculture, industry, bureaucracy and governance of this country. Branding that the Brahmanical society is based on *Culture of Reservations*— keeping education, rule and economy reserved 100 per cent for the Brahmanical castes and relegating the *Bahujans* to service, he wanted to usher in Democratic society based on the *Culture of Representations*. His memoranda to the Southborough Committee, Montagu-Chemsford Committee, Muddiman Committee and his arguments in Round Table Conferences are based on the rights of representation as democratic rights.

Assertion and Equal Citizenship

Babasaheb Ambedkar debunked all those reforms that question only the traditions, but never intended to debase the ideological foundations of those customs as 'sectional reforms' rather than 'social reforms'. It was during the *Mahad Satyagraha* in 1927 that the 'aim' of the movement was proclaimed by Dr. Ambedkar as, "not only removing our own disabilities, but also at bringing about a social revolution that will remove all man-made barriers of caste by providing equal opportunities to all to rise to the highest position and making no distinction between man and man so far as civic rights are concerned." While the *Mahad Satyagraha* focused on "social and legal equality" the Kalaram Temple *Satyagraha* focused on "religious equality". *The Charter of Rights and Demands* of that Dr. Ambedkar presented before the Indian Statutory Commission commonly known as Simon Commission had a wider "*Constitutional significance*" for equal citizenship. While all the participants at the Round Table Conferences were busy with their Communal Representations (Hindu, Muslim, Sikh, Parsi etc.) it was only Dr. Ambedkar who raised the issues of Civic Equality, Adult Franchise and Citizenship to all Indians.

Ambedkar argued that the Brahmins dominated Hindu society and he said that the fundamental principles of Brahminism are :

1. Graded inequality between the different classes.
2. Complete disarmament of the *Shudras* and the untouchables.
3. Complete prohibition of education of the *Shudras* and the untouchables.
4. Ban on the *Shudras* and the untouchables occupying places of power and authority.
5. Complete subjugation and suppression of women.

He suggested the following changes in the Hindu outlook:

1. There should be one and only one standard of Hindu religion, acceptable to all Hindus and recognized by all Hindus;
2. Priesthood among Hindu should be abolished;
3. No ceremony should be allowed to be performed by a priest, who does not hold a legally valid sense;
4. Priests should be servants of the state and should be subject to disciplinary action; and
5. The number of priests should be legally limited according to the requirements of the state.

Annihilation of Caste

Ambedkar was thoroughly convinced that unless a casteless and classless society is created there will be no progress in India. This requires a social reconstruction and Ambedkar was very clear about the means to bring about this change. The caste system was undemocratic and authoritarian in the extreme. The castes constituting the series were hierarchically graded, each caste being considered inferior to those above it and superior to those below it. The status of a man born in a particular caste was determined by the rank of that caste in the hierarchy. Once born in that caste, his status was pre-determined and immutable. Thus, birth decided his status, which could not be altered by any talent he might show or wealth he might accumulate. Ambedkar took-up the reconstruction of Indian society on the foundations of democracy as a "mode of associated living." He asserted that Democracy, properly understood and applied would only be the panacea and initiated his public life in 1916 on this cause. Differing with the Congress and other 'Nationalists', he declared that "social revolution must precede political revolution so as to ensure that every citizen enjoys the benefits of political freedom". Exposing the Jatpat Todak Mandal which aspired to "*Remodel Hindu Society*", Ambedkar stressed that "*Reconstitution of the society*" by annihilating caste and its ideological notions is the cure.

Upliftment of the Status of Women

During the early modern period, the Indian women forced to practice certain social evils such as Child Marriage, *Purdah* System, *Sati* System, Prohibition of Widow remarriage etc. During this period, number of social and political thinkers started movement against such systems and methods. These thinkers aimed at upliftment of the status of women socially, economically, educationally and politically. Of these socio-political thinkers Dr. B.R. Ambedkar, Mahatma Phule, Mahatma Gandhi, Raja Ram Mohun Roy, Ishwar Chandra Vidyasagar, and such others have organized movement for striving equality for *dalits*, backward classes and women. Dr. Ambedkar was not only the champion of the cause of untouchables and depressed classes, but that of the women also. He was convinced that for social justice and progress of the nation it was essential that conditions of women should be improved a lot. He stood for the economic equality of women and vehemently pleaded for the spread of women education. The Hindu Code Bill piloted by him, empowered women to equally inherit property. The Bill also included abolition of the doctrine of rights by birth, provision for inter-caste marriage and divorce. But, the Bill could not be adopted because of the conspiracy of some higher caste Hindu leaders. In protest Ambedkar resigned from Nehru's Cabinet on September 27, 1951.

Ambedkar's Notion of Social Justice

Injustice is everywhere not only Western countries, but in India also. At present some of the contemporary issues are: injustice and caste discrimination. Ambedkar did a movement amongst marginalized communities. His concept of justice generated from thc French Revolution of 1789. Ambedkar's perspective of social justice is based on social democracy which consists of three concepts of justice, namely liberty, equality and fraternity. Ambedkar addressed in Constituent assembly that, the third thing we must do is not to be content with mere political democracy. We must make out political democracy a social democracy as well. Political democracy cannot last unless there lies at the base of social democracy. What does social democracy mean? It means a way of life, which recognizes liberty, equality and fraternity as the principles of life. The movement from 1936 entered a new phase for attaining 'economic equality' along with social, legal, civil and religious equality, by the abolition of caste and class, considering both Brahmanism and capitalism as necessary evils. The formation of "Independent Labour Party" was a new experiment to formulate the government of "labouring classes" who also happen to be the exploited castes in Indian social system. He held the view that ills were not due to machinery and modern civilization; they were due to *wrong social organization* which had made private property and pursuit of personal gain matters of absolute sanctity. These equalities were to be achieved in the trinity of "liberty, equality and fraternity" by Constitutional rights and guarantees, and much more significantly by the reconstruction of society based on this trinity principle. It was due to his thoughts on the above subjects which enabled a Constitutional scheme of Government of India Act, 1935 much ahead of democratic Constitution of Independent India.

The Constitution of India, in order to reconstitute the society on the democratic foundations of equality, liberty, fraternity and justice, incorporated legislations for equality and equal opportunity in all spheres of life. Road map is laid for a democratic and inclusive society through reservations as representations. In order to create social polarization among the victims of the Brahmanical social system, Ambedkar engineered the category "*Backward classes*" would cover three principal components, the Scheduled Castes, the Scheduled Tribes and the Other Backward classes. And he addressed himself to the task of securing social justice for all the Socially and Educationally Backward Classes in the country, under the mandate of a new Constitution. It is to be underlined that the *Idea* is to break monopoly by proportional representations; *Policy* is to bring SC, ST, and OBC on one platform in order to break caste system as representations are for collection of castes, not for individual castes as Backward Classes. The Directive Principles strive to create a Welfare State and a just social order. Making the State responsible for social change, Article 38 contains the essence of these principles: "The State shall strive to promote the welfare of the people by securing and protecting as effectively as it may a *social order* in which justice—social, economic and political—shall inform all the institutions of national life." He announced that the people of India, "Expect to happen in a sovereign and free India is a complete destruction of Brahmanism as a philosophy of life and as a social order." Ambedkar identified the functioning of moral order, observance of Constitutional morality as the conditions for the successful working of democracy. "Society must have either the sanction of law or the sanction of morality to hold it together without either, society is sure to go to pieces."

The social reformers attacked inequalities and separatism and stood for equality and cooperation. They attacked the heredity as the basis of distinction, and law of *karma* as which supplied the religio-philosophic defence of the undemocratic authoritarian caste institution. They called on the people to work for the betterment in the real world. In which they lived rather than strive for salvation after death. They branded the caste system as the powerful obstacles to the growth of national unity and solidarity.

There were different angles from which caste was attacked by different social reform groups, Raja Ram Mohun Roy the founder of *Brahmo Samaj* invoked the authority of *Mahanirvana Tantra*, an old religio-sociological work of the Hinduism, to support his view that caste should no longer continue. The *Brahmo Samaj* opposed the rigid social divisions which caste implied. Rabindra Nath Tagore and Keshab Chandra Sen, who succeeded the Raja Ram Mohun Roy as successive leaders of *Samaj*, were more critical of Hindu scriptures than Raja Ram Mohun Roy. It was Keshab Chandra Sen, who is most unambiguous categorical term, repudiated the caste system without invoking any scriptural authority. The spirit of social revolt, which the Raja inaugurated, reached a climax in the history of the *Brahmo Samaj* under the guidance of Keshab Chandra Sen. The pioneering work of the anti-caste movement first started by *Brahmo Samaj* was continued by other organizations which were subsequently formed in the country. The Bombay *Prarthana Samaj* carried on the propaganda of the repudiation of caste practically on the same lines of the *Brahmo Samaj*. Both *Brahmo Samaj* and the *Prarthana Samaj* under the democratic cultural influence of the West denounced the caste as an institution itself in contract to this attitude, the *Arya Samaj* started by Swami Dayananda Saraswati preached not to repudiation of the caste system. But, the revival of the Hindu society of Vedic period based only on the four castes. The *Arya Samaj*, while crusading against the minute's dissection of the Hindu society into countless sub-castes, aimed at reconstructing it on the original fourfold division. Further, it stood for extending the right to study scripture even to the lowest caste *Shudra*. Thus, while both the *Brahmo Samaj* and the *Prarthana Samaj* were iconoclastic movement with regard to caste, the *Arya Samaj* stood for reforming caste by eliminating all sub-castes. In addition to *Brahmo Samaj*, the *Prathana Samaj* and the *Arya Samaj*, there was other movements, which also carried on a campaign against caste.

Conclusion

Dr. Ambedkar has tried all kinds of strategies during his life for eradicating caste, religion and gender discriminations in India. In the political domain, he promoted separate electorate, party building and public policies like reservations—and did not hesitate to collaborate with the ruler of the time—be it the British or the Congress for having things done. In the social domain, he militated in favour of reforms at the grassroots level—education being his first goal—and reforms by the state—as evident from the Hindu Code Bill. None of his strategies really succeeded during his life time: he could not have separate electorate introduced, he could not build a *Dalit* or a labour party, he could not have the Hindu Code Bill passed—and he became a bitter man. As a result, conversion to Buddhism became the strategy of last resort. But it was not an exit option: Dr. Ambedkar did not take refuge in religion, but looked equality and social reform in religion since Buddhism was likely to endow the *Dalits* with a new identity and a sense of dignity. More than sixty years later, his contribution to the making of modern India is possibly more substantial than that of any other leader of his generation. He has not only prepared the ground for a silent revolution, but has also played a key role in the drafting of the Constitution of India which has set the terms for the development of the world's largest democracy.

References

Bemal Tofan, 2008, "Dr. B.R. Ambedkar, Crusader Against Caste and Untouchabilities of Hindu Social Order", *Orissa Review*, January.

Dash, Siddhartha, 2011, "Dr. B.R. Ambedkar : The Messiah of the Downtrodden", *Orissa Review*, May.

Jaffrelot, Christophe, 2009, "Dr. Ambedkar's Strategies Against Untouchability and the Caste System", Indian Institute of Dalit Studies, Working Paper Series, Volume 3, November 4.

Ranjithkumar, A., 2011, "Ambedkar's Notion of Social Justice—A Different Perspective", *International Journal of Scientific and Engineering Research*, Volume 2, Issue 12, December.

Satya Pal, P.D., 2012, "Dr. B.R. Ambedkar and His Vision for Reconstruction of Indian Society", *International Journal of Multidisciplinary Educational Research*, Volume 1, Issue 2, June.

8

Wage Discrimination in India

Exploring the Impact of Gender

Praveen Mishra

Social Profile of Women

India has long been defined by a strict system of social stratification.[1] India is a society where the male is greatly revered. Therefore, women, especially the young girls, get very little respect and standing in this country.[2] Discrimination against women starts from the day a girl child is born. When a baby girl is born there is a general gloom in the family, contrary to the birth of a baby boy whose arrival on earth is celebrated with much pomp and joy. Because of lack of acceptance from the male dominant society, Indian women suffer immensely. Women are responsible for bearing children, yet they are malnourished and in poor health. Women are also overworked in the field and complete all of the domestic work. Most Indian women are uneducated. Although the country's Constitution says women have equal status to men, women are powerless and are mistreated inside and outside the home.[3] There may be little exception to this, but generally a girl is considered as a liability.[4]

In the realm of employment, hierarchical norms define the types of occupations into which a person might enter, as well as the conditions of employment he or she may expect to encounter.[5] Many industries remain *de facto* segregated by caste and gender.[6]

In the rural areas, women are mainly involved as cultivators and agricultural labourers. In the urban areas, almost 80 per cent of the women workers are working in the unorganized sectors such as household industries, petty trades and services, buildings and construction.[7] Workers in rural India, a majority of whom are illiterate and unskilled, have few opportunities, but to engage in agricultural activities. It appears that while men often manage to move out into other activities or migrate to other areas in search of work, women have fewer options. They remain as a flexible labour force in agriculture—as own account workers, casual agricultural labour or unpaid family workers.[8]

According to the Annual Survey of Industries of 2004-05 the gender pay gap for regular workers in the formal or organized sector was 57 per cent, which is much higher than among casual workers in the formal sector which was over 35-37 per cent. And in agriculture, where an estimated 60 per cent of all operations are handled exclusively by women, the hourly wage rates vary from 50 to 75 per cent of male rates.[9] A survey done by the World Economic Forum (WEF) last year showed that there is a yawning gender gap in the corporate sector too.

The average annual income of a woman is $1,185, less than a third of a man's $3,698 in corporate India.[10] The Government is no better as an employer. Two of its much touted welfare schemes, Integrated Child Development Services (ICDS) and National Rural Health Mission (NRHM) rely on the underpaid work of lakhs of women who are paid "an honorarium" well below the minimum wage. A negative relationship of wages with ratio of female workers in total employment shows that as number of female workers increases the total expenditure of an enterprise on total emoluments declines indicating that females are being paid lower than their male counterparts due to their low quality jobs or due to low bargaining strength. This confirms the general trend of females being underpaid in the unorganized sector of India and so "feminization of poverty".

Thus, in spite of the fact that women constitute a significant part of the workforce in India they lag behind men in terms of work participation and quality of employment.[11] While there has been an improvement in the work participation rate of women, it continues to be substantially less in comparison to the work participation rate of men.

Causes of Wage Discrimination

In India traditionally women bear the primary household responsibilities. Societal and religious norms place the burden of family duties disproportionately on women. Because of this, men are perceived to be more stable in jobs *vis-à-vis* women. Given the higher probability of dropping out of the labour market, employers discriminate against women as they enter into the labour market because they expect future career interruptions. As women move-up the occupation structure and gain job experience, employers become aware of their reliability and therefore, discriminate less.

Child care provisions, maternity leave, voluntary leave and other concessions such as these are certainly not available to the women at the lower end of the wage distribution. Women at the bottom of the distribution who do not get the benefits of such provisions would have a higher probability of dropping out of the labour force or participate less intensely in the labour market and employers could discriminate against them for this reason.[12]

Despite the Government's attempts at improving women's working conditions, inequalities remain. Men are more likely to get promotions than women besides, for men the nature of their jobs often changed with these promotions, unlike women, who usually only got increased responsibility and higher workload. Promotion policies are better in the public sector and unionized companies. However, the provision for facilities at the workplace is inadequate, regardless of whether the company is unionized.[13]

Genesis of Labour Laws

The labour laws of Independent India derive their origin, inspiration and strength partly from the views expressed by important nationalist leaders during the days of national freedom struggle, partly from the debates of the Constituent Assembly and partly from the provisions of the Constitution and the International Conventions and Recommendations.[14] The Labour Laws were also influenced by important human rights and the conventions and standards that have emerged from the United Nations. These include right to work of one's choice, right against discrimination, prohibition of child labour, just and humane conditions of work, social security, protection of wages, redress of grievances, right to organize and form trade unions, collective bargaining and participation in management.[15]

India's International Commitments Against Discrimination

UN Charter: The UN Charter provides in its preamble that there is a need "to reaffirm faith in fundamental human rights, in the dignity and worth of the human person, in the equal rights of men and women."

Universal Declaration of Human Rights: The Universal Declaration of Human Rights (UDHR) which followed and which forms the basis of bills of rights of many national constitutions was equally clear providing in article 1 that, "All human beings are born free and equal in dignity and rights". Article 2 speaks of the entitlement of all persons to the enjoyment of the rights contained within the Declaration "without distinction of any kind, such as race, colour, sex, language, religion, political or other opinion, national or social origin, property, birth or other status." The two instruments coming out of the UDHR, the International Covenant on Civil and Political Rights, 1966 (ICCPR) and the International Covenant on Economic Social and Cultural Rights, 1966 (ICESCR) also so provide equal protection before the law to all.

International Instruments prohibiting specific discrimination include: Convention on the Elimination of All Forms of Discrimination against Women, The Migrant Workers Convention and Convention on the Rights of Persons with Disabilities, 2006.

Governments combat discrimination based on race, gender or ethnic origin by[16]—

(a) Promoting equality of opportunity by outlawing discrimination and making health care and education available to all, and

(b) Seeking equality of results by granting preferences to members of disadvantaged groups. The second approach has been given a variety of labels, including benign quotas, reverse discrimination, reservation policy, employment equity, positive discrimination, positive action and affirmative action.

Constitutional Provisions

The Constitution of India guarantees equality as 'Fundamental Rights' in Articles 14, 15 and 16 under Part III. Article 14 guarantees equality before law and the equal protection of laws. Article 15 prohibits discrimination 'only' on the basis of religion, race, caste, sex, place of birth, or any of them. Article 15 also allows for special provisions to be made for women, children, socially and educationally backward classes of citizens as well as the Scheduled Castes and the Scheduled Tribes (SCs and STs)—such special provisions shall not be considered discriminatory. Article 16 provides for equality of opportunity in matters of public employment. It also allows the state to make reservations in favour of the SC, ST and Other Backward Classes. While the Constitution does not specifically mention reservation for women, the Constitutional (74th Amendment) Act, 1992, brought in provisions mandating one-third reservations for women in local governance bodies. These guarantees apply to state and public institutions.

Other Labour Laws to Combat Discrimination

Under the Constitution of India, Labour is a subject in the Concurrent List where both the Central and State Governments are competent to enact legislations. As a result, a large number of labour laws have been enacted catering to different aspects of labour, namely occupational health, safety, employment, training of apprentices, fixation, review and revision of minimum wages, mode of payment of wages, payment of compensation to workmen who suffer injuries as a result of accidents or causing death or disablement, bonded labour, contract labour, women labour and child labour.

Laws Governing Wages

- The Payment of Wages Act, 1936
- The Minimum Wages Act, 1948
- The Payment of Bonus Act, 1965
- The Equal Remuneration Act, 1976

Against this scenario, it would appear that women are guaranteed equality, equal protection of laws, equality of status and opportunity, thus, redeeming the perambulatory promise of Justice: social, economic and political. The mainstream of Indian society continues to fall short in the realization of full equality for the marginalized groups, particularly women. The disparities in wage earnings between men and women are matched by disparities in employment distributions. employment distribution resembles is characterized by relatively high female representation in low-skilled intensive industries such as garments, food products, beverages, and tobacco, and relatively high male representation in higher skilled and capital intensive industries such as industrial chemicals, glass, iron and steel, fabricated metals, and machinery.[17]

Conclusion and Suggestions

For economic development it is crucial to try and erode this discriminatory social norm by encouraging policies and education that underline the value of women in society and in particular in the labour market. We need to think about targeted policies that change social norms and society's perceptions of what women are capable of. In that sense, our understanding of what policies are effective in shifting deeply embedded cultural norms like gender discrimination is extremely limited.

Notes

1. Vikraman Nair, 2011, The Search for Equality Through Constitutional Process: The Indian Experience, *ACTA JURIDICA* 255, 256 (2011).
2. http://members.tripod.com/global_india1/current.html
3. *Ibid.*
4. Mrs. Indira Nair, Discrimination Against Women, *Central India Law Quarterly.*
5. CTR. FOR HUM. RTS. and Global Just. and HUM. RTS. Watch, *Supra* Note 6, At 55; Surinder Mediratta, Oxford Handbook of Law, Women, and Employment: Policies, Issues, Legislation, and Case Law 2 (2009).
6. CTR. FOR HUM. RTS. and Global JUST. and HUM. RTS. Watch, Caste Discrimination Against *Dalits* or so-called Untouchables in India 54 (2007), *available at* www2.ohchr.org/english/bodies/cerd/docs/ngos/chrgj-hrw.pdf
7. Ministry of Labour and Employment Government of India. Available at http://labour.nic.in/content/division/women-labour.php
8. Sukti Dasgupta and Ratna M. Sudarshan, 2011, "Issues in Labour Market Inequality and Women's Participation in India's National Rural Employment Guarantee Programme", Working Paper No. 98, Policy Integration Department International Labour Office Geneva, February.
9. http://articles.timesofindia.indiatimes.com/2011-03-09/india/28671960_1_gender-parity-equal-remuneration-act-wage-discrimination
10. *Ibid.*
11. http://www.legalindia.in/labour-law-in-india
12. Shantanu Khanna, "Gender Wage Discrimination in India: Glass Ceiling or Sticky Floor?" Working Paper No. 214, Centre for Development Economics, Department of Economics, Delhi School of Economics, Delhi.
13. Berta Esteve-Volart, *Gender Discrimination and Growth: Theory and Evidence from India,* London School of Economics and Political Science, The Suntory Centre, Suntory and Toyota International Centre for Economics and Related Disciplines, London School of Economics and Political Science.
14. Report of the Working Group on Labour Laws and Other Regulation, Twelfth Five Year Plan, http://planningcommission.nic.in/aboutus/committee/wrkgrp12/wg_labour_laws.pdf
15. http://www.caaa.in/Image/19ulabourlawshb.pdf
16. United Nations Expert Group Meeting on Managing Diversity in the Civil Service, United Nations Headquarters, New York, 3-4 May, 2001. Available at http://unpan1.un.org/intradoc/groups/public/documents/un/unpan 000786.pdf
17. *The Impact of Trade Liberalization on Gender Wage Differentials in India's Manufacturing Sector*, Nidhiya Menon, Brandeis University, Yana van der Meulen Rodgers, Rutgers University, December 2006, Women's and Gender Studies Department, Rutgers University, New Brunswick, NJ 08901.

9
Indian State and Annihilation of Caste

Nagesh Chaudhary

Introduction

Indian state is part of the Indian society and the Indian society is built on caste-based social order. That way, State or the Government can do very little to destroy the caste system because as the state is built on the caste and the caste society is controlled by the top castes—the state cannot go against the system even if some among the state runners decide to do so. So, can such a state annihilate caste whichever political party comes to power? Or can anti-caste people become rulers? This has not happened so far since the Independence.

Caste and the Constitution

Dr. Ambedkar had written a paper "Mr. Gandhi and the Emancipation of the Untouchables" in 1942 to be presented in the conference at Quebec, Canada, organised by the Institute of Pacific Relations. In that paper there is a chapter on "Caste and Constitution". This paper was published in a book form in 1943. In the chapter named above Dr. Ambedkar says, "In framing a Constitution the social structure must always be kept in mind. The political structure must be related to the social structure. The operation of the social forces is not confined to the social field.

They pervade the political field also."[1] His emphasis was on political system being according to the social system. In the same paper he demands political rights for the untouchables. Says he, "the only safety against such peoples to have political rights, which the untouchables claim as safeguards against the tyranny of the Hindu Majority defined in the Constitution."[2] Thus, Dr. Ambedkar himself has asked for the safeguards for the *Dalits* in the Constitution. He himself was the Chairman of the Drafting Committee of the Constitution of India which came into operation in 1950, after his above thoughts in the year 1942. The Constitution is meant to run the state or guide the rulers in different branches of the state machinery—administration, judiciary, and legislative bodies. The Constitution of India as it has been drafted by Dr. B.R. Ambedkar, the most vociferous proponent of annihilation of caste one can expect that it contains guidelines to state to annihilate the caste. The Constitution in its Preamble states—"to secure to all its citizens—JUSTICE, social, economic and political, EQUALITY of status and opportunity and to promote among them all FRATERNITY, assuring the dignity of the individual.[3] The Preamble is the resolve and it is not the article of fundamental rights. That is why Preamble is resolved to achieve—secure justice, liberty, equality and fraternity. These resolves under Preamble have not been achieved by the state since the time the Constitution has come into force. The Articles on the Right to Equality: The Articles 14 to 17 are given under the Right to Equality in the Constitution of India. It includes—equality before law (Article 14), prohibition of discrimination on grounds of religion, race, caste, sex or place of birth (Article 15), equality of opportunity in matters of public employment (which includes reservation for backward classes) (Article 16), abolition of untouchability (Article 17). What has been the impact of these articles on the social system? Has untouchability been abolished? Untouchability is very much in vogue today, in the Indian society, in urban as well as in rural India. In the Constitution there is a clear mention that state shall abolish the untouchability. Dr. Ambedkar was also of the view that unless caste system is annihilated untouchability will not go. So, article on abolition of untouchability has no meaning as untouchability still exists. Article 14 states that, "state shall not deny to any person equality before the law or the equal protection of the laws within the territory of India." This article does not mention about equality of castes before law, i.e. society maintains inequality of the castes and the Constitution provides equality before law at personal level and not on caste level. Thus it, under Article 15(1), states, prohibition of discrimination on grounds of religion, race, caste, sex or place of birth or any of them. Section 2 states "no citizen shall on grounds only of religion, race, caste, sex, place of birth or any of them, be subject to any disability, liability, restriction or condition with regard to—(a) access to shops, public restaurants, hotels and places of public entertainment; or (b) the use of wells, tanks, bathing ghats, roads and places or public resort maintained wholly or partly out of State funds or dedicated to the use of the general public. Nothing in this article shall prevent the State from making any special provision for women and children. [Nothing in this article or in clause (2) of Article 29 shall prevent the State from making any special provision for the advancement of any socially and educationally backward classes of citizens or for the Scheduled Castes and the Scheduled Tribes.] This article aims at treating people equally at public places. This article, section 2 prohibits people from discriminatory behaviour and it aims at preventing people from practising untouchability. This article is reinforced by Article 17—Abolition of Untouchability. Only additional provision is observing untouchability is punishable offence. Thus, under fundamental rights articles, the section on right to equality relates mostly to untouchability. The articles do not say that untouchables are equal to other castes. Article 16— equality of opportunity in matters of public employment states that state shall not discriminate in employment based on caste, race, religion etc... Section 3 of this article proposes law for reservation for backward classes. The word used is backward class of citizens. That means the Constitution does not pin-point the existence of caste hierarchy. Because of this lacuna backward class and backward caste relationship had to be got cleared by the Courts and by the Commissions. Kalelkar Commission and Mandal Commission had given the criteria, namely social and economic and then the backward castes have been identified. Scheduled Castes and Scheduled Tribes have been identified for reservation in Article 15(4).

Failure to abolish Untouchability

Though, the Constitution has included in fundamental rights—right to equality, it has failed to establish those rights. The state has failed to abolish untouchability. The untouchability, with a slight change, is in practice in Indian society, both in urban as well as in rural areas. The state, although proclaims abolition of untouchability by law it has failed to infuse that culture in the social behaviour. Who runs the state? The question then arises why the Constitution has not been implemented in words, deeds and spirit? It can be said, as there was need to introduce articles on rights to equality the inbuilt inequality in society was recognised. The class which is running the Indian State according to the Constitution is not doing so as per the spirit of the Constitution. The ruling class is synonymous with upper castes. Is the Indian State identified with upper caste in the Constitution? The provisions in the fundamental rights and in directive principles mean state is giving concessions to the lower castes, S.Cs. and S.Ts. The provisions in the Constitution for reservation and resolve to abolish untouchability means corrective measures adopted by the upper caste rulers. The language would have been different had it been on behalf of the untouchables or backward castes. Had the governing class been SCs, STs or backward castes, the Constitution would have been different, would have been entirely what Dr. Ambedkar wanted it to be or *Dalits*, lower castes, wanted it to be. The upper castes are fooling the *Dalits* today, by saying that Constitution is what Dr. Ambedkar wanted it to be. But, he was not the happy man over the Constitution. He was not satisfied over mere phrasing of right to equality. He wanted social equality, which is a long awaited dream to become reality. Some *Dalits* are taking pride in depicting Dr. Ambedkar as architect of the Constitution. But, they are not as keen as Dr. Ambedkar was for annihilation of the caste system and untouchability. Hence, there is little use of the Constitution for changing the governing class. The Constitution is not the means for systemic change. There is sprinkling of persons from the *Dalits*, tribals, other backward classes, Muslims etc. in the governing class. This sprinkling of personalities (persons) does not constitute the governing class. These personalities do not demand social or systemic change. They cannot go against the dictum of the governing class. The Constitution having provisions for reservation for socially and educationally backward classes means it presupposes—admits it is the governing class which is giving the concessions to the lower strata. Thus, the Constitution admits that the governing class in India is other than the SCs, STs, OBCs and minorities. Had these castes been the governing class, there would not have been the need to demand reservation. The governing class does not demand. It gives. Hence, the governing class in India is giving reservations and filling the quota as it suits that class. Never ever the governing class will fully implement the quota. That class, through, the Supreme Court, has already limited quota to 50 per cent for 85 per cent population but actually representation of reserved category castes is below 10 per cent in the top echelons of the bureaucracy. That shows how the ruling class is using the Constitution for its dominance. Even the 50 per cent reservation is a mockery, as that percentage has not been fulfilled, keeping for itself above 90 per cent services. Thus, in administration it is the governing class which has 90 per cent share. Indian State Administration is thus the upper caste administration. Proportionate share or reservation has not altered the upper caste nature of the Indian state. Till today reservation has done little or no damage to the Brahmanic hold of the Indian state. That shows how Indian state has remained the Hindu state under the Hindu Nation; that is in the grip of upholders of the caste system. Anti-Caste Measures and the State: What are the anti-caste measures? The measures that can bridge the gap between upper and lower castes are to be taken. These measures are enumerated by the anti-caste ideologies in the Indian history. Buddha was the first guiding force behind these measures. He was against *Varṇa* system and the focus of his ideology was to look to the problems of masses. He professed peoples' language as medium of education and not the Sanskrit language. He curtailed the authority of Brahmins. Brahmins or Brahmanism was not the ideology that was followed by Ashoka to Brihadratha. Mass education was adopted by these Maurya rulers. Dr. B.R. Ambedkar says, "... the Maurya period was a period when *Chaturvarṇa* was completely annihilated, when the *Shudras*, who constituted the mass of the people, came into their own and become the rulers of the country. The period of defeat and darkness is the period when *Chaturvarṇa* flourished to the damnation of the greater part of the people of the country."[4] The society became divided entirely after the Maurya rules. That connotes that when the rulers are guided by anti-caste ideology then only the state can be an instrument for breaking caste-*Varṇa* hierarchy. After the Buddhist state, Indian society became caste and untouchability ridden. During Muslim and British rule again the Brahmin power over the rulers was not a binding force. Those rulers had their own set of rules. But, these rulers were not consciously anti-caste. They themselves did not follow caste hierarchy but they were to rule on the foundation of the caste society. British rulers were more harmful than Muslim to the Brahmanic traditions. British brought equality before law and made such laws that were against the caste laws. The measures adopted by the British curtailed the Brahmanic hold. But, the British, as such, were not against the caste system and State Intervention in Religion. Dr. Ambedkar in his thesis, "Annihilation of Caste" suggested—(1) There should be only one standard book of Hindu Religion, acceptable to all Hindus and recognised by all Hindus. This, of course, means that all other books of Hindu religion such as *Vedas*, *Shastras* and *Puranas*, which are treated as sacred and authoritative, must be by law cease to be so and the preaching of any doctrine, religious or social contained in these books should be penalised. (2) ... It should be provided by law that no Hindu shall be entitled to be a priest unless he has passed an examination prescribed by the state and hold a *sanad* from the state permitting him to practise. (3) No ceremony performed by a priest who does not hold a *sanad* shall be deemed to be valid in law and it should be made penal for a person who has no *sanad* to officiate as a priest. (4) A priest should be the servant of state and should be subject to the disciplinary action by the state in the matter of his morals, belief and worship, in addition to his being subject along with other citizens to the ordinary law of the land." He further said in regard to the issue of annihilating caste, "The whole thing is abominable and is due to the fact that the priestly class among Hindus is subject neither to law nor to morality.... It is a pest which divinity seems to have let loose on the masses for their mental and moral degradation. The priestly class must be brought under control by some such legislation.... It will democratise it by throwing it open to everyone it will certainly help to kill the Brahmanism and will also help to kill Caste, which is nothing but Brahmanism incarnate."[5]

Reservation

Reservation measure was brought for the first time by the British rulers. During British period only the personalities like Jyotirao Phule, Dr. B.R. Ambedkar, Periyar Ramasami arose and came to the limelight. This was possible because Brahmins had no power to stop the British from imparting education to backward castes and untouchables. That liberal stand, compared to Brahmin rule, in which *Shudras*, untouchables had no access to education gave an opportunity to non-Brahmins. That measure of British was a cause for rise of personalities like Phule-Ambedkar-Sahu Maharaj who took the cudgels to oppose caste—*Varṇa* system. All these personalities who were anti-caste and supported for the social equality demanded education and reservation for non-Brahmins. Bureaucracy, as we see today, is the creation of British rule and in British period bureaucracy was dominated by Brahmins. So, Brahmins were the ruling clique for the masses and the state was dependent on Brahmins and by corollary the subjects were directly under the Brahmin administration. So, in the British rule, to curtail the hold of Brahmins, demand for education and quota in services was a demand in the right direction. All anti-Caste revolutionaries demanded reservations. These personalities adopted anti-Brahman philosophy. For, example Phule opposed Brahmanic philosophy, their scriptures, the gods and values. He had sown the seeds of Cultural

Revolution. So, was the case of E.V. Ramasami of Madras—South India. Prince of Kolhapur State—Prince Sahu, too, was a staunch anti-Brahmin ruler. As a step to empower the non-Brahmins, he started mass education and brought in a measure of reservation—giving 50 per cent seats to non-Brahmin castes, including Muslims. British rule started reservation for depressed castes and backward castes. That means this anti-caste measure is an outcome of the social revolutionaries like—Phule, Sahu, Periyar and Ambedkar. Of course, some British officials were aware of the overwhelming percentage of Brahmins in administration and they, too, were in favour of reservation.The report of the Backward Classes Commission (generally known as *Mandal Commission Report*, Vol. VII, second part, p. 147, 1980) says, "As far back as 1851, the Madras Revenue Board had entrusted the District Collectors to restrict the number of the Brahmin entrants into the services."[6]

What State can do Annihilate Caste?

At present the Indian state is in the grip of upper caste governing class. The governing class is not same as the ruling class. In India ruling people are from different castes. They represent different castes of both upper and backward including *Dalits* and untouchables. But these people do not make a class with uniform ruling ideology. Over all ruling ideology followed is Brahmanic. Dr. Ambedkar purposely used the word governing class in his book "*What Gandhi and Congress have done to the Untouchables*". He said governing class is the class which controls the sentiments of the people and which controls the administration. Thereby he meant cultural control and bureaucratic control or administrative control. He said governing class in India are Brahmins. Second place he gives to Banias. Can State or the Government change the Brahmin culture which controls the minds of the people? The state follows the established culture. Whichever political party comes to power it cannot bring about the cultural change. If the state is captured by the political force which is against the Brahmanic culture can do that. So, far this has not happened in India. State (government) can change the bureaucratic set-up and make it non-Brahmanic. But, this too has not been attempted fully in India. The ruling party or parties who tried to curtail the hold of upper castes by implementing reservation for lower castes have been dethroned by the governing class. Example is of V.P. Singh Government in 1990. The measure was not for complete change in the bureaucracy it was only a measure which sought 27 per cent jobs for the backward classes. That was not sufficient to alter the entire administrative control of the Brahmins or upper castes. But that was opposed furiously and whole country witnessed an unparallel holocaust in the independent history of India. The state even today is not free from Manu impact. Dr. Ambedkar says, "It might be argued that the inequality prescribed by Manu in his *Smriti* is after all of historical importance. It is past history and cannot be supposed to have any bearing on the present conduct of the Hindu. I am sure nothing can be greater error than this Manu is not the matter of the past. It is even more than a past of the present. It is a 'living past' and therefore, as really present as any present can be."[7] To be in practice by the state how state can be useful to annihilate caste? The philosophy rulers resort today is Manuist. Manu says, "the king should observe four-*Varṇa* hierarchy, i.e. he should do first the work of Brahmins and then of other *Varṇas* in the scale.[8] Is not the state today do what Brahmins want first? Hence, when the rulers will be such that they will completely defy Manu in ruling then only state will be able to annihilate caste system. The ruling ideology will have to be anti-Manu, i.e. free from Brahminic system (the Hindu Nation). The dominant culture in the country will have to be egalitarian. This will be possible not by capturing the state power only, but by creating alternate cultural power, the Bahujan system or Bahujan Nation.

Notes

1. *Dr. Babasaheb Ambedkar: Writings and Speeches*, Vol. 9, p. 423, 1991, Education Department, Government of Maharashtra, Bombay.
2. *Ibid.*, p. 425.

3. *The Constitution of India, The Preamble.*
4. Dr. B.R. Ambedkar, *Annihilation of Caste*, p. 63; *Dr. Baba Saheb Ambedkar: Writings and Speeches*, Vol. I (1979), The Education Department, Government of Maharashtra, Bombay.
5. *Annihilation of Caste*; *Dr. Baba Saheb Ambedkar: Writings and Speeches*, Vol. 1, p. 77, 1979, Education Department, Government of Maharashtra, Bombay.
6. *The Report of the Backward Classes Commission*, Volume I, First Part (1981), Controller of Publications, Government of India, Delhi.
7. *Dr. Baba Saheb Ambedkar: Writings and Speeches*, Vol. 12, p. 719, 1993, Education Department, Government of Maharashtra, Bombay.
8. *Manusmriti*, ch. 4, stanza 23.

10

B.R. Ambedkar on Human Rights and Constitutional Reforms

Kakali Bezbaruah

Dr. Bhimrao Ramji Ambedkar affectionately known as Babasaheb was an Indian social reformer, jurist, political leader, philosopher, and historian. His personality was multi-dimensional. Ambedkar the greatest Indian and thus can be said to be the illustrious son of India. He was born in a family which was a part of the Hindu Mahar caste on 14th April, 1891 at Mhow in present day State of Madhya Pradesh. This caste was considered to be a low caste and was treated as untouchables in the Hindu society.

At an early age, he had bitter taste of caste discrimination and was deprived of socially as well as economically. He had great interest in education and was highly educated. Ambedkar received two doctorates one from Columbia University, New York and other from the London School of Economics. While studying abroad, he mixed with students of other nationalities and races which was an eye opener for him. Some people whom he met there inspired Ambedkar and reinforced his commitment to social reform.

After returning from his studies, despite his foreign education, he was treated differently at work due to his low caste. Ambedkar was humiliated even by his peers. He got firsthand knowledge of the atrocities faced by the untouchables. Such atrocities shook his conscience and gave him inner strength to fight against the prevalent social system. Instead of accepting the oppressive circumstances he began his movement to eradicate caste system and untouchability. He moved into the political arena so that the untouchables can take the advantage of opportunities afforded by British Contitutional Reform. In 1924, he started legal practice in Bombay and founded the Bahishkrit Hitkarani Sabha and Samaj Samanta Sangha to uplift the *Dalit* economically and educationally. In 1927, he led the Mahad march at the Chowdar Tank in Colaba near Bombay for the untouchables so that they can take water from the public tank. In 1930, Dr. Ambedkar launched the temple entry movement at the Kalaram Temple, Nasik. This movement is another landmark in the struggle for human rights and social justice. Through his mass movements, he gave effective expression to the grievances of the rural people. His struggle against the existing land tenure system saved the rural people from extreme economic exploitation. Again to stop the malpractices of moneylenders he presented a Bill in the State Legislative Assembly. Prior to 1935, he led different processions and through caste conferences, campaigns tried to unite the Mahars and other backward sections of the Indian society. He helped the Mahars and the other depressed classes receive reserved legislative seats and jobs. In 1936, he founded the Independent Labour Party and fought for the untouchable workers. As a leader of the depressed classes, Ambedkar attended three Round Table Conferences in London and in those Conferences he championed constitutional safeguards for untouchables. He was the pioneer of human rights advocacy and thus a true champion of human rights. Throughout his life, he put up valiant struggle to help the neglected classes to lead a better life with dignity and self-respect.

He was also known as the chief architect of Constitution of India. He played a significant role in framing the Constitution of India. After Independence, Prime Minister Jawaharlal Nehru appointed Ambedkar as the Chairman of the Drafting Committee of India. He presented the Draft Constitution in February 1948 and it was adopted in 1949. He strongly recommended democracy as the governing principle of human relationship. Along with political dimension, he emphasized social and economic dimensions of democracy and contributed to the understanding of the socio-economic political problems of India. He banned untouchability constitutionally and created constitutional rights that placed the poor people equally among others. He framed the Fundamental Rights and Duties and along with it Direcive Principles of State Policy. He argued for extensive economic and social rights for women. He kept the clauses of the Constitution flexible so that amendments could be changed when situation demands. He provided an inspiring Preamble to the Constitution ensuring justice, liberty, equality and fraternity. Ambedkar used all his experience and incorporated his valuable ideas in drafting the Constitution. Drafting a Constitution is not an easy task. So, Pandit Jawaharlal Nehru remarked that "Dr. Ambedkar had played the most important part in framing India's Constitution. No one took great trouble and care over Constitution-making than Dr. Ambedkar." According to him, Ambedkar is a symbol of revolt.

Thus, his reforms to abolish caste and untouchability, his views regarding women empowerments and the social movements make him a towering figure that fought for the people. In his entire life Ambedkar fought because he wanted to make India a strong democratic nation. India got Independence so many years ago, but still till today in some places *Dalits* are deprived. *Dalits* has to suffer for their basic rights that they need as human beings. So, along with academic education, humanistic education should be provided to each and every human being in order to make the people aware of the fact that we all are equal and we have to respect our fellow human beings. The *Dalits* who are divided on the basis of occupation, community, culture and language etc. should unite and come forward like their leader Ambedkar. We on the other hand can organize *Dalits* by being united for Human Rights. We all are capable of creating a new world but we have to follow the path shown by Ambedkar. He dedicated his life for the people. He was the liberator of all oppressed people. His principles will always guide the nation on the path of justice, liberty, equality and fraternity. His contributions were universally acclaimed, but he was not satisfied for what he had achieved because untouchability persisted in India. The last revolution before his death was that he took refuge in Lord Buddha on 14th October, 1956 along with his 5 lakh followers out of disgust of Hinduism. Ambedkar in his life went on marching ahead without fear and he succeeded in his endeavours. Though he could not completely fulfil his dreams due to narrowness of the society at that time, so it is our responsibility to come forward and complete it. It might be possible by virtue of the broadness of the society.

In this chapter an attempt has been made to explore Ambedkar's contribution towards Human Rights and Constitutional Reform and to examine his philosophy to socially reconstruct India.

11
Human Rights and Constitutional Reforms with Special Reference to Abolition of Untouchability and Role of Dr. B.R. Ambedkar

Chintamani Rout

Untouchability

Untouchability is the practice of ostracising a group by segregating them from the main-stream by social custom or legal mandate. The excluded group could be one that did not accept the norms of the excluding group and historically included foreigners, nomadic tribes, lawbreakers and criminals and those suffering from a contagious disease. This exclusion was a method of punishing lawbreakers and criminals and also protected traditional societies against contagion from strangers and the infected. A member of the excluded group is known as untouchable. The term is commonly associated with treatment of *Dalit* communities, who are considered 'Polluting' among the people of South Asia, but the term has been used for other groups as well, such as the Burakumin of Japan, Cagotus in Europe, or the Al-Akhdam in Yemen. Untouchability has been made illegal in post-Independent India, and *Dalit* subsequently empowered, although some prejudice against them continues, especially in rural pockets dominated by certain other backward caste (OBC) groups.

Reform Movements

The earliest known historical people to have rejected the caste system were Gautam Buddha and Mahavira. Their teachings eventually became independent religions called Buddhism and Jainism. The earliest known reformation within Hinduism happened during the medieval period when the *Bhakti* movements and Ramanuja actively encouraged the participation and inclusion of *Dalits*. Ramanuja took *Dalit* disciples publicly into his fold and even took them into temple. He put forth the *Dalit* born Nammalvar as the Philosophical head of the sect and propagated Nammalvar's work as *Dravid Veda*.

In the nineteenth century, the *Brahmo Samaj*, *Arya Samaj* and the Ramakrishna Mission actively participated in the emanicipation of *Dalits*. While there always have been segregated places for *Dalits* to worship, the first 'upper-caste' temple to openly welcome *Dalits* into their fold was the Lakshminarayan Temple in Wardha in the year 1928. It was followed by the Temple Entry Proclamation issued by the last king of Travancore in the Indian state of Kerala in 1936.

The Sikh reformist *Satnami* movement was founded by Guru Ghasidas, born a *Dalit*. Another notable *guru* was Guru Ravidas, was also a *Dalit*. Other reformers, such as Jyotirao Phule, Ayyankali of Kerala and Iyothee Thass of Tamil Nadu worked for emancipation of *Dalits*. The 1930s saw key struggle between Mahatma Gandhi and B.R. Ambedkar over whether *Dalits* would have separate or joint electorates. Although he failed to get Ambedkar's support for a joint electorate, Gandhi nevertheless began the "*Harijan Yatra*" to help *Dalit* population.

Palwankar Baloo, a *Dalit* politician and a cricketer, joined the Hindu Mahasabha in the fight for independence. Namantar Andolan was part of a 16-year *Dalit* campaign to rename Marathwada University as Dr. Babasaheb Ambedkar Marathwada University. In 1977, the Chief Minister of Maharashtra, Vasantdada Patil, promised the *Dalit* Panthers that a renaming would happen; the Maharashtra Legislature passed a resolution to this effect in July 1978. Thereafter, there were attacks on *Dalits* by non-*Dalits* and upper caste Hindus for a fortnight. A new Chief Minister, Sharad Pawar, postponed implementation and this led to a Long March being organised by *Dalit* leaders and sympathisers, in December 1979 thousands of participants and prominent leaders were arrested. The renaming, involving some compromise, finally took place on 14 January, 1994.

Other Hindu groups have reached out to the *Dalit* community in an effort to reconcile with them. On August 2006, *Dalit* activist Namdeo Dhasal engaged in dialogue with the Rashtriya Swayamsevak Sangha in an attempt to "bury the hatchet". Hindu temples are increasingly receptive to *Dalit* priests, a function formerly reserved for Brahmins. Suryavanshi Das, for example, is the *Dalit* priest of a notable temple in Bihar. Anecdotal evidence suggests that discrimination against Hindu *Dalits* is on slow, but steady decline. Many Hindu *Dalits* have achieved affluence in society, although vast millions still remain poor. In particular, some *Dalit* intellectuals such as Chandrabhan Prasad have argued that the living standard of many *Dalits* have improved since the economic liberalization in 1993 and have supported their claims through large qualitative surveys. In urban India, discrimination against *Dalits* in the public sphere is greatly reduced, but rural *dalits* are struggling to elevate themselves. Government organizations and NGO's work to emancipate them from discrimination, and many Hindu organizations have spoken in their favour. Some groups and Hindu religious leaders have spoken in their favour and also spoken out against the caste system in general. However, the fight for temple entry rights for *Dalits* is far from finished and continues to cause controversy. More recently, *Dalits* in Nepal are now being accepted into priesthood (traditionally reserved for Brahmins). The *Dalit* priestly order is called "*Pandaram*".

Dr. B.R. Ambedkar, before his conversion to Buddhism, had examined Jainism, along with other religions, but he ruled out Jainism because its adherence to non-violence, was too extreme in his opinion. Ambedkar, however, continued to meet Jains to discuss religion, even on the last day of his life.

Government Action in India and the Provision under the Constitution of India

The 1950 national Constitution of India legally abolished the practice of untouchability and provided measures for positive discrimination in both educational institutions and public services for *Dalits* and other social groups who lie within caste system. Those are supplemented by official bodies such as the National Commission for Scheduled Castes and Scheduled Tribes. Article 17 deals with a peculiar problem of our country. Howsoever praiseworthy the caste system in its origin might have been, it certainly proved to be a disgrace to humanity, a threat to unity and a serious hindrance to social, educational and economic progress of our country. The treatment given to Scheduled Castes in India by higher caste Hindus can be comparable to that given to Negros by White people in America at least-up to the middle of the twentieth century; though in the eyes of law Scheduled Castes in India enjoyed slightly better status than Negroes of the United States of America. Mahatma Gandhi and other freedom fighters had realised that equal treatment to these castes was not only necessary for winning freedom for the nation but also for peace and progress of the country after Independence.

The practice of untouchability was, no doubt, prevalent in Hindus on a large scale but it was not altogether absent in other communities. The purpose of the article is to abolish untouchability in all its forms, whether it was untouchability within a community or between various communities. Article 17 abolishes 'untouchability' and forbids its practice in any form. The enforcement of any disability arising out of untouchability is not to be henceforth practiced in any form. If it is so practiced it shall be dealt with as an offence punishable in accordance with the law.

'Untouchability' is neither defined in the Constitution nor in the Act. The Mysore High Court has, however, held that the term is not to be understood in its literal or grammatical sense but to be understood as the "practice as it had developed historically" in this country. Understood in this sense, it is a product of the Hindu caste system according to which particular section amongst the

Hindus had been looked down as untouchables by the other sections of that society. A literal construction of the term would include persons who are treated as untouchables either temporarily or otherwise for various reasons, such as, suffering from infectious diseases or on account of social observance such as, are associated with birth or death or on account of social boycott resulting from caste or other dispute. In either case such persons can claim the protection or benefit either of Article 17 or of the Protection of Civil Rights Act, 1955.

In exercise of the powers conferred by Article 35 Parliament has enacted the Untouchability (Offences) Amending Act, 1955. This Act was amended by the untouchability (Offences) Amendment Act, 1976, in order to make the law more stringent to remove untouchability from the society. It has not been renamed as, "The Protection of Civil Rights Act, 1955." The expression 'Civil Right' is defined as "any right accruing to a person by reason of the abolition of untouchability by Article 17 of the Constitution." Under the amended Act any discrimination on the ground of untouchability will be considered an offence. It imposes a duty on public servants to investigate such offences. It provides that if a public servant, wilfully neglects the investigation of any offence punishable under this act, he shall be deemed to have abetted an offence punishable under this Act. The Protection of Civil Rights Act prescribes punishment which may extend to imprisonment up to six months and also with a fine which may extend to five hundred rupees or both for any one enforcing, on the ground of 'untouchability' religious disabilities like preventing any person from entering any place of public worship or from worshipping or offering prayers therein (section 3) or social disabilities, like (section 7), access to any shop, public restaurants, hotels or places of public entertainment (section 4) and refusing to admit persons to hospitals (section 5) and refusing sell goods or render sevices to any person (section 6) or for other offences, arising out of untouchability.

Role of Higher Judiciary in Removing Untouchability

In Asiad Project Workers case in *People's Union for Democratic*

Rights v. *Union of India*, AIR, 1982 SC 1473, the Supreme Court has held that the Fundamental Rights under Article 17 are available against private individuals and it is the Constitutional duty of the state to take necessary steps to see that these fundamental rights are not violated. It should be noted that Article 15(2) also helps in the eradication of untouchability. Thus, on the grounds of untouchability no person can be denied access to shops, public restaurants, hotels and places of entertainment or the use of wells, tanks, bathing ghats, road and places of public resort maintained wholly or partly out of State funds or dedicated to the use of general public. In *State of Karnataka* vs. *Appa Bala Ingale,* AIR 1993 SC 1126, the respondents were tried for offences under Sections 4 and 7 of the Protection of Civil Rights Act, 1955, convicted and sentenced to undergo simple imprisonment for one month and a fine of Rs. 100 each. The change against the respondents was that they restrained the complainant party by show of force from taking water from a newly dug up borewell (tubewell) on the ground that they were untouchables. The High Court acquitted them. The Supreme Court upheld the conviction. The Court held that the object of Article 17 and the Protection of Civil Rights Act is to liberate the society from blind and ritualistic adherence and traditional belief which has lost all legal or normal bases. It seeks to establish new ideas for society—equality to the *Dalits* as par with general public, absence of disabilities, restrictions or prohibitions on grounds of caste or religion.

In 1989, the Scheduled Castes and Scheduled Tribes (Prevention of Atrocities) Act has been passed by Parliament to prevent the commission of offences of atrocities against the members of the Scheduled Castes and Scheduled Tribes. It provides for special Courts for trial of such offences and matters connected therewith or incidental thereto and duty has been imposed on the State Government to ensure effective implementation of the provisions of the Act. The Act provides for enhanced punishment in cases of subsequent convictions which shall be imprisonment for not less than one year. The Act has been given overriding effect on other laws. Section 18 of the Act provides that Section 438 of the Code of Criminal Procedure shall not apply in relation to arrest under this Act (under Section 18).

National and International Perspective

Dalit is a designation for a group of people traditionally regarded as untouchable. *Dalits* are a mixed population, consisting of numerous social groups from all over India; they speak a variety of languages and practice a multitude of religions. There are many different names proposed for defining this group of people including *Panchams* (fifth-*varṇa*) and *Asprishya* (untouchables). *Dalits* are also found in Nepal, Pakistan, Sri Lanka and Bangladesh. Further wherever immigrants from those countries have left, caste has gone with them. As a result *Dalits* can also be found in the United States, United Kingdom, Singapore, Malayasia and Canada. Mohandas Karamchand Gaṇdhi coined the word *Harijan* and translated roughly as "Children of God" to identify the former untouchables. In addition the terms Scheduled Castes and Scheduled Tribes (SC and ST) are the official terms used in Government of India documents to identify the former untouchables and tribes.

While discrimination based on caste has been prohibited and untouchability abolished under the Constitution of India, discrimination and prejudice against *dalits* in South Asia remains. Since, its Independence in 1947, India has implemented an affirmative policy of reservation, the scope of which further expanded in 1974, to set aside and provide jobs and education opportunities in *Dalits*. By 1995 of all jobs in India, 17.2 per cent of the jobs were held by *Dalits*, greater than their proportion in Indian population. In 1997, India democratically elected K.R. Narayanan, a *Dalit* as the Nation's President. In 2001, the proportion of *Dalit* population was 16.2 per cent of India's population. The *Dalit* population is broadly distributed across Indian States and Districts. In 2001, the State of Punjab and the highest proportion of its population as *Dalit*, at about 29 per cent, and the State of Mizoram had the lowest at nearly zero. The Government of India recognises and protects them as Scheduled Castes and Scheduled Tribes.

Conclusion

The twenty first century, unlike the twentieth century, begins with a bang that is likely to influence the entire course of development of the century. The tragic part of the story is that while the humanity sits on huge wealth—physical and civilization to make everybody's life comfortable, if not decent, it is encountering unprecedented chronic violence, the world-wide unrest on one hand, and the state repression on the other. There are sections of the people who are struggling and asserting for transforming the world peacefully, if possible and necessary with little violence. There is a structural violence at some time, those who are challenging it. The forces working for peace, social harmony, economic justice, equal treatment for every section of the people and enlargement of democratic space are weak, mute and hesitant. It is this historical complexity that calls for positive and conscious intervention of peace loving, democratic minded people willing to strive for a better future for the humanity. It is in this context and these concerns that provided the backdrop for declaration of UN Decade of Human Rights Education (1995-2004).

India is one of those societies among the developing countries, which committed itself to the UN Declaration and took the initiative to encourage and support Human Rights education. As a part of this commitment, it has set-up National Human Rights Commission to monitor the human rights standards and promote human rights educations—NCERT, UGC and the Colleges and Universities were approached to promote human rights education. There is considerable enthusiasm in the form of discussions, seminars, workshops, conferences, regional level debates and academic support to these programmes like equal treatment to all irrespective of caste, colour, race and origin and above all the abolition of untouchability. This is the stage when one can take a stock of situation, discern the trends and directions and draw the lesion from experience to decide about the future of human rights education with regard to have a good, equalitarian civil society.

There are several Acts made by Parliament which give effect to the human rights set out in Parts III and IV of the Constitution.

The most important among them is Article 17 which abolishes untouchability and provides that the enforcement of any disability arising out of untouchability shall be an offence punishable in accordance with law. Parliament has enacted the Protection of Civil Rights Act, 1955 by way of follow-up legislation. Abolition of untouchability is a facet of equality. To secure enforcement of the right conferred by Article 17, it is necessary to invoke the provisions of the 1955 Act wherever necessary to bring equality among the citizens of the country.

References

Agarwal, H.O., 1999, *Human Rights*, Second Edition, Central Law Publications, Allahabad.

Jain, M.P., 2005, *Indian Constitutional Law*, Wadhwa, Nagpur, Maharashtra.

Johari, J.C., 1979, *Indian Government and Politics,* Fourth Edition, Vishal Publication, Delhi-Jallandhar.

Joshi, K.C., 2011, *The Constitutional Law of India*, Central Law Publications.

Journal of National Human Rights Commission, 2005, Volume 4, India.

Pande, G.S., 2009, *Constitutional Law of India,* Eleventh Edition, University Book House, Jaipur.

Pandey, J.N., 2006, *Constitutional Law of India*, C.L.A., Allahabad.

Pylee, M.V., 1998, *An Introduction to the Constitution of India*, Vikas Publishing House, New Delhi.

Rai, Kailash, 2008, *The Constitutional Law of India*, Seventh Edition, C.L.A., Allahabad.

Shukla, V.N., 2004, *Constitutional Law of India*, E.V.C., Lucknow.

12
B.R. Ambedkar's Struggle Against Untouchability

Md. Shah Noorur Rahman

Introduction

This chapter is an attempt to make an in-depth study of Ambedkar's experiences on untouchability and his struggle against it. It also highlights his efforts to do something for the emancipation of the depressed classes and his limitations.

Dr. Bhimrao Ramji Ambedkar (A.D.1891-1956) was one of the most important leaders in modern Indian history who played a major role in Indian politics and society, especially for the betterment and upliftment of the depressed and oppressed untouchables. He rose from a community of untouchables and became one of the major figures in modern Indian politics and society. He was a distinguished economist, a learned educationist, a brilliant lawyer, a reputed author, a great political leader and an immensely champion of human rights and dignity. He was also the founding father of the Constitution of Independent India. He was a champion jurist, a great political leader, a celebrated philosopher, a well-known thinker, an eminent anthropologist, an eloquent orator, a famous editor and an uncompromising revolutionary. But, above all, he left the mark in modern Indian history as to how one could attain the highest glory through self-help, self-respect and self-dignity.

Dr. Ambedkar was born on 14th April, 1891 in an untouchable community known as *Mahar* at Mhow in Madhya Pradesh. Being born into a poor *Mahar* (considered an Untouchable caste) family, Ambedkar spent his whole life fighting against social evils; social injustice, social inequality and social discrimination, the system of *Chaturvarṇa*—the categorization of Hindu society into four *varṇas*—and the Hindu Caste System. He became the representative of the voiceless millions of the depressed untouchables in India in his time.

Untouchability is one of the major problems in India since immemorial times. It has its roots in the Indian society and religion that is based on the caste system. The castes are further divided into so many sub-castes. The people of the lowest caste according to *Manu Smriti,* a Hindu Law Book, are treated untouchables. They do not belong to the fold of Hinduism. Nobody knows exactly about the origin of untouchability or the caste system itself in India. Some historians try to trace the origin of the caste system to the *Vedas,* the ancient religious books of the Hindus. The *Purusha Sukta* in the *Rig Veda* describes the creation of four *Varṇas,* namely the *Brahmin*, the *Kshatriya,* the *Vaishya* and the *Shudra.* The indigenous people of the country were outside the *Varṇa* system.

Experiences of Untouchability

Now, let us describe some of the experiences of Ambedkar faced in his life in the then Upper-caste Hindu dominated society as a son of untouchable family which will inform us the inhuman practices of this system. Ambedkar was brought up in the surrounding of an orthodox and rigid Hindu family that was divided on religious, castes, communal, provincial and regional lines. He complained that the Hindu society was just like a tower, which had several storeys without a ladder. One was to die in the storey in which one was born. There are several instances, which would show the kind of humiliation and injustice Ambedkar, being an untouchable, suffered in his early life. Ambedkar and other untouchable children were segregated and given no attention or assistance by the teachers in the school. They were not allowed to sit inside the classroom. Even if they needed to drink water somebody from a higher caste would have to pour that water from a height as they were not allowed to touch either water or the vessel that contained it. This task was usually performed for the young Ambedkar by the school peon, and if the peon was not available then he had to go without water. Ambedkar states this situation as *"No peon, No Water."*

On a hot summer day, once Ambedkar was going to meet his father along with his nephews at Goregaon, Satara district. They had to arrive at Masur railway station and from there they had to go to Goregaon, which was at a far off distance. The two children sat on a bullock cart and started their journey. But as soon as the owner of the cart came to know that they were *Mahars*, they were ordered to get down from the cart. The children offered double fare. Since, they were untouchables, the owner of the bullock cart did not take their money. In the scorching heat of the Summer the children were denied food and even water though the cart had all the facilities to get these essentials in the course of the journey. We can imagine what scars might have been left on the sensitive heart of a young, intelligent, energetic and precious boy.

Another shock was growing in the mind of Ambedkar. It was indeed a touching scene when he came to know that his hair defiled the purity of the barber who regarded the shaving of a buffalo a better and holier affair than a human being. What a terrible impression these cruel disabilities might have made upon the young mind. But he was quite strong, sensitive and yet very firm. All these maltreatments and ill-treatments created a spirit of patience in the child mind of Ambedkar. All such insulting refusals and ill treatments produced in him a burning hatred for Hinduism and that was quite natural.

The untouchables were prohibited to learn Sanskrit. Being an untouchable, Ambedkar was also compelled to take Persian instead of Sanskrit as the second language in the high school, though he was interested in learning Sanskrit. Sanskrit was the key to the study of the *Vedas.* According to Hindu law the *Vedas* were neither to be heard nor to be read by the *Shudras* and the untouchables. The teacher never touched the notebooks of the untouchable students. Some of them did not even ask them to recite poems or put any question to them for fear of being polluted. But at the same time, there was a Brahmin teacher in the high school who loved this boy very much and even dropped daily a part of his meal of boiled rice, bread, and vegetables into the hands of Ambedkar. But this is exceptional case.

Students from the socially backward communities especially untouchables were segregated and made to sit separately from the other people in schools. They were given gunny bags as mat to sit upon, unlike the others who were provided with wooden planks. The upper caste students and teachers hardly communicated with the students coming from the depressed classes. A blind and foolish tradition made the high caste students believe that even talking to children of the depressed classes would pollute them. This was the feeling of the Hindu society which pained Ambedkar.

The hardships undergone by Ambedkar in Baroda are known to all. The caste Hindus tried their best to prevent him from occupying a house on rent. His peons would not hand over files to him, because he would lose his caste status in the eyes of his colleagues. He would throw official papers on the table of the learned doctor from a distance. He would pour drinking water from the jug without touching him. Life became unbearable for a self-respecting, highly educated and cultured man like Ambedkar. It was a divine grace, which saved Ambedkar's life, which he was to spend in the emancipation of the untouchables from the thralldom of caste tyranny. Ambedkar had come to the firm conclusion that the social problems of the country required a political solution. So, he decided to fight the evil of untouchability all alone at any cost under any odd circumstances.

The Movements of the Untouchables

The movement of the untouchables against the injustice of the Hindu social order has a long history behind it. This history falls into two stages. Petitions and protests marked the first stage. The second stage is marked by open revolt in the form of direct action against the established Hindu religion.

The Government tried to discourage them by declaring that all public utilities and public institutions are open to all citizens including the untouchables. But, the untouchables were not satisfied with the only declaration of the policy of the Government. They began their movements that included several cases of direct action aiming at the demolition of the Hindu social order by applying dynamite to its very foundation. That is why, they started their fight against untouchability.

Burning of the *Manu Smriti*

The burning of the *Manu Smriti* took place at Mahad on December 20, 1927 by the untouchables. The function was a part of the campaign for establishing the right to take water from the Choudar tank. The burning of the *Manu Smriti* took place publicly and openly in a conference of untouchables. It was a deed of great daring and courage. It was an attack on the basic tenet of Hinduism. The *Manu Smriti,* that contains the Hindu codes, is insulting to persons of low castes. It deprived them of the rights of human-beings and crushed their personality. The conference felt that it was apt to lay down the goals of untouchables. The conference proclaimed that the untouchables wanted a complete overhauling of the Hindu social system. It further affirmed that this reconstruction must not be based on the old foundation of *Shastras.* It maintained that whatever be the character of the new foundation, it must be consonant with justice and equality between the Hindus and the *Shudras*. The *Manu Smriti* is the sacred scripture of the Hindus. Being scared it is infallible to them. Every Hindu believes in its sanctity and obeys its fundamental injunctions. Manu not only upholds caste and Untouchability, but also gives them a legal sanction. The *Manu Smriti* embodies the spirit of inequality. It keeps the untouchables outside of the Hindu fold because it did not acknowledge the fifth *Varṇa*. The untouchables were not at all happy with the principles of the *Manu Smriti.* Thus, they burnt it in front of the Brahmins. The burning of the *Manu Smriti* by the untouchables at Mahad in 1927 is a significant event in the history of the caste-ridden society in India. It has same significance and importance in the history of the emancipation of the untouchables in the country.

Refusal of Untouchables to Carry Dead Bodies

One of the duties of the untouchables is to remove the skin of and carry the dead animals of the Hindus in the villages. If the untouchables refused to perform these duties to the Hindus the land on which they lived is liable to be confiscated. They had to choose between doing the dirty work and facing starvation.

The important thing to note is that the conference of the untouchables, which met in Mahad, resolved that untouchables would neither remove the skin of the dead animals of the Hindus nor carry it or eat the carrion. The minor and major objectives of these resolutions were to foster among the untouchables self-respect, self-esteem and to strike a blow at the Hindu social order. It aimed at making the Hindus do their own works.

Temple Entry

Ambedkar carried out his fight on political as well as religious fronts. He wanted the untouchables to have the right to enter a Hindu temple, which was banned for them by the Hindu Law giver. So, in 1929, the Parvati temple entry *Satyagraha* was organized at Poona wherein the unarmed untouchables and caste Hindu participants were attacked and injured. Among them were the untouchables' Chamber leaders, Pandurang Nathuji Rajbhoj and N.V. Gadgil. N.V. Gadgil was popularly known as Kakasaheb Gadgil. After this there was a famous Kalaram temple entry at Nasik. The *Satyagraha* was carried out from 1930 to 1935, but when obduracy of the orthodox Hindu did not relent, Ambedkar made it clear before the public that though he was born as a Hindu, he would not die as a Hindu. He fulfilled this promise by embracing Buddhism. And till his death he was a Buddhist. The main aim of the temple entry *Satyagraha* was to make the entry possible in the temple for the untouchables. Indeed it was a herculean task in the context of time and space in the contemporary Hindu dominated society.

Choudar Tank Incident

It is true that Ambedkar's politics of agitation started with the Mahad march to the Choudar Tank. In 1925, the Municipality passed a resolution to keep open its tank to the depressed classes. In pursuance of the resolution, Ambedkar led a march to take water from the tank. The powerful majority of the conservative society was unwilling to part its hold and the power structure had to be confronted. The march was successful but after having fetched water from the tank, rumours were spread that the untouchables were also planning to enter the temple of Vireshwar situated in Mahad. Instigated by such rumours a large crowed of high caste Hindus armed with bamboo sticks attacked the untouchables. Delegates of the untouchables went to Ambedkar's bungalow and asked for a green signal to hit back. Ambedkar was not an extremist. He, like Gandhiji, preached and practiced peace and non-violence. He said: "We do not want to fight a physical battle where we can hurt only few individuals; we will fight a ferocious battle where we can fight with the enemy of casteism." Like a law-abiding citizen, he lodged complaint to the police and in spite of the advantages, which the caste Hindu hooligans had; five of them were sentenced for four months rigorous imprisonment because of the untiring efforts of Ambedkar. While Congress was waging the Quit India Movement in 1942, Ambedkar did not participate in the movement. He was politically and socially disillusioned and was quietly working for the betterment and upliftment of the untouchables. He was described as a traitor and as a stooge of the British Government in India by his opponents. But he took all these accusations on his shoulders and continued to do his splendid work. He did not bother for it.

Rejection of Hinduism

Dr. Ambedkar rejected Hinduism from his life. Born as an untouchable, Ambedkar was not an exception to face and experience the same humiliation and difficulty, which every untouchable had to face on those days. He was humiliated in school, college, institution and every sphere of life in the society.

He struggled continuously to face poverty and untouchability. In his own words: "Owing to the poverty of my father I did not have the opportunity to enjoy any of these luxuries. Till late in life I suffered excessively and laboured very hard." Ambedkar struggled a lot to get the answer regarding the sufferings of a particular section of people in a big society. He blamed Hinduism, which, he thought, was the reason for this plight. He believed that the Hinduism was based on inequality and injustice. It divided men cruelly in the name of caste. In its fold some people became untouchables and slaves. It never encouraged them to develop their minds and to advance in life. It suppressed the enthusiasm and inspiration of the students of the downtrodden class of people. He realized intensely that the Hindu religion did not appeal to his conscience, and did not appeal to his self-respect. So, as long as the downtrodden remain in the Hindu fold, they cannot lift their heads-up and move fearlessly. To quote him: "This religion and the social order had ruined us. But this is not going to stop here. This would ruin the Hindus themselves and ultimately India." So, he decided not to live any more in the Hindu fold. Though by chance he was a born Hindu, he did not want, at least, to die a Hindu. Since, then he went on constantly thinking and searching for the most appropriate form of religion that touches the heart to the grief stricken humanity. Ambedkar wanted that Hinduism should be reorganized and Hindu thought should be revitalized on the basis of social equality, liberty, fraternity, and democracy, both for the sake of Hinduism and the Indian nation. He said: "Caste has had a bad effect on the ethics of the Hindus. It has killed public spirit, destroyed sense of public charity and narrowed down public opinion has respected man's loyalty to his caste, made virtue and morality caste rider." Finally, he embraced Buddhism in protest of rigid casteism of the Hindu religion.

Significance of Buddhism in Ambedkar's Life

In spite of all the atrocities that he had gone through, Ambedkar was not against religion. He considered it essential for the proper development of mankind. He did not agree with those who said that religion is parasite or is an opiate. Religion instills hope in human-beings and drives them for activity. Buddha's religion was based on proper reflection and reason. He asked his disciples not to follow him blindly, but accept him only after testing his words with reason. Ambedkar felt that modern civilization needed such a rational religion. He wished to have the religion in the sense of morality, which remains the governing principle in every society. It must be scientific. As a social code of morality it must recognize the fundamental tenets of liberty, equality and fraternity. The most important aspect is that it has to enrich the lives of people mentally and materially. Morality is the essence of religion and society. It protects their dignity, value and self-respect. Ambedkar found that Buddhism was the only religion that satisfied all these requirements. At the age of sixteen Ambedkar was fascinated by the book called *Buddha Charita* in Marathi. He realized that Buddhism was the greatest of all the religions in the world as it was not merely a religion, but a great social doctrine. His research-oriented mind was fully convinced by the logical, empirical, humanistic and pragmatic teachings of Buddha. He observed that besides *Ahimsa,* Buddha taught many other things, such as social freedom, intellectual freedom, economic freedom and political freedom. Ambedkar emphatically says that Buddhism is the most appropriate religion in which there is no place for the distinction of high or low, rich or poor, caste or colour etc. It is the religion based on equality and universal brotherhood.

Ambedkar embraced Buddhism on October 14, 1956 at Nagpur along with many of his followers. After his initiation into Buddhism he gave the following message to his fellow Buddhists:

> "Having embraced Buddhism, the responsibility of following it sincerely rests on you. Try to elevate the nobility of this religion by your own behaviour. Try to spread the message of Buddha and liberate the people not only of your own country, but also of the world. Keep-up the dignity of the religion you have embraced."

Ambedkar says that the struggle of the downtrodden is not

simply for economic progress, but for honour and self-respect. He said:

> "For a man it is his birthright to lead an honourable life. To achieve this aim, we must do our utmost. We are prepared to make the greatest sacrifice for achieving this. We are struggling for human dignity. We want to make our life as full and wholesome as possible. We have started this movement to develop and educate our mind."

One needs confidence, courage and will to rise. Ambedkar believed that Buddhism as humanistic religion provides all these things. The essence of Buddhism lies in working practically for one's freedom—economic, social and political. Buddha was the torchbearer of democracy and an ardent exponent of liberty, equality and fraternity. It is only in Buddhism, he insisted, that human persons can have freedom.

Another interesting observation made by Ambedkar in Buddhism was the equal treatment of women. It is true that the Buddha did advise his disciples not to make it a habit to visit families of lay disciples for fear of human weakness yielding to frequent contact with women. But, he did not forbid such visits nor did he express any regard about women as inferior to men. He wanted to treat them and regard them as mothers, sisters and daughters depending on their age. He knew that women were fully capable of realizing his doctrine and discipline. That is why he maintained *Bhikkuni Sangha* along with *Bhikku Sangha*. *Bhikkuni Sangha* has been opened for all classes of women, married, unmarried, widowed and even for prostitutes. All could acquire merit, freedom, dignity, and equality along with men.

Dr. Ambedkar says that it is the duty of every Buddhist to visit *Buddha Vihara* on every Sunday and listen to the discourses. Unless this is done, the neo-Buddhists will not be able to understand Buddha properly. He also suggested his men not to encourage violence, work hard and educate themselves and face any problem with calm and peaceful way, without fear in mind. The untouchables have been trying to break-up the Hindu social structure. Though the leading member of the untouchables, Ambedkar is not here, but his movements are very much active. As a result, people have become aware of their rights and they fight for their rights.

Means for the Emancipation of the Untouchables

Ambedkar was devoted to the welfare of the untouchables. The emancipation of the untouchables began by establishing an association called the *Bahishkrit Hitkarani Sabha* (Depressed Classes' Welfare Association) on 20th July, 1924 at Parel in Bombay. The aim of this association was to make the untouchables aware of their miserable plight, their legitimate rights and to arouse among them consciousness of their rights. In pursuance of this aim, Ambedkar gave them a three-pronged: "Educate, Organize and Agitate".

His direct participation and commitment to the movement for the upliftment of the untouchability is very important and significant. He took different means for their emancipation which helped the untouchable in course of time.

Education: A Means for the Emancipation

Ambedkar was convinced that education alone could emancipate the untouchables. For the education of the untouchables he set-up some educational institutions. The establishment of the Siddharth College in Bombay in 1945 and the Millind College at Aurangabad in 1951 stand witness to his endeavour to make higher education not only available to the depressed classes, but also to put the rails of the administration of such educational institutions in their hands. Ambedkar realized that the significance of organized activity to carry forward his movement. He considered education to be essential for all men and women irrespective of their social and economic status. All men and women must get at least the minimum education, so that, they may know how to read and write. The primary education caters to the minimum essential need of educating the masses.

Education provides strength and opportunity for them to fight against poverty, disease, and backwardness. According to him the purpose of education was to help the students to study the situation critically. Therefore, education should be scientific, detached, and impartial in character. In the realm of higher education, Ambedkar was in favour of giving teachers necessary freedom to frame their own syllabus and assess the performance of their students. He was opposed to prescribing and following a rigidly structured syllabus.

He gave emphasis on promoting education and research in universities rather than converting them into conducting examination and degree distributing bodies. He founded people's Education Society on 8th July, 1945 with a view to advancing the educational interest of the downtrodden sections of the Indian society in general and the Scheduled Castes in particular. He considered education the most powerful agent for bringing about desired changes in society. For him education was as instrument to liberate the *Dalits* from illiteracy, ignorance and superstition and thus enable them to fight against all forms of injustice, exploitation and oppression. He believed that untouchables had to attain political power. They had to have training in political participation and the electoral politics. With this objective, he established the Independent Labour Party in 1936 and the Scheduled Caste Federation in 1942. He contested elections on the plank of these political parties. He gave the call "be a ruling class". It is good for a community if it is a part of the ruling class.

Social Emancipation

It was Ambedkar who ultimately succeeded to give legal rights of equality and social justice to millions of suffering masses of the untouchables and the exploited. This unique achievement was largely due to Ambedkar's efforts, and he, therefore, rightly can be called the liberator of the helpless untouchables and the tribes of India, who were treated for centuries no better than so many sects of condemned sub-humans. Ambedkar was, on occasions, found to be too aggressive, arrogant, and extremely uncompromising in his attitude. He deliberately preferred to keep himself away from the mainstream of the freedom movement, as its leadership appeared to him to be exclusively in the hands of the people who predominantly belonged to the upper castes. He also published a paper as the mouthpiece of his organization on 21 January, 1920. It was first named *Mooknayak* (Dumb-Leader) and then *Bahishkrit Bharat* (Outcaste India). He, in his weekly paper, *Mooknayak* (the leader of the Dumb or the voice of the Dumb) wrote:

> "It is imperative to suggest ways and means to redress the wrongs done to the depressed classes, and to discuss the measures for their upliftment. A journal reaching the mass is the best means to achieve this end."

In this way Ambedkar took upon himself the responsibility of rousing the conscious of the people.

He was not unaware of the social movements organized by Raja Ram Mohun Roy, Swami Dayananda Saraswati, and Swami Vivekananda for reforming the caste-character of the Hindu society. But it appeared to Ambedkar that the approach for religious reformation of the Hindu society for elimination of caste-events and giving the status of social equality to the untouchables or the depressed classes would not be more effective than the political approach to deal with this deeply entrenched caste-conservatism among the Hindus. He, therefore, decided to organize his movement primarily along political lines. Through the medium of his journals like *Janata* renamed as *Prabuddha Bharat,* Ambedkar endeavoured to educate the people on social, political, historical, religious, educational, economic, and other problems of the downtrodden people of India. His writing's breathed rationalism and humanism, and they revolutionized the outlook of the untouchables, completely as never before.

Ambedkar adopted a two-fold programme for his movement. The first programme was meant to propagate the cause of the untouchables and unite them under the banner of an organization and question the very religious concept and justification of the caste system. Though as an untouchable, he was not allowed to study Sanskrit in his school days; nevertheless, in later days, he himself definitely mastered the Sanskrit language to study the Hindu-religious books, particularly those *Shastras* that justified the system of caste stratification of the Hindu society. He wrote a number of books like *Annihilation of Caste*, *Who were the Shudras* and *how they came to be the fourth Varṇa in Indo-Aryan Society? The Untouchables, who are they and why they became Untouchables?* He, thus, daringly challenged the religious validity and the precepts behind the caste system at its very *Shastric* root. This created immense self-confidence among untouchables, who were made to suffer from a crippling inferiority complex.

He asked the Scheduled Castes and the Scheduled Tribes to forget all about the sins of their ancestors and strongly pleaded with them not to wait for their fictitious rebirth for the alleviation of their sufferings. He urged them that their social liberation must be ensured in this very life.

Political Movement

Ambedkar believed that by getting the recognition of the Depressed Class as a separate minority community like the Muslims from the British Raj, it would be easier to gain political power and consequent legal rights of equality and social justice for the untouchables and the outcaste. He, therefore, decided not only to ask for legally recognized status of minority community for the Depressed Class, but also for introducing the system of separate electorate for choosing their representations to legislature. For this purpose he submitted a memorandum to the Indian Statutory Commission, which was set-up by the British government in 1928. In 1930 the Round Table Conference was convened by the British Rule for Indian Administrative Reform. Ambedkar was nominated by the British Government to this conference for representing the interests of the Depressed Class before it. In the Round Table Conference, Ambedkar claimed a separate minority state with right for separate electorate for the Depressed Class. Ambedkar gave the evidence in a written statement to the Franchise Committee, on 27th January. He pleaded for communal representation, saying: "Communal representation is a device to ward off the evil effect of the division." By the words, "evil effect of the division", he clearly meant the evil effect of caste and untouchabilitiy. He further stated that the interests of the untouchables can be represented by the untouchables alone. There is distinctly their own interest and none else can truly voice them.

The British Prime Minister Ramsay MacDonald readily accepted the demand of Ambedkar and announced it in the Communal Award of 1932. He was of the opinion that the untouchables should be regarded as citizens. According to him, citizenship means a bundle of rights such as personal liberty, personal ideology, personal security, right to hold private property, equality before law, liberty of conscience, freedom of opinion, speech, right of assembly, right of representation in a country's government and right to hold office under the state. Urging the Depressed Class to participate in the politics and legislatures of the country, Ambedkar said: "I am in a situation in which Tilak was once placed. As long as the opponents curse me; it is taken for granted that my work for you is on the right lines and is justified. During the last two thousand years never was such an attempt made to annihilate untouchability." The untouchables are now convinced that the demand for *Swaraj* and the cause of the Hindus will suffer for want of support from the depressed classes. Ambedkar said that whatever the Hindus do for you is not out of charity or mercy. They do it for their own welfare as well. The mission of our movement is to fight out tyranny, injustice and false traditions, and to undo all privileges and release the harassed people from bondage. Our cause has gained recognition, because of our ceaseless struggle. Addressing the women he said:

> "Never regard yourselves as untouchables. Live a clean life. Dress yourselves like the touchable ladies. Never mind if your dress is full of patches, but see that it is clean. None can restrict your freedom in the choice of your garments and in the use of the mental for your

> ornaments. Attend more to the cultivation of the mind and the spirit of self-help."

Ambedkar recommended to the Minority Committee of the Round Table Conference that the Depressed Classes could not consent subjecting themselves to majority rule in their present state of hereditary bondsmen. Before majority rule is established their emancipation from the system of untouchability must be an accomplished fact. It must not be left to the will of the majority. The Depressed Classes must be made free citizens entitled to all the rights of citizenship in common with other citizens of the state. Ambedkar writes:

> "In slavery the master at any rate had the responsibility to feel cloths, and house the slave and keep him in good conditions lest the market value of the slave should decrease, but in the system of untouchability, the Hindus takes no responsibility for the maintenance of the untouchables."

Untouchability is not only a system of unmitigated economic exploitation, but it is also a system of uncontrolled economic exploitation. That is because there is no independent public opinion to condemn it and there is no impartial machinery of administration to retain it. There is no appeal to public opinion, for whatever public there is, it is the opinion of the Hindus who belong to the exploiting class and as such favour exploitation.

The Communal Award was a great triumph for Ambedkar. However, for Gandhiji it was a threat to divide the Hindu community with a sinister imperialist design to weaken the main base of the freedom movement. The Mahatma, who was then imprisoned, started fast unto death to save the unity of the Hindu society by preserving the system of joint electorate for all Hindus. The whole country was anxiously waiting for a positive response from Ambedkar, who was in a dilemma either to yield to the moral appeal of the Mahatma or stick to the political gains that he thought he had achieved for the Scheduled Castes. Ultimately, he agreed to give-up the claim for separate electorate for the

Scheduled Castes and consented to retain the system of joint electorate along with the other communities of the Hindu society. Gandhiji on his part liberally conceded to increase the number of reserved seats for the Scheduled Castes from 78, as it was fixed in the Communal Award to a much higher figure of 148. This settlement between Gandhiji and Ambedkar is known in history as the Poona Pact.

Ambedkar later wrote concerning why he succumbed to the moral appeal of Gandhiji. "There was before me a duty, which I owed as part of the common humanity to save Gandhi from sure death. I responded to the call of humanity and saved the life of Gandhi by agreeing to alter the Communal Award in a manner satisfied to Gandhiji." Till that time Ambedkar was looked upon as a sectional leader of the Depressed Class only, but after the Poona Pact everybody expected him to play the role of a national leader by joining national movement for India's freedom. However, Ambedkar thought it to be more prudent to rely on the gesture of the British Raj for enhancing the interests of the Scheduled Castes, although his policy was not wholly supported by his own community in recording their verdict in the General Election of 1937. Ambedkar might have been criticized for showing an obsession on issues pertaining to the interests of the Scheduled Castes. But he could never be accused of not being a true Indian and a genuine nationalist. He was no doubt a nationalist.

Constitutional Safeguard

In his changed evaluation of the new political realities Ambedkar decided to enter into the Constituent Assembly for making efforts to safeguard the interests of the Scheduled Castes by using this highest forum of democratic decision-making. In his maiden speech, he made a remarkable critical analysis of the discourse of Pandit Nehru when the latter moved the main resolution on the aims and objectives of the Constituent Assembly. Ambedkar's style of delivery, Constitutional acumen, moderate approach, and nationalist perspectives deeply impressed the Members of the Constituent Assembly. He was soon appointed a member of the

Seven-Member Drafting Committee for the preparation of the Constitution and then made its Chairman. It was not an act of any concession to assuage the sentiments of the Scheduled Castes that this highest position in the preparation body of the Constitution was given to Ambedkar. It was done in genuine appreciation of his exceptional ability to handle the stupendous task of framing the Constitution of India.

It has been admitted by all that Ambedkar played the role of the principal architect of the Constitution of free India. He was advised, assisted and guided on many issues by two other architects, namely Pandit Nehru and Sarder Patel who conceptualized the basic principles, provisions and objectives of the Constitution. It was the moment of highest achievement and happiness for Ambedkar, when the resolutions on Directive Principles and Fundamental Rights, Constitution declare:

> "The State shall not discriminate against any citizen on grounds only of religion, race, caste, sex, place of birth or any of them." Article 21 says: "No person shall be deprived of his life or personal liberty except according to procedure established by law." Again Article 17 of the Constitution states: "Unotuchability is abolished and its practice in any form is forbidden. His enforcement of any disability arising out of untouchability shall be an offence punishable in accordance with law."

It is indeed like a charter of legal rights of liberty for the untouchables. A Scheduled Caste member of the Constituent Assembly significantly observed after the adoption of the Constitution:

> "It is an irony of fate that the man who was driven from one school to another, who was forced to take his lesson outside the classroom, has been entrusted with the great job of framing the Constitution of free and Independent India, and it is he who finally dealt a fatal death-blow to the custom of untouchability, of which he was himself a victim in his younger days."

After the adoption of the Constitution, all the Members of the Constituent Assembly showered lavish praises on Ambedkar. In reply, he said in all humility:

> "I came into the Constituent Assembly with no greater aspiration than the safeguard of the interests of the Scheduled Castes. I had not the remotest idea that I would be called upon to undertake more responsible function. I am grateful to the Constituent Assembly and Drafting Committee for reposing so much trust and confidence in me and giving me."

Legacy and Relevance

Ambedkar's legacy as a socio-political reformer had deep effects on modern Indian society and politics. In post-Independent India his social and political thoughts have acquired respect across the socio-political spectrum in the country. His initiatives have influenced various spheres of life of the people and transformed the way India today looks at socio-economic policies, educational programme and positive action through socio-economic and legal incentives. His reputation as a scholar led to his appointment as Independent India's first Law Minister, and Chairman of the committee responsible to draft a constitution for free India. He passionately believed in the freedom of the individual and criticized equally both orthodox casteist Hindu religious societies. His condemnation of Hindu religion and its foundation of caste system, made him controversial, although his conversion to Buddhism sparked a revival in the interest in Buddhist philosophy in home and abroad.

Ambedkar's political ideology has given rise to a large number of *Dalit* political parties, organizations, publications and workers' unions that remain active across the country, especially in Maharashtra. His promotion of the *Dalit* Buddhist Movement has created interest in Buddhist philosophy in many parts of India and abroad. Mass conversion ceremonies have been organized by *Dalit* activists in modern times in India, emulating Ambedkar's Nagpur Ceremony of 1956.

Some scholars took the view that the British were more even-handed between castes, and that continuance of British rule would have helped to wipe out many evil practices. This political opinion was shared by quite a number of social activists including Jyotirao Phule.

Many scholars and common individuals question the continued institution of reservations initiated by B.R. Ambedkar as outdated and anti-meritocratic. However, such arguments have always been dismissed by the *Dalit* intellectuals and masses. They express that the opposition of Caste-based reservations in India, primarily comes from the antagonism rooted in the Hindu society towards the *Dalits*. In fact, that the Caste-based reservations in India, have become the uplifting of *Dalits* in the post-colonial period. At the end of the 1990s, some Hungarian-Rumanian drew parallels between their own situation and the situation of the *Dalits* in India. Inspired by Ambedkar's approach, they started to convert to Buddhism.

Limitations

But Ambadkar was also not beyond criticism. He had also no doubt some limitations. Narayan Rao Kajrolkar criticized him because he believed that he was biased to spend government on his own caste, the Mahar, rather than divide the funds equally among others such as the Chambars and the Mangs. Ambedkar was also criticized by Sitaram Narayan Shivtarkar on the same ground at the Chambar conference held at Khond at the Ratnagiri District on 27 October, 1937. Even at the "First Chambar Conference" held at Ratnagiri in December 1937, chaired by S.G. Songaonkar, echoed this yet again.

In spite of all criticisms we can say that Ambedkar adopted several ways and means for the upliftment and betterment of the untouchables. Institutions like Bahishkrit Hitkarani Sabha (Depressed Classes' Welfare Association). Siddharth College and Millind College are imparting education based on equality for all the people of all sections. Even today, his dream of classless society is being carried through such institutions in India.

References

Primary Sources

Dr. Baba Saheb Ambedkar: Writings and Speeches, 1989, Vol. 5, Mumbai, Maharashtra Education Department.

Dr. Baba Saheb Ambedkar: Writings and Speeches, 1990, Vol. 7, Mumbai, Maharashtra Education Department.

Secondary Sources

Dhananjoy Keer, 1990, *Dr. Ambedkar: Life and Mission,* Bombay: Popular Prakashan.

D.R. Jatava, 1997, *Dr. Ambedkar: Social Philosophy*, Jaipur: Rawat Publications.

Eleanor Zelliot, 2001, *From Untouchables to Dalit,* New Delhi: Manohar Publishers.

K.N. Kadam, (ed.) 1991, *Ambedkar and the Significance of His Movement,* London: Sangam.

K.S. Chalam (ed.) 1993, *Relevance of Ambedkarism in India*, Jaipur: Rawat Publications.

P. Arvind Nirmal, 1991, *Dr. Ambedkar: A Centenary Tribute,* Madras: Gurukul Theological College.

Robert Deliege, 1997, *The World of the Untouchables*, New York: Oxford University Press.

S.K. Dhanwan, 1991, *Dr. Ambedkar: A Select Profile*, Delhi: Wave.

Sudarshan Agarwal, (ed.), 1991, *Dr. Ambedkar: The Man and His Message,* New Delhi: Prentice-Hall of India.

Suresh Dalal, 1998, *Dr. Ambedkar: Life and Mission*, Madras: University of Madras.

V. Chandra Mowli, 1990, *Dr. Ambedkar: Man and His Vision*, Sterling.

13

Thought of *Bhagavadgītā* and *Savarṇa* in Contemporary *Dalit* Discourse

A Rejection of Legacy of Ambedkar

Binod Kumar Agarwala

Introduction

The aim of this chapter is not to be critical and dismissive of contemporary *dalit* discourse. I take that discourse as it comes to me very seriously and I have made an attempt to understand it. But in the very understanding of the contemporary *dalit* discourse I discern its weakness which is preventing the *bahujan samaj* from reaching social goal which they think is within their grasp and reach. Because, there is democracy and they, the *bahujan samaj*, are in majority, they should have reached and grasped the social goal towards which they embarked with Dr. B.R. Ambedkar. This is the constant refrain of *dalit* discourse. And yet even after more than sixty years the goal, which appears so easy and within the possible reach and grasp, is always receding like a mirage and ever appears so far. This frustration in achieving the social goal is making the *bahujan samaj* angry, that comes out clearly in the *dalit* discourse. When the emotions like anger cloud a collective discourse it loses track of reason, starts looking for scapegoat, who can be blamed for preventing them from reaching the easily graspable goal. The scapegoat of the *dalit* discourse is obviously the *savarṇas* with their ideology of *varṇa dharma* as propounded in *Bhagavadgītā*, as clearly discerned by Dr. Ambedkar and constantly emphasized by *dalit* discourse ever since. In this discernment they are both right and wrong but more wrong than right. They discern correctly the strength of *savarṇas* that it has something to do with their grasp of *Bhagavadgītā*, which gives them an edge, not merely an edge, but puts them far ahead of *bahujan samaj* in spite of their numerical strength in modern democratic institution. But, they immediately go wrong the moment they identify the strength of *savarṇas* with their ideology of *varṇa dharma* as it finds expression in *Bhagavadgītā* or the moment they identify the strength of *savarṇas* with the perseverance of old caste structure or the old caste mechanism even into the modern democratic institutions. This false trail on which the *dalit* discourse is put serves the interest of *savarṇas*, as the secret of their strength still remains hidden from *dalit* like a magic potion to which only *savarṇas* are privy, which gives them the strength to be far ahead, and the *bahujan samaj* following the false trail goes on the garden path of impossible goal of removing the *savarṇas* from modern institutions or using the old structures entrenching it in political arena indulging in angry rhetoric sans logic which can lead no where but can keep the illusion alive that the goal is near within grasp so that they keep on proceeding on the false trail when *savarṇas* keep enjoying their superiority undisturbed. There lies the weakness of *dalit* discourse: it is so *self-absorbed* that it is only interested in weaving discourse around centuries of their oppression, or continued position of *theirs* in the old structures that survives, articulating *their* goals, articulating how *their* goal is graspable and how *their* goal is eluding them, trying to find out who is responsible frustrating the strength of their majority etc. They discuss nothing else; they try to find out nothing unless it somehow relates to them directly. So, the only thing they bother to know about *savarṇa* is their *varṇa* ideology, the only thing that attracts them is the reference to *varṇa* in *Bhagavadgītā*, the thing that catches attention is the old caste structure and techniques, intrusion of these into modern institutions because this is what *they* can relate *themselves* with. But the strength of *savarṇas*, which they derive because of their grasp of *Bhagavadgītā*, which gives them an edge, not merely an edge but puts far ahead of *bahujan samaj* in spite of their numerical strength in modern democratic institution, is of no concern of the latter.

I shall discuss below that only fourteen verses out of seven hundred verses of *Bhagavadgītā* contain reference to *varṇa* directly or indirectly. *Savarṇas* do not derive their strength from these fourteen verses which refer directly or indirectly to *varṇa*, as these are only contextual references, which could be replaced by other references which need not have any connection even remotely to *cāturvarṇyam*, and yet the teaching of *Bhagavadgītā* will remain same unaltered, giving the same strength to live in the world that present *Bhagavadgītā* gives. This secret of *Bhagavadgītā*, that gives the magic potion to *savarṇas*, which puts them ahead and continues to put them ahead, whatever be the time, whatever be the institutional arrangement, whatever be the circumstances, that is completely missed in the *dalit* discourse. If they want to find their way, if they want to participate in action that will be successful, they have to grasp this secret (*rahasya*, *guhya*) teaching of *Bhagavadgītā*.

Even if the *bahujan samaj* perceives the *savarṇas* as adversaries in their struggle, the first principle of adversity being that you respect your adversary and discern the real strength of your adversary, they need to discern the real strength of their perceived adversary, i.e. *savarṇas*, and not remain satisfied with smug confidence that *savarṇas* derive strength from ideology of *varṇa*. In the Second World War Montgomery, the British General, and Patton, the American General, had the greatest respect for their enemy Rommel, the German General. "Monty kept a portrait of the German in his command caravan while Patton studied Rommel's book on tactics. Rommel returned the compliment: 'Montgomery never made a serious strategic mistake … [and] in the Patton Army we saw the most astonishing achievement in mobile warfare'."[1] So, the *bahujan samaj* in its discourse needs to understand the real thinking of *savarṇas*, which the latter derive from the secret (*rahasya*, *guhya*) teaching of *Bhagavadgītā*, which has nothing to do with *varṇa*, or caste order or intrusion of caste order into modern institutions.

The present essay has two components. In the first part I try to understand the contemporary *dalit* discourse which exposes its weaknesses, hence, this part may sound critical, but the primary aim is to understand not to criticize, but the very understanding appears as a critique. In this part there are three theses regarding *dalit* discourse: (1) *Dalit* Discourse has rejected the legacy of Dr. B.R. Ambedkar, by becoming a discourse to achieve a political agenda that is against his legacy; (2) the reason for this is that the *dalit* discourse even in academic platforms refuses to adhere to reason both theoretical and practical, in its zeal to become a discourse for a political agenda; and (3) Dr. Ambedkar himself set erroneous standards of discourse, which was emulated by his followers.

In the second part after the discernment of weakness in contemporary *dalit* discourse I try to find out with the help of secret (*rahasya*, *guhya*) teaching of *Bhagavadgītā* the way of overcoming the weakness of *dalit* discourse. Only when the secret (*rahasya*, *guhya*) teaching of *Bhagavadgītā* is discerned as the strength of *savarṇas* by the *dalit* discourse, the *bahujan samaj* will realize that they are capable of participation in emerging institutional arrangement on equal terms with others without there being any adversary perceived or real.

1. Understanding Contemporary Dalit Discourse

1.1. Rejection of the Legacy of Dr. B.R. Ambedkar

Let me begin with explanation of first work that *Dalit* Discourse has rejected the legacy of Dr. B.R. Ambedkar, by becoming a discourse to achieve a political agenda that is against his legacy. To understand the first work we have to understand what Dr. Ambedkar's legacy is. His greatest legacy is the Constitution of an arrangement of institutions—political, economic and social, which unites all the people of India into a modern state on the basis of principles, which find mention in the preamble to the Constitution of India. As chairman of the drafting committee of the Constitution of India he was not merely filling pages with alphabets of a language, he was not merely spelling out a vision, but giving shape to the institutional arrangement of the State of India, which included all people irrespective of religion, caste and gender, which embodied principles of liberty, equality, fraternity etc. This is the legacy of Dr. Ambedkar.

My claim in the form of first work is that this legacy of Dr. Ambedkar is completely rejected and a different political agenda finds favour in the contemporary *dalit* disourse. In fact there is no contemporary *dalit* discourse to defend or accept the legacy of Dr. Ambedkar. *Dalit* discourse is woven round a political agenda that completely rejects the legacy of Dr. Ambedkar. But what is contemporary *dalit* discourse? First of all *Dalit* discourse is by the *dalits* themselves. And secondly, *dalit* discourse is that discourse by *dalit* leaders and scholars which is in public domain. I am not talking about the discourse in the classroom by *dalit* scholar as that is a discourse by a teacher in a classroom and not a discourse by *dalit* in public. Thirdly, *dalit* discourse is that discourse by *dalit* in public domain that is dealing with social issues. Fourthly, for the present work contemporary *dalit* discourse is that discourse that has emerged with Independence struggle of India and is being continued now. Only when these four conditions are satisfied by a discourse then it is contemporary *dalit* discourse for the work under consideration. If one surveys *dalit* discourse with above four characteristics in mind then one will notice that all contemporary *dalit* discourse is woven round the perceived issues, real or imaginary, of suppression of the *dalits*, or denial of rights of *dalits*, or hurt sentiments or pride of *dalits*, i.e. hurt by others etc., which reveals the aspiration of those carrying on that discourse even if it does not explicitly articulate demand of any kind like that for some change in the structure or demand for intervention in the situation or demand for stoppage of some process that is already going on etc. Our definition of *dalit* discourse is neither meant to cover nor covers the discourse by such great *dalit* saints like, Ramanuja, Ekanatha, Chokhamela, Ravidas (Raidas), Kabir, Namadeva, Sant Gyaneswar (Dhyaneshwar), Sant Tukaram, and others who also rejected existing system of *Vedas* supported *chaturvarṇas* in their own ways.

Let me illustrate my work by two examples. Consider the contemporary *dalit* discourse regarding hurt sentiments and hurt pride of the *dalits* due to the presence of cartoon of Ambedkar sitting on a tortoise with Nehru standing behind him with a whip. This discourse was an articulation of an aspiration of *dalits* that rejected Dr. Ambedkar's legacy. The cartoon was published at a time when the drafting committee of which Dr. Ambedkar was chairman was perceived to be slow in drafting the Constitution and Nehru was goading the chairman to hasten the work. There is no recorded history prior to the recently generated *dalit* discourse that it was found offensive by Ambedkar or anyone else, or that it is not protected by the fundamental right of freedom of speech and expression etc. It shows that the legacy of Dr. Ambedkar in the form of fundamental right of freedom of speech finds no favour in *dalit* discourse, which articulated the hurt sentiments and hurt pride of *dalits* at the sight of presence of such cartoons in text books.

Consider the discourse on centuries of oppression; a discourse carried even now leading to demand for perpetual caste based reservation of seats in educational institutions, government jobs, even private enterprises, or proportional political representation etc. under Scheduled Caste category or the euphemism of backward classes etc. This kind of discourse is nothing but an attempt to entrench caste distinctions in the arena and scope of electoral politics, which amounts to complete rejection of the legacy of Dr. Ambedkar which he left in the form of vision of democracy embodied in arrangement of democratic political institutions.

The essence of democracy embodied in arrangement of democratic political institutions is not the so-called majoritarian principle which requires that every decision is made by majority; rather it is discussion, knowledge and judgement. Discussion with others checks our partiality and widens our perspective; we are made to see things from diverse standpoints and the limits of our vision are brought home to us. The benefits from discussion lie in the fact that we are limited in knowledge and ability to reason. No one knows everything the others know, or can make all the same inferences that people can draw in concert. Discussion is a way of combining information and knowledge and enlarging the range of arguments. Hence, discussion enables us to arrive at sound judgement. But this lesson is rejected in *dalit* discourse. The very coining of the term '*bahujan*' indicates that the *dalit* discourse equates democracy as majoritarian principle only and likes to project itself as the majority and likes to entrench itself as the majority in the electoral politics. It rejects all other principles of democracy that circumscribe majoritarianism. The majoritarian principle is always a subordinate principle circumscribed by the requirements of essence of democracy, i.e. free discussion. But, overturning the essence of democracy there is a gradual ascendancy and entrenchment of the majoritarian principle as essence of democracy in thinking manifested in *dalit* discourse. This development started in seventies and still continues. This development is linked to the transformation and consolidation of religions, castes, and ethnicities into political vote banks. The social forces, which were leading towards ascendancy and entrenchment of majoritarian principle, were also behind creation of permanent political vote banks to consolidate their position in the body politic. Diverse religions and castes and ethnicities always existed in India, but it is only a recent development that these are transformed into factions pitted against each other through politics of vote banks. The electoral politics of democracy, when transformed into politics of vote bank, transforms the essence of democracy. Essence of democracy is transformed from free discussion to majoritarianism in *dalit* discourse. Once this happened it is easy to see that knowledge as the essence of discussion got replaced by propagation of *dalit* opinion as the essence not only of political campaign and dissemination of views through *dalit* mass media but also of *dalit* discourse emanating from academia.

At a much deeper level the working of democracy through its electoral campaign and dissemination of views through mass media on issues confronting the electorate has been subverted by *dalit* discourse. Our intellectual tradition going back to ancient times had a conception of discussion captured in the Sanskrit term *adhikaraṇa*. In this conception of discussion one is expected to discuss all the possible views on the topic under consideration with all the best supporting reasons for each possible view so that pro- and contra- are evenly matched to be taken seriously in the discussion. With further investigation and consideration if one succeeds in tilting the balance of reason in favour of one view and is able to rebut the reasons and evidence in support of the opposing views than one is said to have acquired knowledge of the topic under discussion. In this conception of discussion the essence of knowledge consists not merely in judging something correctly but also, at the same time and for the same reason in excluding what is wrong. In the mass media and the electoral campaign by the *dalit* discourse knowledge in this traditional sense has been discarded altogether. *Dalit* discourse in electoral campaign and mass-media aim not at knowledge but creation of opinion. Gadamer, a famous German thinker, in his study found that opinion has a curious tendency to propagate itself.[2] Every opinion would always like to be the general public opinion. It is interesting to note that the word ancient Greeks used for opinion was "doxa". This word meant the decision made by the majority in the council assembly. Therefore, opinion has great power. Opinion has the support of majority that wields power. So, the power of opinion easily defeats the power of knowledge that derives power only from reason and discussion and not from the support of majority. In *dalit* mentality in matters social the feeble power of knowledge has given way to the strong power of majority opinion under the euphemisms of '*dalit* sentiment', '*dalit* perception' and 'political correctness'. It is this change that gets reflected in academic *dalit* discourse now.

1.2. Dalit Discourse Emanating from Academia

By *dalit* discourse emanating from academia I mean the scholarly discourse woven round *dalit* issues by *dalit* academicians in institutions of higher learning like universities for presentation in public. It is my second work that the *dalit* discourse emanating from academia, i.e. academic platforms for public dissemination, refuses to adhere to reason both theoretical and political, in its zeal to become a discourse for a political agenda and hence ceases to adhere to standards of knowledge and produces only *dalit* opinion without any backing of reason theoretical or practical.

A national seminar on "Dr. B.R. Ambedkar's Ideas and Thoughts" was organized during (March 11 & 12, 2013) in the Permanent Campus of North-Eastern Hill University, Shillong. A *dalit* scholar, Dr. Anoop Kumar, a scholar from JNU, New Delhi, introduced himself as a young *dalit* political activist and delivered a key note address whose topic was "Caste Discrimination in Higher Education System in India". The address was woven round the issues of suicide of Scheduled Caste students in higher institutions of learning in medicine and technology. He merely emphasized the suicide of Scheduled Caste students in these institutions without comparaing the data of same kind regarding students from higher castes. He did not establish by any data any statistical correlation of rate of suicide among Scheduled Caste students with the membership of the students to Scheduled Caste group discounting other factors that may be operative, nor did he establish by any data that there is less or zero statistical correlation of suicide among higher caste students with membership the students to the higher caste discounting other factors that can be contributory factor for suicide. It was an *a priori* assumption that the suicide of Scheduled Caste student means that it must be due to caste discrimination by teachers and fellow students, majority of whom belong to upper castes. His lamentation was that there is no evidence to link suicide with caste discrimination. His lamentation was that it is so difficult to prove caste discrimination in suicide cases of scheduled caste students. So, *in lieu* of evidence of correlation between caste or caste discrimination and suicide in the cases of suicide by Scheduled Caste students, the group of young *dalit* activist scholars have started producing documentaries, he informed us. He in fact showed a documentary which was woven round post-suicide pathos of the family and friends and their recollection of how bright he was, what hopes the family had pinned on him etc. It was a movie of twenty minutes calculated to arouse pathos in favour of the bereaved family and the çaste. One failed to understand how the documentary established the correlation of suicide with caste discrimination in the case of the Scheduled Caste students who had committed suicide.

After the movie ended he resumed his talk and discussed the discourse of merit *versus* reservation introduced by upper caste students and intelligentsia, which he said is nothing, but a discourse to continue the centuries of oppression by dubbing those who come through reservation as less meritorious. His contention was that students coming through reservation are no less meritorious than the students who come through general competition. In his view this is what emerges from the movie he had shown. It was a little surprising to hear this, for there was no statistical data anywhere in the movie or his lecture to establish correlation between merit and reservation or absence of correlation of merit with general competition. In an academic discourse how can one make such categorical statement that suicide of *dalit* student implies caste discrimination if he is not ready to rescind it if he cannot establish that there is correlation, as he himself admitted that it is difficult to prove or establish that a suicide is due to caste discrimination. How can one say that the students coming through reservation are as meritorious as those coming through open competition and yet continue to advocate caste based reservation? If they are as meritorious as those coming through open competition than where is the need for reservation and if there is need for reservation than they are not as meritorious because they are not ready for competition on equal terms.

But, if it is still claimed that the students coming through reservation are as meritorious as those coming through open competition and yet, it is also claimed that there is need for caste based reservation, then the argument presupposes that there are structural bottlenecks for the entry of Scheduled Caste students. But this presupposition cannot directly justify reservation unless it is argued that the structural bottlenecks for Scheduled Tribe students cannot be removed otherwise. But, there was no discussion regarding the issue. He did not even mention or examine that structural bottlenecks can be removed by strengthening or making the institutional arrangement left as a legacy by Ambedkar, by removing corruption or malfunctioning of that institutional arrangement. But, as I have made it clear in the first work there is no taker of that legacy as far as *dalit* discourse academic or otherwise. This shows that there is lack of rigour of theoretical reason in academic *dalit* discourse.

When it is claimed that the students coming through reservation are as meritorious as those coming through open competition and it is also claimed that there is need for caste based reservation, then the argument through the presupposition of existence of structural bottlenecks for the entry of Scheduled Caste must, first logically move to demand for removal of the structural bottlenecks by strengthening or making the institutional arrangement left as a legacy by Ambedakar, which can be done by removing corruption or malfunctioning of the institutional arrangement. But, the issue is why does *dalit* discourse not move in that direction of demanding removal of bottlenecks, but demand reservation for easy entry? Of course, the theoretical reason is not adhered to, but more than that practical reason is also not adhered to. Issues are obfuscated violating theoretical reason and prescriptions are formulated in violation of practical reason in *dalit* academic discourse.

Let me give another example to illustrate the point. When the anti-corruption movement of Anna Hazare was at its peak, an essay written by Dr. Viveka Kumar, Associate Professor, CSSS/ JNU, New Delhi, who is a *dalit* academic voice, was circulated by e-mail (Monday, 22 August, 2011 16:15:40 IST). Viveka Kumar defines corruption: "Corruption can be defined as a mechanism by which, a numerically small section of society denies majority of its people a plethora of rights and privileges whether it is 'Human Rights for dignified existence', 'equality: economic, political and social', 'liberty of occupation,' 'residence and religious practices, fraternity' etc. By doing this numerically smaller group monopolizes religious, political, economic, educational and judicial institutions etc. Historically, this mechanism is created, at the inception of the society, through religious texts and sanctions. Later they are legitimatized socially by theories of *Dharma* and *Karma*. The traditional structures created, in this fashion; do not die in modern times. But, they remain alive changing their form and style of functioning and influence keeping the monopoly of the numerically small section of the society intact. The existing dominance in and composition of modern institutions of governance, production, and education in India amply prove the point." So, naturally and logically one expect that he will make a demand to remove corruption, by separating the traditional structures from the modern institutions of governance, production, and education in India and that he will ask for the destruction of traditional structures of oppression, so that the modern institutions can function properly and a numerically small do not have the mechanism left to deprive the majority a plethora of rights and privileges. But that is not what he argues for. But, contrary to natural and logical expectation Viveka argues for leaving the modern structure intruded by the traditional structure intact as it is. The traditional structures, which he will like to continue to function in modern institutions, are the structures legitimatized socially by theories of *Dharma* and *Karma*, i.e. early *varṇa* system which later metamorphosed to *jati* (caste) system. The rationale is present but hidden in Viveka's definition of corruption given above but which is easily missed because the reader is thinking as per theoretical and practical reason, while his hidden ground will come to the fore if the reader assumes that the theoretical and pratical reason is suspended in Viveka's writing. Let us recollect that according to Viveka a 'mechanism' is 'corruption' by definition when a *numerically small section* of society *denies majority of its people* a plethora of rights and privileges by using that mechanism. Now, if the reader assumes that Viveka has given farewell to reasons theoretical and practical, and allows them not to colour thinking in his writing, then it automatically and obviously implies that *the mechanism, mentioned in the definition of corruption by Viveka, ceases to be corruption when a numerical majority uses that mechanism to deny a minority of upper castes plethora of their rights.* In Viveka's definition, the problem of corruption lies not in the mechanism, but lies in who uses the mechanism. The problem of corruption is when the mechanism is used by minority of *savarṇas* to deny majority its right, but the same mechanism is used by majority to deny minority of *savarṇas* its right then it is not corruption by definition. It is now any body's guess how far

Viveka is exhibiting reason, theoretical or practical, in his discourse. The entirety of the long discourse of Viveka after he gave his definition of corruption, through a multiple tour *de force*, is for drawing the conclusion which was apparent to me the moment I read his definition of corruption.

How this old structure of *varṇa*, which later metamorphosed to *jati* (caste), functions and what is its mechanism has been studied by eminent sociologists Andre Beteille. I will give a very very simplified account. *Jati* system operated in four areas: recognition of hierarchical position, purity-impurity, occupation determination and marriage. Firstly, as *jatis* were hierarchically ordered, from *jati* of a person one could find out where he stood in the hierarchy and what is due (goods, services, and respect etc.) to him because of his *jati* in the hierarchy. Secondly, it worked in determination of purity and impurity. If food is touched by a particular *jati* then it became impure not to be eaten by some other *jati*. There were rules of this which *jati* can eat food from which *jati*'s house and cannot eat food from which *jati's* house etc. This in its extreme case took the form of untouchability, i.e. a person of a specific *jati* is himself impure and he is untouchable for persons of other *jatis* to the extent that sometimes even the shadow of the former was considered pollutant. Thirdly, *jati* determined occupation. If one is born into cobbler *jati* he has to take-up the work of cobbler etc. And lastly, according to *jati* system *jati* deremined, whom one can marry and whom one cannot marry. There were again elaborate rules regarding which *jati's* person can marry the person of opposite sex from which *jati*. These were the four areas in which old order was functioning.

After Independence and coming of democratic institutions and electoral politics, advancement in education and change in economy and urbanization the old structure started losing its strength gradually even if it had not become sufficiently weak to die or go out of existence. Democratic politics and openness of modern institutions started reducing the strength of *jati* hierarchical order even if it did not die completely. Because of mobility, urbanization, increase in the size of floating population, and coming-up of hotels in large numbers in cities, the issue of impurity and purity started losing its strength even if it did not become sufficiently weak to die completely. With the coming of modern and new economy with unheard of services and production *jati* started losing its strength in job selection by the person and hiring by firms even if its influence did not become sufficiently small to declare it as dead as a dodo. Lastly, due to many factors like education, mobility, inter-mixing of the opposite sexes in educational institutions, work places etc. and increase in love marriages, which started making caste consideration less important in marriage even though it was not completely gone out or become sufficiently weak to declare it a thing of the past.

When the caste consideration were becoming less important in its traditional areas of operation then why does the *dalit* discourse even refuses to recognize the trend? Why does the *dalit* intellectuals merely weaves discourse around the remaining strength of the caste system and insists on its "changing", "form and style of functioning and influence," that too not to make a demand to dismantle it? The reason is simple and is just below the veneer of words of Viveka, "Who were the people who monopolized the institutions of governance, education, and production? Of course, the so-called upper castes! And hence, they were responsible for a corrupt social order from its inception which was inequal and devoid of equality, liberty and fraternity (*Dr. Babasaheb Amedkar: Writings and Speeches,* Vol. 3, pp. 96-115). If that was the case in ancient period what is the condition in the present situation? Who are the people who dominate and monopolize the modern and secular institutions, viz. Polity, Judiciary, Bureaucracy, Industry, University and Media? Again the answer is the so-called Upper castes! ... Bureaucracy, Judiciary, and Polity are main centres of corruption and hence have to be brought under Lok Pal. But here also when we analyse the composition of these three institutions on the basis of available data... in these institutions again so-called upper castes are directly responsible for corruption." So, issue is not *corruption as action done* in modern institutions, rather the issue is *corruption of institutions by presence of people of upper castes* in the modern and secular institutions, viz. Polity, Judiciary, Bureaucracy, Industry, University and Media. So, for Dr. Viveka Kumar agenda is not proper functioning of the modern institutions by removing possibility of corrupt action, nor is it the destruction of old structures and mechanisms from modern institutions, nor is the removal of intrusion of old structures and mechanisms from the modern institutions. He needs all these, as it is then only, his agenda can be achieved. His agenda is removal of people of upper castes from the modern institutions and induction of scheduled caste people in their place. Not only Vivek does not want the destruction of old structure and mechanism, he does not want their intrusion to be removed from the modern institutions. That was the way of domination of minority on the majority, so the same mechanism has to be utilized to establish the domination of majority (of *Bahujan*) on the minority (of *savarṇas*) for that is sanctified by majoritarian principle which is democracy in his view. He is quite clear that democracy is just the majoritarian rule, it is the route through which reservation can be made to arrive in the modern institutions, and then it will be easy to perpetuate the same dominance, but this time dominance of *bahujan* on the minority of *savarṇas* through the same old mechanism. So, he needs the intrusion of old structure and old mechanism into the modern institutions. Once this state of affairs is achieved, it will be a corruption free society, as corruption is *corruption of institutions by the presence of savarṇas*. Corruption is when *savarṇa* minority dominates, but it is not corruption, but perfect democracy, when the majority of *bahujan* dominates. The problem is neither old structure, nor its mechanism, nor the intrusion of these two into modern institutions, rather the problem is the presence of *savarṇas*, who are in minority, in institutions modern or old in the position of power and dominance, but presence of *bahujan* in position of power and dominance is perfect democracy, as they are in majority.

These are conclusions of his argument in my words. Let us hear his conclusion in his words: "So, what are the conclusions we can draw from the above analysis of structures and mechanisms of corruption?" he asks. He answers, "Why this movement has left corruption in private, religious and social sectors untouched is best known to the leaders of the movement. Or is it a political ploy to target only government where now we have stated witnessing arrival of erstwhile excluded communities like SCs, STs and OBCs?" Conclusion in the interrogative is a curiosity unless it is a rhetorical question which contains its own answer. Since, these are conclusions of argument, these are to be understood as rhetorical questions containing statements as their answers. What is that statement which is the real conclusion? The statement in these two rhetorical questions read together is: this movement has left corruption in private, religious and social sectors untouched because it is a political ploy to target only government where now we have stated witnessing arrival of erstwhile excluded communities like SCs, STs and OBCs. The use of expression 'arrival' makes it sound as if he is saying as we SCs, STs and OBCs have started 'arriving' at the table there is a ploy by *savarṇas* to take the plate away under the name of anti-corruption movement. So, SCs, STs and OBCs are arriving in the government sector to indulge in eating whatever is eatable, after all, their implicit argument is that that was what upper caste people were doing, so they have no right to complain. So, structures of corruption must be retained, both old and new for 'arrival' of SCs, STs and OBCs. The table should be laid and ready for them too as their 'arrival' has started.

The conclusion banks on the coincidence of arrival of the Scheduled Castes and other minorities with the rise of voice against corruption, but in his eagerness to establish the correlation between the two phenomena from the coincidence of timing Viveka has not taken into consideration other coincident phenomena which give a different perspective to what is happening. The increase in the brazenness of corruption leading to easy culpability, increase in number of incidents of corruption leading to easy detectability and sting operations, increase in size of quantum of each corruption crossing the tolerance limit of the public, rise in mass media leading to wide publicity of corruption, rise in the number of NGOs crusading for various causes including corruption are also coincident phenomena. How is Viveka discounting these other coincident phenomena to advocate a theory of conspiracy of *savarṇas* to take away the laid full plate from the dinning table where the Scheduled Castes have just arrived? One can easily establish any work by merely selecting favourable phenomena and turning a Nelson's eye at unfavourable phenomena.

Another conclusion of Viveka states, "The present movement does not highlight the fact that corruption is an upper caste phenomenon." It means corruption is presence of certain castes, i.e. higher castes, in modern institutions and absence of corruption is absence of higher castes and presence of lower castes in modern institutions. Next conclusion is stated, "So, when the corruption is high caste phenomenon then this on-going movement against corruption is for correcting the wrongs of the so-called upper castes only. Where does the nation and other population figure?" Its illogicality and irrationality is apparent. If the corruption is high caste phenomenon requiring correction of the wrongs of the upper castes then it is the business of the nation or lower castes to stop the upper caste from corruption. So, lower caste should have a stake in removal of corruption and not be a mere bystander as Viveka envisages. But why is Viveka not able to see his illogicality? What is going on in his thinking which is preventing him from seeing that there is illogicality here? It is easy to see what is going on in his thinking. The crux of his thinking lies in the expression "*correcting the wrongs of the so-called upper-castes only*." The issue of corruption is "correcting the wrongs of the so-called upper castes only." Any normal thinking person, with a modicum of reason, will interpret Viveka's expression for removal of corruption, i.e. "correcting the wrongs of the so-called upper castes only" as saying that correction is required in the wrongdoing, which of course is here done by upper castes. But that is not his meaning. His meaning of removal of corruption intends of course to correct something, but that something, which needs correction, is not the so-called wrong doings. He is using the expression "so-called" explicitly with upper castes many times, but the upper caste is not merely so-called for him they are real and real adversary, they are not illusory, hence, they are not merely so-called upper castes. So, he is implicitly reading the expression "so-called" with wrong doings. Wrong doings are not real, they are so-called wrong doings, and in fact these are mere doings not wrong doings as these are merely so-called wrong doings. Hence, these wrong doings being merely so-called wrong doings require no correction. But something is really wrong and that requires correcting nonetheless. What is that? It is the presence of people of upper castes that is wrong, it is precisely because doings are doings of people of upper castes present in modern institutions that is why the doings appear as wrong, and hence, these are merely so-called wrong doings. So, what needs correction is the presence of people of upper castes in modern institutions which is wrong. So, correction required is not in the so-called wrong doings, but the correction of the population manning the modern institutions. At present the population manning the modern institutions is that of upper caste, remove them, make the population that man the modern institutions that of lower castes, it will become right, and even if we have the same doing in the same modern institution under the impact of old structure and mechanism it will cease to be wrong doing. So, by definition wrong doing is a doing if done by person of upper caste, the same doing if done by person of lower caste it ceases to be wrong doing. So, the rhetorical question "Where does the nation and other population figure?" is an implicit statement which says that the anti-corruption movement was a movement for correcting the 'doings' labelled as 'wrong doings' in which only upper caste people participated, since, it was not a movement for correction of the population manning the modern institutions which predominantly is that of upper castes, which needed to be corrected, hence the other population (i.e. lower castes) and nation did not participate in it.

So, Viveka states his next conclusion: "Hence, to argue that they have organized this movement for and on behalf of the nation is a big farce." It means it was a movement organized not by the nation as lower castes did not participate in it who are a majority, it was merely a movement organized by upper castes to modify 'doings' labelling them as 'wrong doings' which really required no correction. If read together with what he had said earlier it becomes clear why it was a 'farce' organized by upper castes only. It was a farce, because when they were the only population manning the government and bureaucracy they indulged in these doings, but now that lower caste people have started arriving in government and bureaucracy, they are labelling these doings as 'wrong doings' and want these doings to be stopped. It is a farce. The doings must continue, they should not be labelled 'wrong doings', and these doings should not be stopped because we, the lower castes, have started arriving to indulge in these doings, which by definition is going to make them good doings.

So, naturally it follows: "Hence, this movement does not represent the majority of the population belonging to SCs, STs, OBCs and Religious Minorities." SCs, STs, OBCs and Religious Minorities do not want the so-called wrong doings to be stopped, for it is their chance to indulge in these doings, only upper castes want these so-called wrong-doings to be stopped when it is our chance to indulge in doings. Hence, the anti-corruption movement does not represent the majority etc.

Behind this is a wrong understanding of democracy by Viveka in which democracy means majoritarianism and majoritarianism is the highest value that sanctifies and legitimizes everything, every doing in democracy. There is a second false assumption too that he belongs to a group that is the permanent majority, consisting of SCs, STs, OBCs and Religious Minorities. So, implicitly from these two false assumptions he draws the conclusion that nothing is justified unless it is consented to by this majority group. Hence, with this principle in mind Viveka makes last three observations regarding the anti-corruption movement. "This movement does not represent all also because *we did not elect the leaders and the issue* of this movement.... Hence, the leaders of the on-going movement are self-styled and self-appointed leaders.... What an irony undemocratically elected leaders are talking about saving democracy." (Italics are added by the present author to highlight how strong is his equation of majoritarianism with democracy and how strong is his belief that he belongs to a permanent majority, so as to make such a statement whose implication is that nothing is justified without the consent of the 'we' with whom he identifies himself with.) Now, we can see why Viveka wants to retain the old *varṇa* and caste order, without discarding it. By majority, in a modern democratic polity, the lower castes with similarly placed groups of other minorities, can invert the caste system, by making themselves politically superior in power to the upper castes and can use that power for other advantages too and do the same to upper castes what upper castes did to them in past by the caste system. The continued division and distinction of castes and *varṇas* is essential to his political agenda.

Let me advise Viveka with three quotations from James Madison, a great leader of American Democracy, who was also one of the founding fathers of American Democracy, who also inspired Dr. Ambedkar, whose legacy Viveka is rejecting. James Madison wrote in *Federalist* No. 10: "*In Republics, the great danger is, that the majority may not sufficiently respect the rights of the minority.*"[3] Tyranny of majority over minority, advocated by Viveka, is no less dangerous than the tyranny of minority over majority, which he is questioning. James Madison wrote in a letter, "There is no maxim, in my opinion, which is more liable to be misapplied, and which, therefore, more needs elucidation, than the current one, that the interest of the majority is the political standard of right and wrong."[4] Viveka, therefore, needs to do his homework on democracy a little more. James Madison also claimed, "If we are to take for the criterion of truth the majority of suffrages, they ought to be gotten from those philosophic and patriotic citizens who cultivate their reason."[5] If Viveka is to be part of the suffrage that determines the truth (not mere opinion or *doxa*), he has to cultivate his reason and patriotism a little more as a sober citizen, rather than abandoning himself to the heat of the passion of the moment as a factional activist. Let me end this discussion of Viveka's views on *dalit* agenda by a quotation from Dr. Ambedkar himself, "If the social forces are to be prevented from contaminating politics and preventing it to the aggrandizement of the few and the degradation of the many then it follows that the political structure must be so framed that it will contain mechanisms that will bottle the prejudices and nullify the injustice which social forces were likely to cause if they were let loose."[6] This as much applies to Scheduled Castes/*dalits* now as much it applied to *savarṇas*/Hindus once.

I am not interested in criticizing Viveka or his writings. I am making an effort to understand the representative sample of the scholarly *dalit* discourse. But unfortunately, the representative discourse turns out to be very poor when judged by standards of theoretical as well as practical reason. This representative sample of *dalit* scholarly discourse is a perfect example of what *Bhagavadgītā* terms as *tāmasika buddhi* (dark intellect). *Bhagavadgītā,* XVIII.32: defines *tāmasika buddhi* (dark intellect): *adharmaṁ dharmamiti yā manyate tamasāvṛtā / sarvārthān viparītāṁśca buddhiḥ sā pārtha tāmasī //* —"That which, enveloped in darkness, sees wrong as right and all things as inverted, that intellect, O Pārtha, is *Tāmasika.*" In this representative sample of *dalit* discourse "wrong doing" (i.e. corrupt act) is right doing but presence of people in an institution simply because they happened to be upper caste which is not wrong in itself but is perceived as wrong is clearly an example of *tāmasika buddhi* (dark intellect). In dark intellect everything appears as its opposite, right as wrong, wrong as right, good as bad, bad as good, beautiful as ugly, ugly as beautiful, something that is mirthful like a cartoon appears as something hurtful and what is hurtful appears as mirthful etc. The world of *dalit* discourse is really the *verkehrte Welt* 'inverted/perverted world' described by Hegel in the chapter on 'Forces and Understanding' in the *Phenomenology of Spirit.*"[7] In inversion-perversion something appears as its opposite. In the *verkehrte* 'inverted/ perverted' world everything is the reverse of the right world whose inversion-perversion it is. In such an inverted/perverted world revenge is justice, justice is revenge, punishment is pardon, pardon is punishment, infliction of injury is well-doing, well-doing is infliction of injury, what is not culpable is culpable, and what is culpable is not culpable etc. No doubt to the *dalit* intellect what is in their grasp appears as remote and what is remote appears as in their reach and in both situation the illusion they have fallen into makes them frustrated and angry.

1.3. Ambedkar's Erroneous Standards of Discourse

The *dalit* scholastic discourse is following a paradigm of faulty discourse. Anoop Kumar in his discourse appealed to Ambedkar. Viveka too appeals to Ambedkar's discourse. Hence, my third work is that it is Ambedkar himself who is responsible for setting an erroneous paradigm of *dalit* discourse which is emulated and copied by the subsequent present generation of *dalit* scholars which is really leading to rejection of his real legacy in *dalit* discourse. I have chosen his discourse on *Bhagavadgītā*, for multiple reasons. According to one scholar, "It is ... natural that Ambedkar, who was a serious scholar and critic of Hindu religion and society, should take cognisance of this great book. Ambedkar was a champion of the *Shudras* and *ati-shudras* in our society. He, therefore, has evaluated the *Gītā* in an entirely different way. His comments on the *Gītā* essentially summarise, his critique of Hindu religion and society."[8] Ambedkar's evaluation of *Gītā* follows the pattern of scholarly discourse and it is *dalit* discourse on all parameters, i.e. it is by a *dalit* thinker himself and it is woven round issues of *dalit* concern which is the ideological support *Bhagavadgītā* gives for maintenance of an order of caste that keeps oppressing the *dalits*. So, the first reason is that it is a fitting example which the *dalit* scholarly discourse emulates. Secondly, it is available for evaluation objectively. Ambedkar's views on the *Gītā* are available in an unfinished manuscript entitled *Revolution and Counter-revolution in Ancient India*, the text of which was included in Vol. 3 of the *Dr. Baba Saheb Ambedkar: Speeches and Writings* published by the Government of Maharashtra. Not only his comments are available in black and white, these can be evaluated objectively by comparing with the text of *Bhagavadgītā* which was available to him to come back again and again to validate his comment and which is available to us also to check and recheck the validity of his comments.

Ambedkar's major comments on *Bhagavadgītā* are as follows: (1) It is a philosophical defence of the counter-revolution.[9] By counter-revolution he means restoration of Brahminism during Gupta period, especially during the reign of king Balāditya. It is counter revolution because it took place after moral and social revolution ushered in by Buddhism during Mauryan empire especially during the reign of King Ashoka was over. The *Bhagavadgītā*, says Ambedkar, was composed to give ideological and moral support to this counter-revolution. During counter-revolution *varṇa* was turned into caste. The Brahmins brought about a system of graded inequality based on birth.

(2) *Bhagavadgītā* consists of four separate parts.[10] (3) Kṛṣṇa offers a philosophic defence of war and killing in war.[11] (4) *Bhagavadgītā* offers a philosophic defence of *caturvarṇya*. The soul of the *Bhagavadgītā* seems to be the defence of *caturvarṇya* and securing its observance in practice.[12] (5) The *Bhagavadgītā* offers a philosophic defence, Ambedkar continues, for the *karma mārga*. By *karma mārga* the *Bhagavadgītā* means the performance of the observances, such as *yajña* as a way to salvation.[13]

1.3.1. Is Bhagavadgītā Counter-revolutionary?

Let me examine each of these comments by referring to what is written in *Bhagavadgītā* itself. I will not take help of any conjecture regarding history, as the factuality of *Bhagavadgītā* as the product of and for early Gupta period is questioned on historical grounds, as Jayant Lele and Romila Thapar find it as a product of the early post-Maurya period, which was a period of crisis and transition of social system.[14]

Let us evaluate first Ambedkar's claim that *Bhagavadgītā* is a philosophical defence of the counter-revolution. By counter-revolution he means restoration of Brahminism. It is counter-revolution because it took place after moral and social revolution ushered in by Buddhism was over. The *Bhagavadgītā*, says Ambedkar, was composed to give ideological and moral support to this counter-revolution during which *varṇa* was turned into caste. The Brahmins brought about a system of graded inequality based on birth.

I shall evaluate it on the basis of first chapter of *Bhagavadgītā* itself. In the first chapter Arjuna's confusion regarding *varṇa dharma* comes out clearly when he formulates his anxiety regarding fighting in the war. The war will destroy many families. In I.39-43 Arjuna articulates his anxiety keeping in view the possible destruction of families. He says: *kulakṣaye praṇaśyanti kuladharmāḥ sanātanāḥ / dharme naṣṭe kulaṁ kṛtsnam adharmo bhibhavatyut // adharmābhibhavātkṛṣṇa praduṣyanti kulastriyaḥ / strīṣu duṣṭāsu vārṣṇeya jāyate varṇasaṁkaraḥ // saṁkaro narakāyaiva kulaghnānāṁ kulasya ca / patanti pitaro hyeṣāṁ luptapiṇḍodakakriyāḥ // doṣairetaiḥ kulaghnānāṁ varṇasaṁkarakārakaiḥ / utsādyante jātidharmāḥ kuladharmāśca śāśvatāḥ // utsannakuladharmāṇāṁ manuṣyāṇāṁ janārdana // narake niyataṁ vāso bhavatīty anuśuśruma* // "On the extinction of a family, the immemorial *dharmas* of that family disappear, when the *dharmas* disappear, *adharma* overtakes the whole family. By the prevalence of *adharma*, O Kṛṣṇa, the women of the family become corrupt. Women corrupted; there will be intermingling of *varṇas* (*varṇa-saṁkara*), O descendant of *Vṛṣṇīs*. Intermingling of *varṇas* leads the family of these destroyers also to hell; for, their forefathers fall (down to hell), deprived of the offerings of *piṇḍa* (rice-ball) and water. By these evil deeds of the destroyers of families which cause the intermingling of *varṇas*, the eternal *dharmas* of castes and families are subverted. We have heard, O *Janārdana*, that necessary is the dwelling in hell of the men whose family *dharmas* are subverted." Conclusion is that as Arjuna does not want to go to hell he does not want to fight in the war.

In the above argument Arjuna's confusion regarding *varṇa dharma* is complete. He is not able to make a distinction between *kula* (family linease) *dharma*, *jāti* (caste) *dharma* and *varṇa dharma*. He is confusing one with the other and using *kula*, *jāti* and *varṇa* interchangeably throughout. The reason is that he has linked *varṇa* to birth. This is the confusion we all suffer from even today. But, that is not the only confusion we all share with Arjuna. But, there are deeper confusions about *dharma* that will emerge as we analyse the relevant verses of *Bhagavadgītā*.

When *Kṛṣṇa* discusses *dharma* he never talks about *kula* (family) *dharma* or *jāti* (caste) *dharma*. He only talks of *varṇa dharma*, *svadharma*, *paradharma* or *dharma* in general or *śāśvata/śātvata dharma*. This shift in terms used by *Kṛṣṇa* is very significant. He is dissociating *varṇa* from birth. So, the claim of Ambedkar, that *Bhagavadgītā* was composed to give ideological and moral support to counter-revolution during which *varṇa* was turned into caste is completely unsupported by the text, rather it is the other way round; *varṇa* is dissociated from *jati* as well as birth by Kṛṣṇa in *Bhagavadgītā*.

Not only is Kṛṣṇa dissociating *varṇa* from birth but also signalling a shift in the social order that is taking place and going to take place completely through the war is cognized and presented in the first chapter of *Bhagavadgītā*. Social organization before *Mahābhārata* war was clan, which was based on relation through birth and alliance. *Kurus* (*Kauravas*), *Pāñcālas*, *Vṛṣṇīs* etc. were such clans. All such clans were wiped out by the end of the war except *Vṛṣṇīs*, who annhilated themselves completely by internal fight later. Only *Pāṇḍavas* survived annihilation, but they were not a real clan as their blood line was broken as they neither had a common father nor a common mother. In a way they stood as persons with respective merits and yet organized together.

The conflict between importance of relations of birth and alliance in social organization and importance of the merit of the person in social organization comes out clearly in the first chapter of *Bhagavadgītā*. When Duryodhana the representative of Kaurava clan speaks to *Droṇa* he introduces the members of his army and opposite army either by name or by definite description involving their merit. I.2-9—*dṛṣṭvā tu pāṇḍavānīkaṁ vyūḍhaṁ duryodhanastadā / ācāryamupasaṅgamya rājā vacanamabravīt // paśyaitāṁ pāṇḍuputrāṇām ācārya mahatīṁ camūm / vyūḍhāṁ drupadaputreṇa tava śiṣyeṇa dhīmatā // atra śūrā maheśvāsā bhīmārjunasamā yudhi / yuyudhāno virāṭaśca drupadaśca mahārathaḥ // dhṛṣṭaketuścekitānaḥ kāśirājaśca vīryavān / purujitkuntibhojaśca śaibyaśca narapuṅgavaḥ // yudhāmanyuśca vikrānta uttamaujāśca vīryavān / saubhadro draupadeyāśca sarva eva mahārathāḥ // asmākaṃ tu viśiṣṭā ye tānnibodha dvijottama / nāyakā mama sainyasya saṁjñārthaṁ tānbravīmite // bhavān bhīṣmaśca karṇaśca kṛpaśca samitiñjayaḥ / aśvatthāmā vikarṇaśca saumadattistathaiva ca // anye ca bahavaḥ śūrā madarthe tyaktajīvitāḥ / nānāśastrapraharaṇāḥ sarve yuddhaviśāradāḥ //* "Having seen the army of the *Pāṇḍavas* drawn up in battle-array, king Duryodhana then approached his teacher and spoke (these) words: "O teacher, look at this grand army of the sons of Pāṇḍu, marshalled by your talented pupil, the son of Drupada. Here are heroes, mighty archers, equal in battle to Bhīma and Arjuna—

Yuyudhana, Virāta, and Drupada, the master of a great *ratha* (*mahāratha*), Dhṛṣṭaketu, Chekitana, and the valiant king of Kāśi, Purujit and Kunti-Bhoja and that eminent man Saibya; the heroic Yudhamanyu and the brave Uttamaujas; the son of Subhadrā and the sons of Draupadī, all masters of great *rathas* (*mahārathas*). But know, O best of the twice-born, who are the most distinguished among us, the leaders of my army; these I name to you by way of example: yourself and Bhīṣma, and Karṇa, and also Kṛpa, the victor in war, Aśvatthāmā and Vikarṇa, and also Jayadratha, the son of Saumadatta; and many other heroes who are ready to give-up their lives for my sake, fighting with various weapons, all well-skilled in battle." Duryodhana is quite modern in outlook and has an individualistic perspective. He is looking at the merit of each indidividual fighter even in the opposing army. He is evaluating each individual fighter in his own standing without taking into consideration his lineage, which is used if at all only for identification of the individual but not for attribution of merit to him.

But when Arjuna representing *Pāṇḍavas* who were not a real clan looked at the army on both sides he saw only relations mostly of birth and alliance. I.26-27—*tatāpaśyat sthitān pārthaḥ pitṝn atha pitāmahān / ācāryān mātulān bhrātṝn putrān pautrān sakhīṁstathā // śvaśurān suhṛdaścaiva senayorubhayor api / tān samīkṣya sa kaunteyaḥ sarvān bandhūn avasthitān //* "Then the son of Pṛitha saw arrayed therein both the armies fathers and grandfathers, teachers, maternal uncles, brothers, sons, grandsons and comrades, fathers-in-law and relatives." In I.33-34 Arjuna himself speaks: *yeṣāmarthe kāṅkṣitaṃ no rājyaṁ bhogāḥ sukhāni ca / ta ime 'vasthit yuddhe prāṇāṁstyaktvā dhanāni ca // ācāryāḥ pitaraḥ putrāstathaiva ca pitāmahāḥ / mātulāḥ śvaśurāḥ pautrāḥ śyālāḥ sambandhinastathā //* "They for whose sake dominion, enjoyments and pleasures are sought by us are here standing, having staked their life and wealth: teachers, fathers, sons as well as grandfathers; maternal uncles, fathers-in-law, grandsons, brothers-in-law as also (other) relatives." This repetition of list of relations first through the mouth of *Sañjaya* as a third person description of what Arjuna saw and then through his own speech in first person is very significant. The author of *Bhagavadgītā* through repetition is trying to emphasize this fact regarding what Arjuna saw as if he is underlining it. This is made more emphatic, as if the author is adding *italics*, by making Arjuna refer to the people assembled to fight as *svajana* (own people) four times in four different verses, i.e. verses I.28, I.31, I.37, and I.45. This is put in greater relief, as if put in bold face, by putting it in contrast to what Duryodhana saw. So, this fact is important in understanding and interpreting *Bhagavadgītā*, as it underlies the confusion of Arjuna and makes him *dharmasaṁmūḍhacetāḥ* "confused in mind regarding *dharma*". Similarly, the long list of warriors by name or definite description through the mouth of Duryodhana is put deliberately by the author of *Bhagavadgītā* and it is meant for recognizing the principle operative implicitly in the mind of Duryodhana as it is put in contrast to what Arjuna saw when he looked at the same warriors. The contrast highlights that Duryodhana is not seeing warriors on both sides as related by birth or alliance, but as persons with personal merit. This fact is also important for interpretation of *Bhagavadgītā*.

It is surprising that it is the representative of Kaurava clan, i.e. Duryodhana who is already attuned in his thinking unawares for the new kind of social organization that is opposite to what he really represents. In contrast Arjuna's despondency is as much for the relatives as much it is for the death of old social order he is familiar with, i.e. clan.[15] The significance of the opening scene of the dialogue in the first chapter is that it dramatically highlights through the words of the two heroes Duryodhana and Arjuna the transition of social order, i.e. the transition of social order of clans based on relations through birth and alliance to more inclusive social order based on person's merit and nature without depending on relations through birth and alliance.[16] That transition is taking place is clearly indicated the way the two kinds of concerns: concern for more inclusive social order based on person's merit and nature without depending on relations through birth or alliance, and concern for social order of clans based on relations through birth and alliance, are introduced. The forty seven verses of the first chapter are divided equally by the twenty fourth verse which is the middle verse. The first twenty three verses are written with a view to represent the upbeat mood of Duryodhana and Arjuna, with both the protagonists bristling with enthusiasm to fight. And in the context of this upbeat mood the theme of concern for the more inclusive social order based on person's merit and nature without depending on relations through birth or alliance is brought in implicitly. But, from verse twenty five onwards the upbeat mood all of a sudden gives way to despondency of down cast Arjuna, who starts lamenting the possible demise of social order of clans based on relations through birth and alliance. The middle verse, i.e. twenty fourth verse is very telling: *evamukto hṛṣīkeśo guḍākeśena bhārata/ senayorubhayormadhye sthāpayitvā rathottamam //* "O descendant of Bhārata, Hṛṣikeśa (Kṛṣṇa) thus addressed by Guḍākeśa (Arjuna) stationed that excellent car between the two armies..." The verse tells as much about placing of the physical charriot in middle of the two physical armies, as it tells about the placing of the entire carriage of discussion in the middle of the conflicting inclusive social order based on person's merit and nature without depending on relation through birth or alliance presented in upbeat mood and the social order of clans based on relations of birth and alliance presented in the mood of despondency.

The opening chapter of the *Bhagavadgītā* has been neglected in the context of determination whether it is revolutionary or counter revolutionary text. Ambedkar merely takes note of first chapter only to highlight the battle context of the dialogue to declare *Bhagavadgītā* as a dialogue to justify war. This kind of reading misses the hermeneutic significance of the opening scene of the battle field in the first chapter of *Bhagavadgītā* which is the context of the dialogue.

Kṛṣṇa is reinterpreting the existing *varṇa* theory dissociating it completely from birth to suit the emerging social order based on recognition of merit and he had to find new basis for *dharma*. The new basis far *dharma* is better suited for more inclusive society that was emerging than what existed which was based on relations of birth and alliance, a kind of tribe. This new basis, as it will be shown later, prepared the basis for possible criticism of *varṇa dharma* in future, to even make possible further transition from it to a newer organization as the new realities demand. The *varṇa dharma* was just a contingent temporal realization of a more general idea of *dharma* which could be realized through social system other than the *cāturvarṇyam* as far as *Bhagavadgītā* is concerned. *Bhagavadgītā* goes on to develop a general theory of *dharma* also suitable to the emerging new social organization based not on descent or alliance but on relations which are inclusive, inclusive of persons on their merit independent of descent or alliance. So, one can conjecture that the author of *Bhagavadgītā* was after all not in favour of *status quo* rather had reformist intention in reinterpreting *varṇa dharma*. It was a revolutionary text and not a counter revolutionary as Ambedkar projects on historical grounds, but internal textual evidence shows it to be revolutionary, assisting a transition from clan based social system to merit based inclusive open society.

1.3.2. Vivisection of Text by Modern Mind and Its Faulty Hermeneutics

Bhagavadgītā even though not confused in itself can be confusing for and has confused many modern readers including Ambedkar. This is because the classical Indian way of thinking has withdrawn from our consciousness because our thinking in modern times is completely fixated on objectivity, on overcoming the resistant character of the object in a percipient certainty of ourselves as subjectivity.

Modern thinking has its roots in classical Greek thinking. The classical Greek thinking characterized the craftsman, the expert, the creator of new shapes and forms, the *technites*, the man who masters a technique and at the same time finds proper place to exercise this technique. He required the discovery of a free space for creative production that will be available to him in the middle of a pre-given nature, a wholeness of the world that orders itself in shapes and forms. Thus, thinking during the Greek awakening is the thoughtful becoming aware of the enormous exposure of human-beings within this tiny field of free space that the ordered whole of the course of nature allows for human will and ability. It is precisely in this exposure that thinking becomes conscious of the confrontation between the intelligible world and masterable world. What fascinated the modern thinking was the masterable world. Therefore, modern thought that began in the seventeenth century, turned the intelligible world into the object (of subject-object dichotomy of Western philosophy) of methodical inquiry by means of the mathematically conceived and abstracted and isolated question frame of modern experimental science (undertaken by the subject), and thus, collapsed the distinction between intelligible and masterable world by absorbing the intelligible world in the masterable world and turning the earlier technique into modern technology.

But classical Indian thinking knew of no such masterable world. The self (*ātman, puruṣa*) though conscious was devoid of activity. The activity was in the *prakṛti* in the presence of self, even as *jīvātman kartā* he merely participated in the activity of the *prakṛti*. So, the question of mastery of the world never arose for the Indian thought. Classical Indian thought is geared for unravelling the metaphysics of belonging, i.e. belonging to the world, settling in the world. But this aspect of the classical Indian thought is taken as conservatism and advocacy of *status quo*. While to think of the world including the social practice as masterable and hence deliberately changeable to make it conform to preconceived ideal is understood as revolutionary. This is the reason modern mind like that of Ambedkar gets confused by thinking present in *Bhagavadgītā*. Ambedkar's comments are based not only on not reading the text closely violating the principle of reason required in textual hermeneutics, but also not being able to follow the logic of development of the topic. This comes out more clearly in his second comment.

Let us examine the second claim regarding *Bhagavadgītā* by Dr. Ambedkar that it consists of four separate parts. The four parts are as follows: first part is the original core which is just a heroic tale of how Arjuna was not prepared to fight and how Kṛṣṇa forced him to engage in battle, how Arjuna yielded and so on. The second part is the first patch on the original core, which is the part in which Kṛṣṇa is spoken of as *Iśvara*, the god of the *Bhāgavata* religion. This part is embedded in those verses of the text which are devoted to *Bhakti Yoga*. The third part is the second patch on the original core, which is the part that introduces the *Sāṁkhya* and *Vedānta* philosophy as a defence of the doctrines of *Pūrva Mīmāṁsā* which they did not have before. This philosophical portion was a later intrusion. The fourth part is the third patch on the original core, which consists of verses in which Kṛṣṇa is elevated from the position of *Īśvara* to that of *Parameśvara*.

Bhagavadgītā is a poetic statement. All historical-occasional element not found in the poetic text do not belong to it and have no bearing on the meaning of such text. This limits the value of historical information that comes not from the text but from some other place. Such information cannot be a criterion for correct interpretation. What matters in the determination of the meaning of a poetic text is what the text itself says. Not even the author's intention has any authority here, for what one wants to understand is a particular text and not the intention that the author had in producing the text. Even if the author of *Gītā* had an intention of legitimizing a particular historical practice that fact does not control the meaning. *What determines the meaning is what the text says to the reader or listener in his context and that is the function of the overall unity of the text. It is the anticipation of unity of meaning of the text that controls the understanding of the text.* Texts like *Gītā* address people from all strata in all ages and are not meant for teasing and provoking the learned society of Marxists or *Dalits* or otherwise in any way. Its meaning is not dependent upon any sophisticated historical knowledge to which only Marxist or *Dalit* or other scholars have a privy.

But how does one understand what the text says? The understanding comes only from the repeated reading of the text, i.e. by *abhyāsa* and not by following any kind of technique sanctioned by a theory like Marxists theory or Critical theory or analytical theory. If knowledge prevents us from learning anything from the poem that knowledge is useless. Marxist and *Dalit* knowledge of history of production of *Gītā* is such knowledge and hence has no bearing on what it says.

Historically, it may be possible to show that *Gītā* is a late composition and it is interpolated in *Mahābhārata* later. What impact does this fact have on its interpretation? Ambedkar finds *Bhagavadgītā* as an interpolation by some obscure authors wishing to hide their own identity or to claim a greater credibility for their work who adopted some well known author's name, such as that of Vyāsa, as their pen-name. But does that really matter and how?

Gītā is embeded in a larger text of epic *Mahābhārata*, yet tradition has generally read *Gītā* as an independent text, i.e. independent from its being embedded in epic *Mahābhārata*. What is the significance of this fact? This fact requires that we may have to *clarify* an embedded intellectual creation like the *Bhagavadgītā,* with respect to some substantively important feature, with recourse only to larger text or context in which it is embedded. And yet it is a self-contained whole. That means that we should interpret important substantive feature of it by knowledge of sources mentioned in it like *Sāṁkhya*, *Yoga* etc., and yet having recourse to help of other texts it has to be interpreted as a self-standing unitary text in its own right and not as appendage to, extension of, or part of another system of thought, or a un-unified syncretic putting together of divergent views to appeal to every section of society. Vivisection of *Gītā* to suit one's preconceived ideological interpretation as advocated by Ambedkar violates the essential guideline of any textual interpretation. A text has to be read as a coherent unified text standing by itself.

The words of a poem have the unity of a speech, unity of a text. It requires not only understanding of the individual words, but also determination of the significance of a word within the unity of meaning formed by the text itself. The polyvalence of the word needs to be made determinate in completing the meaning of the unified text. Since, a poem like *Gītā* is self-standing it cannot be measured by any thing that exist prior to or independent of it. Hence, sublation of positivity of signifying and naming level of meaning of words has to be achieved by seeing it as a rejoinder, i.e. as an answer to a question. This question is not said explicitly in the text yet is audible as a presupposition of expectation of meaning awakened by the poem. Referential function of words is realized not through the posited reality independent of the text of the poem, rather the referential function of the word is for the service of hearing the question to which the text is an answer.[17] Through the referential function of words the question is audible as the unsaid of the text. Since, the text of a poem does not posit a reality to which it refers and by which it can be measured it is completely self-contained unity. So, determination of meaning of a text is not a historical quest for an independently posited reality but a determination of the question to which the text is an answer.

Gītā itself declares the truth that what it declares is not on the surface, at the level of word meaning which can be available to any one. Rather its truth is *guhya*, hidden in the cave (of the heart) to be discovered by the reader himself, who has the requisite capacity to delve into the deeper recesses of the text and words, who have the firm belief that such truth is there, so that they do not give up the task of harmonizing text by mere surface meaning of word and finding them contradictory leading to vivisection of the text.

The literary form of *Bhagavadgītā* is not only that of metric verse, but also that of mythical dialogue. The maxim of interpretation of dialogue is that every dialogue is intelligible, even if not necessarily *adequately* interpretable, in terms of its own totality. It is impossible to understand a dialogue like *Bhagavadgītā* without at the same time making the effort to understand on one's own the subject matter to which it is devoted. Here, we have to keep in mind that a dialogue is guided by the topic to which it is devoted. The logic of the connections in *Bhagavadgītā*'s analysis of the topic is more concealed than apparent and can be uncovered only by having recourse to the logical order of the subject matter itself. Speaking more generally, we would be poor readers of *Bhagavadgītā* if we did not allow this dialogue to lead us to the things, the facts of the matter themselves or if we did not try to retrace as questioners the course of questioning that the dialogue presents and to describe the direction in which the Dialogue proceeds. Accordingly, we have to take as our point of departure the phenomena as they show themselves to us laying aside all our scholarly knowledge and only subsequently to bring scholarly knowledge to conceptualize it in a manner to make it accessible in contemporary idiom.

The common error that obstructs one's way to the poem is the error of trying to read it on the basis of something external to the poem, something brought in from the outside, even one's subjective impressions regarding the poem. The correctness of an interpretation depends on how far the interpretation tightens-up the text and increases the coherence of the text and also to the extent that the interpretation itself has cohesion. If the coherence does not extend to the full text, the interpretation has the potentiality of going wrong. If the unity of the text is made visible and comprehensible in the interpretation then a certain criterion of correctness is achieved. The closed unity of a poem like *Gītā* is very stringent and it does not allow itself to be redefined by a larger context as it happens with other kinds of unities of speech, whose true meaning is provided by the context. But unfortunately Ambedkar has failed to read *Gītā* as a unity or a unified text. Vivisection of the text of *Bhagavadgītā* to suit one's preconceived ideological interpretation as advocated by Ambedkar is an implicit admission of inability to read the text as a unity and implicit admission of ones inability to understand the logic of development of the topic, but a simultaneous overt refusal to do so and cover-up one's inability by projecting it as a faultlines in the composition of the text, like the faultline between core and interpolation or faultline between multiple patches. Intellectual honesty demands that one should declare that one has not been able to see or discover coherence in a text if he has not been able to read it as such and not project it as a scholarly discovery if the text has a long tradition of being read as a unitary text while vivisection is only a recent phenomenon due to withdrawal of classical thinking from modern mind like that of Ambedkar. Not only withdrawal of classical thinking, but also excessive self-obsession prevents a scholar from listening to the question to which the text is an answer. When we listen to the question audible in the text to which the text is an answer and let the *the overall unity of the text to determine the meaning or what the text says to the reader or listener* then the unity of theme emrges and becomes visible in the unity of text. When we follow the correct principles of hermeneutics we find that the entire discussion of *Bhagavadgītā* from the very first chapter is carried keeping in mind the conflict between inclusive social order based on person's merit and nature without depending on relations of birth or alliance, which is presented in upbeat mood, and the social order of clans based on relations of birth and alliance, which is presented in the mood of despondency. And Kṛṣṇa is reinterpreting the existing *varṇa* institution dissociating it completely from birth to suit the emerging social order based on recognition of merit to find new basis for *dharma*. The new basis for *dharma* is better suited for more inclusive society that was emerging than what existed which was based on birth relation, a kind of tribe. *Bhagavadgītā* goes on to develop a general understanding of *dharma* that can fit into human practice of any institution and also develops a theory of institutional revision. This new understanding prepared the basis for possible criticism of *varṇa dharma* in future, to even make possible further transition from it to a newer organization as the new realities demand. It was his excessive self-absorption in his personal experience that prevented Ambedkar from really getting the message of *Bhagavadgītā*. Had he been able to get the message of *Bhagavadgītā* his experience would have been different and not so self-absorbing and he would have been a far more successful leader and not a mere lately discovered symbol for a *dalit* identity that denies his legacy and conceives its goal not institution building or reformation of institutions but as a wholesale replacement of entire population, depending on caste, manning institutions as if social reformation is a war of one section of population with another to displace and dispossess them and not a co-operative effort to move with the times. This aspect of Ambedkar's thought comes out in his third comment.

1.3.3. Is Bhagavadgītā a Philosophical Justification of War and Killing?

His third comment on *Bhagavadgītā* is that in it Kṛṣṇa offers a philosophic defence of war and killing in war. This is a very facile reading of war setting of *Bhagavadgītā* in the first chapter. Let us read the first chapter to find out when and why the discussion of *Bhagavadgītā* began. It begins after the two armies are assembled to fight and the battle-conches had blared out to declare readiness for war. This war was already collectively decided to be fought. So, where was the scope for discussion to decide whether war is to be fought or not to be fought? That issue was already decided and was over much before the discussion of *Bhagavadgītā* began. So, by no stretch of logic can it be claimed that Kṛṣṇa offers a philosophic defence of war and killing in war in *Bhagavadgītā*.

One must then ask why this most intricate three hour abstract discourse on philosophy of praxis is set as delivered after the battle-conches had blared out to declare readiness for war, a war which is already collectively decided to be fought. Is it not obvious that it is highly improbable that such a discourse will take place in a battle-field? What is the significance of the fact that this improbability of discourse is made so obvious in the text itself? Firstly, it highlights the mythic nature of the dialogue. It is only a mythical dialogue not a real dialogue. Secondly, the exegetical significance of the obvious improbability is that the text is not to be read merely as reasoning to incite someone to fight a battle in the war as the text does not befit the battle context. That is to say the text has meaning that transcends the battle context. Yet, the text is artificially embedded in the battle context to highlight the requirement that one cannot interpret it unless this context of war is taken as the starting point. That is to say even though a meaning is to be found that transcends the situation yet that meaning cannot be found if we do not interpret the text starting from the context of the battle which is already decided to take place and allow the universal meaning to be controlled by this context.

Here, we have to dwell a little longer on the context of war in which the dialogue of *Gītā* has its setting. Why is the context of war the starting point for *Gītā*? Why this extreme limit situation of mass death provide context for *Gītā*? The phenomenon of war is the strangest discovery of the twisted nature of man. Man appears to be a contradiction within nature itself. Nature has produced a type of being that can turn against itself in a particular way unknown to any other species in nature. Man in a planned and organized fashion attacks, destroys, or maims fellow members of his own species. So, war points to fundamental instability of human nature, which is unique in the realm of nature. No other species of being exhibits such instability of its nature. To stabilize man's nature there is greatest need to stabilize norms of conduct in the sense of right and wrong. In the kind of being that man is, whose needs and goals have become complex and even contradictory, there is a need for enlightened choice, just deliberation, and right conduct for common objective. This is a first step toward what we call practice (praxis).[18] The object of *Gītā*'s discourse is the human practice (praxis) and war is the limit of the practice. Let me emphasize once again that a strange being called man has emerged within the chain of the formations of nature or creation. In nature every other living creature is interlocked in its instinctual schemes and this scheme's relation to the preservation of the species. Man is the only being that has turned away from the natural interlocking of its instinctual schemes and its relation to the preservation of the species. Essentially, human being's vital instinct has been atrophied and this makes him stand out in contrast to everything else in the animal realm. The specificity of atrophied instinct in man is that he has the in-built capacity to think beyond his own life in the world, to think about death. Setting of the dialogue of *Gītā* in the context of war is to highlight this capacity of man to think beyond his own life, to think about death, testified by Arjuna's *karuṇā* and *viṣāda* for others. War itself exhibits a contradiction, a breakdown of practice and also the continuance of the practice. To think of death amidst the war is also indicative of the human practice of treatment of the dead in the war, be that practice be of burial or the cremation. The practice of treatment of the dead, the funerary practice, is perhaps the fundamental phenomenon of becoming human. Man does not let death have the last word. The most elementary significance of this fact is that it fundamentally constitutes human being. So, from the last rites of the dead derives the specific sense of human practice. No doubt in his argument from *kula dharma* and *jāti dharma* Arjuna refers to the specific last rites of the dead. The rites of the dead are conduct of life that has spiraled out of the order of nature due to atrophied instinct of man. In nature we observe instinctual ignorance, indifference or shunning of dead members of the species. In contrast to what happens in nature instinctually in other species, humanity has even turned against this natural vital instinct of survival and has begun the practice of rites of the dead. But what is practice? That is the question *Gītā* asks and answers. *Gītā* no doubt discusses the practice in general through the specific practices but its main topic is not the specific practice. It is the practice in general that *Gītā* is interested in.

The dialogue of *Gītā* is placed at the beginning of the war, and not at the end of the war. It deals with the issues confronting Arjuna's thinking before he starts fighting in the war that has arrived, not with thinking at the end of the fight. This perspective on action before the commencement of the action is to be distinguished from the perspective on action after it has begun or it has ended. The modern thinking on action is from the point of view after the action has begun or ended. So, in modern thought the emphasis is on attributing the action to individual or individuals. We look for what makes the action an act of some one or some person. We look for who is responsible for what on what ground. Even in the corporate act attempt is made in modern thought to lift the veil of corporation to find the individual responsible for the action. In the modern thought perspective is that of punishment after the act is performed. Who is to be blamed?, who is to be held responsible?, and who is to be punished?, such are the prime questions. If the action is such that no one is responsible then it is not an act at all. It is only an event in nature. But, *Gītā*'s perspective on action is exactly the opposite. It is thinking on action before its commencement in a context where requirement of action has already arrived. We as agents are always *in a situation like arrival of the war* as the praxis in the family, profession, society, and state has already arrived for each one of us. How is one to act so that no one even notices that an agent has performed an action, it appears so natural, as if the institution is functioning by itself. To put it differently, the question is: How is one to participate or not participate so that the blame does not come to the person who performs his conduct at the arrival of the praxis? This is the prime question. What is the correct initiative of action so that it becomes a corporate act or natural act so that the responsibility and blame does not come to the person who performs it? The action is noticed and the issue of blame arises when we do not decide correctly and do not act correctly. Modern thought blames individual without telling him how he is to act so that blame does not come to him? Mere avoidance of conditions of *post facto* blame and responsibility does not tell us how to act. That is the problem with thinking on action by moderns. But the classical Indian thought especially, in *Bhagavadgītā*, tells how to initiate action so that the question of *post facto* blame and responsibility do not arise. Right initiation of action (*samārambha*) makes it a natural or corporate act according to *Gītā*. If there is *samārambha* of action then it is so easily distributed as action over collectivity that nobody even notices who has performed the action. Such, is the nature of true action, an institutional action according to *Bhagavadgītā*.

Is *Bhagavadgītā* a philosophical justification of killing in war as Ambedkar claims? War itself is a practice, but a practice at a limit point, where solidarity and reason of institutional practice is about to break or broken. It is an ambiguous point. So, war is a practice, where every other way of practice like the practice of dialogue has failed, to restore institutional practice. So, it has its own *dharma* as practice. Its *dharma*, its essence, and its ideation is nothing to do with killing or being killed. It is an accidental extra added in the situation of war to the ideation of war. This is presented in the figure of Bhīṣma who cannot be killed as he is portrayed as some one who can die only if he himself wishes. If essence of war is to kill and be killed, then Bhīṣma being the commander of one army is a logical contradiction in war. What this contradiction is meant to highlight is that killing and be killed, dying and causing death is not the *dharma* of war. In the first chapter itself the presence of Bhīṣma in the war was underlined. His presence in the war is mentioned thrice by Duryodhana in I.8, I.10, I.11 as if the author is underlining this fact as relevant to understanding *Bhagavadgītā* and its claims. Even that was not enough Sañjaya emphasizes presence of Bhīṣma by mentioning him thrice in I.12 as *kuruvṛddha pitāmaḥ* (eldely *kuru* the grandfather), in I.25 by name Bhīṣma, in I.26 as *pitāmaḥ* (grandfather). Author is still not satisfied he wants to emphasize Bhīṣma's presence in war even more so that there is no misunderstanding of the war context of the dialogue. So, Arjuna also acknowledges Bhīṣma's presence in war twice in I.34 as *pitāmaḥ* (grandfather) and in the beginning of chapter two in II.4

by name. When the presence of Bhīṣma, who can die only if he himself wishes in war, is emphasized it is meant to discount the idea that killing is essential to war or that killing is *dharma* of war. Then what is *dharma* of war? The *dharma* of war is not to kill or harm the enemy, but to set him right by force, to use force to restore practice, to use force to prevent him from breaking the practice. *Yuddha* is *saṁgrāmaṃ*, i.e. forceful settlement. Plato also accepts this point in his *Republic* where he makes Socrates refute Polemarchus by claiming that the justice of war is not in hurting the enemy but in setting enemy right with force.[19] Even when Bhīṣma could not be killed, he could still be forced out of war for settlement of the issue, but not for settling the scores as *dalit* mentality makes it out to be. So, by no stretch of imagination is *Bhagavadgītā* a philosophical justification of killing in war as Ambedkar claims. Killing is accidental not essential to war even for *Bhagavadgītā*. Ambedkar had no hermeneutic principle which could help him distinguish what is essential from what is accidental.

The so-called arguments for immortality of soul from chapter II on which Ambedkar relies to show that *Bhagavadgītā* is a philosophical justification of killing in war are not arguments for immortality of soul at all. The first chapter of *Bhagavadgītā* introduces the intense grief of Arjuna at the very thought of imminent possibility of so many of his own people being killed in the war. Kṛṣṇa responds in the second chapter by telling Arjuna that he is grieving for those who should not be grieved for and yet he is speaking like the learned (II.11): *aśocyānanvaśocastvaṁ prajñāvādāṁśca bhāṣase/gatāsūn agatāsūṁśca nānuśocanti paṇḍitāḥ //* The expression *prajñāvādāṁśca bhāṣase* "speaking like the learned" is a reproach that controls the meaning. What Kṛṣṇa is saying is that Arjuna is speaking like a *jñānin,* but he does not really know how to speak. Similarly by saying of Arjuna *aścyān anvaścas* "grieving of the ungrievable" which implies "thinking of the unthinkable" *Kṛṣṇa* wants to find fault with the intensional (and also intentional) structure of his thinking, i.e. the intended object of thought do not fit the intension of the thought at all. There are things which are not fit object of grief or thought; these are the dead (whose life breath is gone) as well as the living (whose life breath has not gone away). Wise men do not treat them as objects of grief or thought. Here, by a single arrow Kṛṣṇa wants to do away with grief of Arjuna and also to make Arjuna realize how to speak and think by realizing correctly the intensional (and also intentional) structure of thought and speech. Hence, by a single arrow Kṛṣṇa wants to kill two birds. Or to say it the way Gārgī puts it in *Bṛhadāraṇyaka Upaniṣad* 3.8.2: *pāśyo vā vaideho vograputra ujjyaṁ dhanurdhijyaṁ kṛtvā dvau bāṇavantau sapatnātivyādhinau haste kṛtvopottiṣṭhedevameva*—"as a man of Benares or the King of Videha, scion of a warlike dynasty, might string his unstrung bow and appear close by, carrying in his hand two bamboo-tipped arrows highly painful to the enemy"—Kṛṣṇa spoke with the intention to make Arjuna realize how to speak and think by realizing correctly the *intensional* structure of thought and speech and the *intentional* structure of action implied in it. Both the structures need to be corrected simultaneously to do away with grief of Arjuna and to make him fight in the war. What Kṛṣṇa says answers the following possible question which emerges from what he says: Why do the wise men not treat either the dead or the living as objects of grief? With answer to this question begins the answer to the question: why is intensional structure of Arjuna's thinking and speech wrong? The answer is given by Kṛṣṇa in the form of explanation for immortality of the soul which aims to remove Arjuna's grief not by proving the soul to be immortal, but by correcting the intensional structure of his thinking and speaking. Kṛṣṇa's so-called arguments for the immortality of the soul are really the clarification of the structure of intensionality of thought that prevents both whose life breath is gone and whose life breath is not gone from becoming the intensional object of thought and speech. Kṛṣṇa's so-called arguments for the immortality of the soul are not meant for licence to kill as Ambedkar thinks. His reading is very inadequate because of absence of any sound principle of textual hermeneutics.

1.3.4. Is Bhagavadgītā a Philosophical Defence of cāturvarṇyam?

No doubt this absence of hermeneutic principle to distinguish the accidental from essential in the mind of Ambedkar is highlighted by his fourth comment on *Bhagavadgītā* that it is a philosophic defence of *cāturvarṇya*. Can we accept that *Bhagavadgītā* offers a philosophic defence of *cāturvarṇya* as Ambedkar claims? Can we accept that the soul of the *Bhagavadgītā* seems to be the defence of *cāturvarṇya*? Can we accept that the aim of the *Bhagavadgītā* seems to be securing its observance in practice as claimed by Ambedkar?

Let me answer the second question first. There are not more than fourteen verses out of seven hundred verses which directly or indirectly deal with *varṇa* or *varṇa dharma*. These verses are: I.41; 43; II.31-33; IV.7; 8; 13; IX.32;33; XVIII.41-44. So, not more than 2 per cent verses in *Bhagavadgītā* deal with *cāturvarṇya* directly or indirectly. Is it sufficient to declare that *Bhagavadgītā* offers a philosophic defence of *cāturvarṇya*? Yes it can be sufficient provided it is shown that these verses state the work and rest of *Bhagavadgītā* build argument for the thesis. But self-admittedly Ambedkar is unable to unify the text. So, how can he unify the text to show that it is a philosophical defence of *cāturvarṇya*? It is only a superficial biased motivated reading. It must be kept in mind that at no place in *Bhagavadgītā* it is mentioned that people are divided into four *varṇas* on the basis of birth. But there is a division of all people born into two groups. The entire sixteenth chapter of twenty four verses is devoted to bipartite division of people. The bipartite division of people is stated in XVI.6 in these words: *dvau bhūtasargau loke'smin daiva āsura eva ca* "there are two creations of beings in this world, the divine and the demoniac", those of *āsuraṁ bhāvam* and *devaṁ bhāvam*. From the fact that only fourteen verses which are scattered are devoted to division of people into four *varṇas*, but entire twenty four verses of one chapter are devoted to bipartite division of people can we not reasonably infer that discussion of four *varṇas* is not as important as the discussion of division into those of *āsuraṁ bhāvam* and those of *devaṁ bhāvam*? Can we not reject the claim that the soul of the *Bhagavadgītā* seems to be the defence of *cāturvarṇya*? The answer to both the questions is in the affirmative. In fact it will be shown that all references to *varṇa* or *varṇa dharma* in *Bhagavadgītā* are contextual an accidental references. All references to *cāturvarṇya* can be replaced by reference to appropriate institutions without altering the meaning and truth of teaching of *Bhagavadgītā*.

The first group of verses uttered by Arjuna I.41 & 43 refer to *varṇa* and I have already shown how it presents the confusion regarding *varṇa dharma* in the mind of Arjuna to be removed by Kṛṣṇa's message to him.

The second group of verses II.31 to II.33 also refers to *varṇa dharma*. But how is reference to *varṇa dharma* utilized in them? Let us find out. Kṛṣṇa in *Bhagavadgītā* II.31 to II.33 brings in *varṇa dharma* to develop argument why Arjuna should fight in the battle: *svadharmamapi cāvekṣya na vikampitumarhasi / dharmyāddhi yuddhācchreyo'nyatkṣatriyasya na vidyate // yadṛcchayā copapannaṁ svargadvāram apāvṛtam / sukhinaḥ kṣatriyāḥ pārtha labhante yuddhamīdṛśam// atha cet tvamimaṁdharmyaṁ saṁ grāmaṁ na kariṣyasi / tataḥ svadharmaṁ kīrtiṁ ca hitvā pāpamavāpsyasi //* "Having regard to your own *dharma* also you ought not to waver. For, to a *Kṣatriya*, there is nothing better than a war of *dharma*. Happy are the *Kṣatriyas*, O son of Pṛitha, who find such a war as this, which has come of itself, as an open door to heaven. Now, if you will not fight this battle of *dharma*, then, having abandoned your own *dharma* and fame, you will incur sin." In them reference to *varṇa dharma* is made use of in a way that highlights its contextual nature. Since, *cāturvarṇyam* was already in existence with its early understanding with which Arjuna was familiar, Kṛṣṇa makes reference to it. If any other social practice were in existence, for example the practice of modern state the argument will be equally valid. One only has to rethink of the opening scene with armies of two modern states facing each other and one of the brigadiers of one of the army after assuming the command of the brigade and having entered the battle-field refuses to fight out of despondency because of impending death of his comrades in arms. Here, the argument from his *dharma* as member of the army and also argument from fame will be equally valid. The opening scene can be changed even further to a scene in examination hall in a university where student leaders are sitting as examinee well known for their hooliganism and history of copying and if caught tearing the copies of other examinees in the hall. An invigilator having collected the bundle of blank answer sheets and question papers enters the examination hall, but seeing such student leaders refuses to invigilate out of compassion for the innocent examinees fearing certain disturbance of their writing the examination and destruction of their answer scripts. Here, also the same argument from *dharma* and fame—this time *dharma* will be the *dharma* of one as teacher of the university—will be equally applicable. So, the argument of II.31 to II.33 makes contextual reference to *varṇa dharma* but the argument as such transcends *varṇa dharma*. *Dharma* could have been that of *śatavarṇyaṃ*, *sahasravarṇyaṃ*, *śatasahasravarṇyaṃ* or any other social practice without any *varṇa* here, the argument would still be valid provided the similar situation arises in that practice. In fact, it would be shown later that *Bhagavadgītā*'s understanding of *dharma* transcends that of *cāturvarṇyam*.

The third group of verses that refer to *varṇa* are IV.7, 8 & 13. In IV.7-8 *Kṛṣṇa* claims *yadā yadā hi dharmasya glānirbhavati bhārata / abhyutthānamadharmasya tadātmānaṁ sṛjāmyaham // paritrāṇāya sādhūnāṁ vināśāya ca duṣkṛtāṁ / dharmasaṁsthāpanārthāya saṁbhavāmi yuge yuge //* "Whenever there is a decline of *dharma*, O Bhārata, and an ascendency of *adharma*, then I manifest Myself; for the protection of the good, for the destruction of evil-doers, for the firm establishment of order, I am born in age after age." The context in which it is stated is not the context of discussion of *varṇa dharma* but the context of discussion of his multiple births from ancient times and why he is born again and again. But in the same chapter in the context of discussion of how he is not agent yet has become a creator agent in IV.13 he says *cāturvarṇyaṃ mayā sṛṣṭaṁ guṇakarmavibhāgaśaḥ / tasya kartāramapi māṁ viddhyakartāramavyayam //* "The system of fourfold *varṇas* has been created by me according to the division of *guṇas* and *karmas*; though I am the agent thereof, know Me non-agent and imperishable."

Can we facilely interpret these verses as claiming that god is born again and again to restore *varṇa dharma* whenever it weakens, that god created *varṇa dharma* and hence, it is permanent and sanctified, as does Ambedkar? The issue of interpretation of these verses is not so simple as Ambedkar and Ambedkarites think. First, we have to harmonize these verses with the injunction that is given in XVIII.66 after the discussion is carried through little more than fourteen intervening chapters: *sarvadharmānparityajya māmekaṁ śaraṇaṁ vraja / ahaṁ tvāṁ sarvapāpebhyo mokṣayiṣyāmi mā śucaḥ //* "Abandoning all *dharmas*, go for surrendering solely to me; I will liberate you from all sins; do not grieve."

There is a problem here. If the *Bhagavadgītā* is a philosophical justification of *varṇa dharma* as it is claimed by Ambedkar then what does the concluding injunction of *Bhagavadgītā* mean? *Sarvadharmān parityajya* means abandonment of all *dharma* including the *varṇa dharma*. If the aim of *Bhagavadgītā* is to justify *varṇa dharma* how can it advocate abandonment of all *dharma*? Since, abandonment of all *dharma* is the conclusion of the entire *Bhagavadgītā*; we have to give greater credence to it. And yet, no one can deny that *Bhagavadgītā* introduces consideration of *varṇa dharma* to develop arguments to convince Arjuna to fight in the war. So, the real position of *varṇa dharma* is quite complex in the philosophy of *Bhagavadgītā* which is not discerned by a superficial reading as has been done by Ambedkar. As mentioned before Ambedkar could not read *Bhagavadgītā* as a unified text. He read XVIII.66 as advocating *bhakti yoga*, which is a later addendum while the discussion of *varṇa* and *dharma* is main aim of the original *Bhagavadgītā* which is counter revolutionary. If one is not ready to harmonize all parts of the text then one can give any meaning to what is said in a text by neglecting what is in the context or even what is there in the sentence itself. One can very well refuse to take note of presence of even the words in the sentence as does Ambedkar as it will be shown. Vivisection of text has no limits; it can go to the extent of vivisection of sentence altering the meaning of what is there in the sentence. This is what Ambedkar does while interpreting verse IV.13.

Is Kṛṣṇa speaking of *dharma* in general or is he speaking of *varṇa dharma* in the context of IV.7 & 8 ? And whatever be the sense in which *dharma* is spoken of there why should he protect *dharma* if the injunction is to abandon all *dharma* as mentioned above? The Ambedkar's tendency at worst is not to give credence to the exhortation of XVIII.66 or at best is to read it with secondary meaning, i.e. metaphorically as exhortation for *bhakti* and to read IV.13 as telling that *varṇa dharma* is created by God forgetting that at the same breath he has been declared to be a non-agent. But both the readings miss the significance of the injunction to abandon all *dharmas* and hence miss the significance of the entire verse. So, the real position of *dharma* or the *varṇa dharma* in the philosophy of *Bhagavadgītā* is not as apparent as Ambedkar and Ambedkarites claim while criticizing it. Since, the colourless figure of Arjuna in the entire mythic dialogue is like a shadow in which each reader is meant to recognize himself or herself *dharmasammūḍhacetāḥ* (II.7) represents the kind of deluded understanding we have of *dharma*, which needs to be enlightened. That is because we all like Arjuna have *kārpaṇyadoṣopahatasvabhāvaḥ*, i.e. we have become incapable of using resources of our *svabhāva* like a miser. One should not forget here that from the very beginning, i.e. the beginning of the question regarding *dharma* (II.7), the author of *Bhagavadgītā* had put a warning against reading *Bhagavadgītā* as advocating *bhakti*. Only *kārpaṇyadoṣopahatasvabhāvaḥ... dharmasammūḍhacetāḥ... tvāṃ (Kṛṣṇaṃ) prapannam*. Only when one finds himself incapable of using resources of his *svabhāva* like a miser and is confounded about *dharma* one goes for surrendering to Kṛṣṇa warns the author of *Gītā*. Injunction of the author is to treat it as warning and not to treat it as an injunction for *bhakti*. Arjuna was already *prapanna* to Kṛṣṇa, there was no need of any injunction of *bhakti* to him. So, the injunction has to be other than *bhakti* for Arjuna. It will be shown that the message of *Bhagavadgītā* is to enable one to use the infinite resources of his *svabhāva* liberally to get out of confusion regarding *dharma* to determine how to conduct oneself in the world so that there would be no more need for such *prapatti* to Kṛṣṇa. So, XVIII.66 needs to be interpreted properly to determine the significance of abandonment of all *dharmas* which in turn determine what the final invitation of Kṛṣṇa is for in that verse.

In spite of it being declared that *cāturvarṇyam* is created by god it does not highlight any sanctity or permanency. It is impermanent like other things in the world which are also created by god. The god's creation of *cāturvarṇyam* is meant to highlight that it is not man's creation, only a natural evolutionary phase in the human practice which will eventually be superceded in time by new forms of practice. Hence, it indicates that institution is not an object of human action. It cannot be created, modified or manipulated as an object of human action. Men cannot create institutions, like table and chairs, it is the creation of God. That is to say that institutions are natural creations like other natural creations. When Kṛṣṇa is declared in IV.13 to be "*kartāram*", i.e. the doer and yet he remains "*akartāram avyayam*", i.e. non-perishable non-doer in the context of creation of *cāturvarṇyam,* it indicates in conformity to modern thought the apparent contradiction in the very conceptions of personality of the institution. Institutional personality never acts by itself, strictly speaking only members of the institutions act by themselves. And yet the institutions are actors, institutional personality is an actor, i.e. actions are attributed to institutions and hence to institutional personality. The example of creation of *cāturvarṇyaṃ*, a classical institution, is given precisely to draw attention to the institution with its apparent contradictory nature; to highlight that Kṛṣṇa represents the person of institution with its apparent contradictory aspect. As the institution by its very nature cannot act yet we do say that institutions act. In the same way even if Kṛṣṇa is *kartā* as a creator of *cāturvarṇyam* yet he is essentially *akartā*, because he is the institutional person.

Bhagavadgītā goes on to develop a general understanding of *dharma* that can fit into human practice of any institution. But unfortunately the critics of *cāturvarṇyam* like Ambedkar and Ambedkarites never understood the real understanding of *dharma* advocated in *Bhagavadgītā*.

The fourth reference to *varṇa* is in IX.32 & 33. The verse IX.32 is one of the most criticized verses in *Bhagavadgītā*. It says: *māṃ hi pārtha vyapāśritya ye'pi syuḥ pāpayonayam / striyo vaiśyāstathā śūdrāste'pi yānti parāṁ gatim //* "for finding refuge in Me, they also who, may be of a sinful birth—women, *vaiśyas* as well as *śūdras*—even they attain to the Supreme Goal." Ḳedar Joshi finds such verse as satanic.[20] D.D. Kosambi criticizing this verse writes, "We hear from the mouth of Kṛṣṇa himself (*G*.IX.32): "For those who take refuge in Me, be they even of the sinful breeds such as women, *vaisyas*, and *śūdras* ..." That is, all women, and all men of the working and producing classes are defiled by their very birth, though they may in after-life be freed by their faith in the god who degrades them so casually in this one."[21] As I have argued *Bhagavadgītā* is revolutionary in intent. What it says is that those who are traditionally taken as of sinful birth like women, *vaisyas* as well as *śūdras* are capable of achieving the highest goal of *karma saṁnyāsa* as preached by him. Otherwise, the use of word '*syuḥ*' meaning "may be" in the verse cannot be explained. One attributes to the author of *Bhagavadgītā* on the basis of IX.32 the categorical statement that "all women, and all men of the working and producing classes are defiled by their very birth" as done by Kosambi by neglecting the occurrence in the verse the word '*syuḥ*'. The author of *Bhagavadgītā* doubts such claim but says may be all women, and all men of the working and producing classes are (as others say) defiled by their very birth yet they can also follow the revised *dharma* on equal footing unlike the earlier unrevised *dharma*, which in fact was no *dharma*. Taking refuse in Kṛṣṇa is to follow his revised *dharma* of *karma saṁnyāsa* according to *Bhagavadgītā*.[22] If the so-called defiled class can perform action achieving the highest goal of *karma saṁnyāsa* then Kṛṣṇa in IX.33 declares, *kiṁ punarbrāhmaṇāḥ puṇyā bhaktā rājarṣayastathā / anityamasukhaṁ lokamimaṁ prāpya bhajasva mām //* "What again [to repeat regarding] the merited *brāhmaṇās* and devoted royal saints! Having reached this transient joyless world do thou worship Me." The contrast between the people mentioned in the former verse and the latter verse is not being advocated by Kṛṣṇa. The contrast is already there in the minds of people of the times of composition of *Bhagavadgītā*. The advocacy of Kṛṣṇa is to overcome the contrast that is there in the culture. This contrast will vanish if people take recourse to the *dharma* of *karma saṁnyāsa*. In this advocacy he did not need to convince the people of so-called defiled birth as they were already convinced, but he needed to convince the people of so-called knowledgeable *brāhmaṇāḥ* and knowledgeable *Kṣatriyas*, i.e.

rājarṣayas and hence the syntax and semantics of these two verses fit well with this revolutionary intent of *Bhagavadgītā*.

The final group of verses that deal with *varṇa dharma* are XVIII.41-44. Here, the basis of division of *karmas* of four *varṇas* is explained by Kṛṣṇa in the four verses XVIII.41-44: *brāhmaṇakṣatriyaviśāṁ śūdrāṇāṁ ca parantapa/karmāṇi pravibhaktāni svabhāvaprabhavairguṇaiḥ//śamo damastapaḥ śaucaṁ kṣāntir ārjavamevaca/jñānaṁ vijñānamāstikyaṁ brahmakarma svabhāvajam//śauryaṁ tejo dhṛtirdākṣyaṁ yuddhe cāpyapalāyanam/dānam īśvarabhāvaśca kṣatrakarma svabhāvajam//kṛṣigorakṣyavāṇijyaṁ vaiśyakarma svabhāvajam/ paricaryātmakaḥ karma śūdrasyāpi svabhāvajam//*"Of *brāhmaṇa*, *kṣatriya* and *vaiśyas*, as also of *śūdras*, O Parantapa, the *karmas* are divided according to *svabhāva* by the *prabhāva* of *guṇas* (strands). Serenity, self-restraint, austerity, purity, forgiveness, and also uprightness, knowledge, wisdom, faith— these are the *karmas* of the *Brāhmaṇas*, born of *svabhāva*. Heroism, lustre, perseverance, dexterity, Non-retreating from battle, generosity and rulership are the *karmas* of the *Kṣatriyas*, born of *svabhāva*. Ploughing, cattle-rearing, and trade are the *karmas* of the *vaiśyas*, born of *svabhāva*; and of the nature of service is the *karma* of the *śūdra*, born of *svabhāva*."

The first point that needs to be noted is that these verses are not concerned with division of people, the persons who are born. Where the issue is the division of the people who are born *Bhagavadgītā* uses the term *abhijāta* "those who are born". And we have already seen that *Bhagavadgītā* divides people who are born only into two kinds which is independent of four *varṇas*. The context of the discussion in chapter XVIII is the discussion of distinctions of various kinds of *jñāna*, *karma*, *kartā*, *buddhi*, *dhṛti*, *sukhaṁ* etc., which all are abstract things. It is in this context that the distinction of four kinds of *svabhāvajaṁ karma* of four *varṇa* is brought in. Be it noted that it was a division of *karmas* into four kinds that is introduced and not division of people who are born. So, the division of four *varṇa karma* is to be understood as the division of something abstract like the earlier items. But there is a difference in treatment of *jñāna*, *karma*, *kartā*, *buddhi*, *dhṛti*, *sukham* etc. each of which is divided into three kinds. But all of a sudden division of *varṇa karma*, which are *svabhāvajaṁ karma*, was introduced and *varṇa karma* which are *svabhāvajaṁ karma*, were divided not into three kinds in line of the division of earlier items, rather were divided into four kinds. This difference in treatment of division of *jñāna*, *karma*, *kartā*, *buddhi*, *dhṛti*, *sukhaṁ* on the one hand and *varṇa karma* which were *svabhāvajaṁ karma* on the other hand highlights that *jñāna*, *karma*, *kartā*, *buddhi*, *dhṛti*, *sukhaṁ* all of which are internal to the living person who is born, differ from *varṇa karma* in that it is not internal to such person, rather it is external to him. So, it must be something abstract but external. Naturally, it refers to abstract external public institution, i.e. *cāturvarṇyam* and public role in it. So, this division of *svabhāvajaṁ karma* is not the division of *svabhāvajaṁ karma* of the particular person (a flesh and blood human being) who is a *brāhmaṇa* or a *kṣatriya* etc. Rather, it is a division of *svabhāvajaṁ karma* of the abstract and general *brāhmaṇa* or a *kṣatriya* etc. in the public institution of *cāturvarṇyam* that is discussed.

The reason why it cannot be division of the *svabhāvajaṁ karma* of individual persons who is born who may be *brāhmaṇa* or a *kṣatriya* etc. is that there are too many variations to be covered by the four divisions and if it is so conceived it is false even according to *Gītā* as it gives another division of *karma*s of the person born by referring to them as *abhijāta*. A person born may have *svabhāva* that is not only that of *kṣatriya,* but also *āsurā* at the same time making his *svabhāvajaṁ karma* as different from that of *kṣatriya* only. Such, a person's *svabhāvajaṁ karma* cannot be accepted as *dharma* or *kartavya* by *Gītā*, as actions emerging from *āsurā svabhāva* are prohibited. Secondly, *Mahābhārata* recognizes many human beings who are not covered under the four *varṇas* like the group of people to which *Hiḍimbā* belonged, *sabaras*, *niṣādas* etc. If the division of *karmas* are not understood as *karmas* of person as mere abstract and general *brāhmaṇa* or a *kṣatriya* etc. and it is understood as division of *kartavya*s of individual person who is born as that individual then the argument of Kṛṣṇa in II.33 *atha cettvamimaṁ dharmyaṁ saṁgrāmaṁ na kariṣyasi / tataḥ svadharmaṁ kīrtiṁ ca hitvā pāpamavāpsyasi //* "now if you will not fight this battle of *dharma*, then, having abandoned your own *dharma* and fame, you will incur sin," makes no sense. Especially, troublesome is reference to *kīrtim* fame or publicity. Publicity of action is a requirement of a public institution. It is not a private person's requirement. Although private/public, individual/institutional—such distinctions were not available at the time of *Mahābhārata* that is why the argument as well as the distinction is made in a vocabulary that makes it appear as if one is speaking about division of actions of a flesh and blood person and not that of abstract and general institutional role. *Bhagavadgītā* is trying hard to conceptualize institutional action. So, the aim was not to discuss *varṇa dharma* or justify it, but to utilize the existing understanding of *varṇa dharma* to clarify a point regarding how institution in general function whatever that institution be. Here, too the reference to *varṇa dharma* was only contextual and not essential or primary.

The verses XVIII. 41-44 have been misunderstood by scholars like Dr. Ambedkar as advocating that a person's *svabhāva* determines his *svadharma*. This kind of reading is a complete travesty of relation between *svadharma* and *svabhāva*. The claim that *svabhāva* is determinant of *svadharma* may be true if *dharma* is understood in a morally neutral way as quality of a person, like the *svadharma* of *agni* if at all we can talk of *svadharma* in this way. But *dharma* understood as moral category translated as duty or *kartavya* it is simply false that *Bhagavadgītā* accepts that *svabhāva* determines a person's *svadharma*. *Bhagavadgītā* recognizes *āsurī svabhāva* of people, but action determined by that *svabhāva* are not recognized as *dharma* or *svadharma* of such people. Strictly speaking *svabhāva* can lead to both *dharma* and *adharma* according to *Bhagavadgītā*. The theory of *svabhāva* in *Bhagavadgītā* is too complex to admit of such simplistic reading as *svabhāva* is determinant of *svadharma*.

If as I have argued *svabhāva* of the individual person who is born is not determinant of *dharma*, then how come the *svabhāva* of the abstract and general institutional persona as *brāhmaṇa* or *kṣatriya* etc. determine its *svadharma*. That is because the *cāturvarṇyam* is already taken as part of the cosmic order and unity. What imparts the quality of *dharma* to the actions of abstract *brāhmaṇa* or *kṣatriya* etc. as such which emerge from their *svabhāva* is that the division of the four types of institutional role and their respective *svabhāva* is already determined keeping in view the order and unity of the institution of *cāturvarṇyam*. It is like an unified institution like university with different abstract general persona like professor, reader, lecturer, deputy registrar, assistant registrar with their qualifications, and the unity of the institution gives legitimacy to the action that emerge from such persona because of their qualifications. The requirement of performance of *svadharma* and prohibition of *parādharma* is not merely a requirement of division of labour but a requirement of unity of the institution. Only when the persons performs his *dharma* oriented way from that class of persona orienting and committing himself to the unity of the institution as a whole that gives ethical quality or *dharma* to his action. This is the meaning of performing action for *lokasaṁgraha* and *karma saṁnyāsa*, i.e. action has to be performed without desire and its ownership has to be given of to divinity as representing the unity of cosmos to which the institution belongs. Even if a person performs actions of the general abstract persona yet oriented exclusively to this persona and oriented and committed away from the institutional unity his action born of *svabhāva* will loose ethical quality or *dharma*, as it happened in the case of Duryodhana in *Mahābhārata*. And in this way of looking at the *cāturvarṇyam* as part of the cosmic order and unity contains seeds of its destruction. For everything in the cosmic unity is transitory except the cosmic unity as a whole. Maintaining the permanency of order and unity of cosmos everything else comes and goes in cosmos including *cāturvarṇyam*. The advocacy of *Bhagavadgītā* is that even when you have different institution, other than *cāturvarṇyam*, say modern liberal egalitarian political arrangement, then also as a person manning that institution you will be required to perform action oriented away from your group identity keeping in mind the unity of total institution, and you will be required to perform action not as your personal action, but as the institutional action, giving the ownership of action performed by you to the institution and this is what *karma saṁnyāsa* is and that is the *dharma*, the highest *dharma* advocated by Kṛṣṇa. So, the conception of *dharma* in *cāturvarṇyam* is neither linked to *cāturvarṇyam* nor to birth as it transcends both. All reference to *cāturvarṇyam* are contingent, contextual reference to make a general point and reference to *cāturvarṇyam* was neither essential nor meant to state a point regarding that specific institution, rather taking for granted an understanding of an existing institution, Kṛṣṇa tries to explain the functioning of institution in general whatever that may be.

And in the context of making distinction of institutional persona the author of *Bhagavadgītā* states in XVIII.47 *śreyānsvadharmo viguṇaḥ paradharmātsvanuṣṭhitāt/ svabhāvaniyataṁ karma kurvannāpnoti kilbiṣam //* "Better is one's own *dharma* (even if) destitute of merits, than the *dharma* of another well performed. Doing the *karma* ordained according to *svabhāva* one acquires no sin." Here, *svadharma* refers not to the *dharma* of person as born, but to the *dharma* of the person occupying a role in the institution.

Does *Bhagavadgītā* seem to be securing the observance in practice of *dharma* of *cāturvarṇyam*, as claimed by Ambedkar? Ambedkar's argument is based on III.26. In this Kṛṣṇa says in his interpretation that a wise man should not by counter-propaganda create a doubt in the mind of an ignorant person who is a follower of *karma kāṇḍa* which, of course, includes the observance of the rules of *chaturvarṇya*. In other words, you must not agitate or excite people to rise in rebellion against the theory of *karma kāṇḍa* and all that it includes. Let us, find out if what he says is true. In III.26 Kṛṣṇa says: *na buddhibhedaṁ janayedajñānāṁ karmasaṅginām/joṣayetsarvakarmāṇi vidvān yuktamaḥ samācaran //* "Let no wise man create a division (confusion) in the minds of the ignorant who are attached to action; he should make them do all actions, himself rightly doing them being harnessed." As I have been trying to show there is only contextual and accidental reference to *varṇa dharma*. The chapter III does not refer to *varṇa dharma* at all. It is only a general discussion of how action is performed in an institution whatever that be III.26 is a conclusion of an argument that begins at III.20 and ends at III.25. So, III.26 needs to be interpreted in light of what Kṛṣṇa says from III.20 to III.25.

III.20 states *karmaṇaiva hi saṁsiddhimāsthitā janakādayaḥ/ lokasaṁgrahamevāpi sampaśyaṅkartumarhasi* // "By action only, indeed, Janaka and others did attain right success. Even with a view to *lokasaṁgraha* (gathering of people in a unity), you are fit to act." Here, the phrase "with a view to *lokasaṁgraha*" is very important. *Lokasaṁgraha* is not a purpose external to action to be achieved by it. If it were so it would be *karmaphala*, which it is not. We perform action belonging to the *loka* that is already *saṁgṛhita* and our action further maintains that *saṁgṛhita loka*. Hence, action is performed with a view to *lokasaṁgraha*, but not taking *lokasaṁgraha* as external purpose. The later would mean that before the action there was no *saṁgṛhita loka* and the *saṁgṛhita loka* will come into existence after the action has been performed. But such is not the case. The context of action is the *saṁgṛhita loka*, even if the context is the limit of *saṁgṛhita loka*, which is the context of war. War is not chaos but an organized conflict [*saṁgrāmam* (*Bhagavadgītā,* II.33)] to resolve some issues by force, which could not be solved in any other way, that is to say that *saṁgrāmam* is a forceful settlement. How can we say *lokasaṁgraha* is both origins for action as well as model for action. The duality is inherent in the very idea of cycle mentioned in Verse III.16. In III.15 cycle is that of *brahman-action-yajña-brahman*. So, *Brahman* is both the origin of action as well as model to be established in *yajña* by action. This dual role of *Brahman* is transferred to *lokasaṁgraha* in the present *śloka*. Both *lokasaṁgraha* as well as *Brahman* refer to some kind of unity, which is the institutional unity, which is both origin of as well as model for action. The reference to Janaka is to bring to fore another aspect of action with a view to *lokasaṁgraha*. *Lokasaṁgraha* as origin of and model for action does not provide any decision procedure for ascertaining the definite action to be performed. There is no such decision procedure that can be learned and followed for ascertaining action to be performed in a situation. So, here one depends on precedent and examples. One ascertains what action to perform by following (but not imitating) the examples of people who have attained perfection, maturity or ripeness in performing action, like the ones of Janaka. Why following an example is not mere imitation? It is answered in the next *śloka*.

Gītā, III.21 says—*yadyadācarati śreṣṭhas tat tad evetaro janaḥ/sa yat pramāṇaṁ kurute lokastad anuvartate //* "Whatsoever a great man does, that alone the other men do; whatever he sets up as the standard that the people follow." Great men are exemplars. What action they perform the lesser men also perform the same action. This may give an impression that the lesser mortals imitate the exemplars. But this is not a correct reading. Hence, in the very next line the possibility of this error is removed. The people follow the standard or measure they set-up (*yat pramāṇaṁ kurute*). To use an analogy from the modern law we say that following the precedent of a higher court by lower courts does not amount to imitation of the past judgement of the higher court, what is accepted by the lower court, which is binding, is the *ratio decidendi*, the reason on which the case was decided. Similar thing happens when lesser mortals follow the great men. Following their precedent does not amount to imitation of their external action. What is accepted as binding by the lesser mortals is the reason on which the great men decide the action for performance. That ratio (*pramāṇaṁ*, measure) is followed. The need for exemplar and measure of action arises because the kind of action *Bhagavadgītā* is speaking about cannot be decided on the basis of any external goal taking into account the efficiency of the action in achieving the goal as these actions have no external goal. The action performed in an institution does not relate to unity of the institution as a means to an external end.

In III.22 to 24 Kṛṣṇa presents himself as the exemplar for action and argues: I have no work whatsoever to perform in the three worlds nor is there anything un-obtained that should be obtained; yet I engage in action. For, should I not ever engage in action, unflaggingly, men would in all respects follow my path. These people would be ruined if I should not perform action; I would be the agent of chaos, and would be destroyer of these beings born. Here we must ask the question: what is the purpose of giving this second example when the example of Janaka is already given? In II.61 Kṛṣṇa innocuously identifies himself with the *sat tattva*, which was designated variously as *puruṣa*, *dehin* or *śarīriṇa*, which was established to be eternal, permanent and immortal, without any *bhāva vikāra* (modification), which is declared to be something that can neither act nor be acted upon, i.e. it can neither be the agent nor the patient of action. Now in III.22 declares: *na me pārthāsti kartavyaṁ triṣu lokeṣu kiñcana/ nānavāptamavāptavyaṁ varta eva ca karmaṇi //* "I have nothing whatsoever to achieve in the three worlds, O son of Pṛthā, nor is there anything unattained that should be attained; yet I engage in action." This highlights that the *sat tattva*, is the institutional personality, as institutionl personality it lacks nothing yet it engages in action. What is being highlighted from III.22-24 is that strictly speaking institutional personality never acts by itself, yet the institutional personality acts, if institutions stop acting, which is the same as institutional personality not acting, and then it would lead to chaos and ruin the persons. The perspective of *Bhagavadgītā* is quite advanced and ahead of its times. It recognizes the apparent contradictory nature of the institution, i.e. the institution cannot act by itself yet institutions act. If institutions do not act then it will lead to chaos and ruin mankind. This apparent contradiction will be resolved only in the eighteenth chapter. But an indication is given regarding the solution of the problem.

In III.25 concludes: the wise man, as he belongs to the institution, should act unattached from an objective of *lokasaṁgraha*. After having argued for performing action without desire, but performing it only for the objective of gathering people into a unity, finally in III.26, as mentioned above, it is concluded with respect to higher ups in institutions that they being wise should not create confusion in the minds of the ignorant who are attached to action, by setting wrong examples of action himself. He should make them do all actions by setting himself as an exemplar which he can do by himself rightly doing all actions being harnessed to actions as required by *yoga*. This holds good for any modern institution even today. So, it was not really a counter revolutionary injunction, but a revolutionary injunction, that understood ahead of its time how any institution, what ever that may be functions and requires its higher ups to act in what manner, a lesson which was not remembered by Ambedkar, even if it was part of his legal education, how *ratio decidendi* of judgements of judges of higher courts binds the judgement of judges of lower courts as precendents.

1.3.5. Is Bhagavadgītā a Philosophical Defence of Ritual Actions for Salvation?

The evaluation of the fourth claim of Ambedkar has already exposed the weakness of his fifth claim regarding *Bhagavadgītā* that it offers a philosophic defence, for the *karma mārga*, which means the performance of the observances, such as *yajña* as a way to salvation. Well Ambedkar simply failed to understand what *yajña* is in *Bhagavadgītā*. *Yajña* is the early conceptualization of institution even when men had not seen any thing as complex as modern institution. Since, *Bhagavadgītā* is developing its theory of institutions at a time when institutions were just taking shape and were at very rudimentary stage, the specific *yajña* (institutions) mentioned in IV.24-30 like *deva yajña*, *tapoyajña*, *yogayajña* etc. may not be very relevant today. But, out of the various kinds of *yajña* mentioned in IV.24-30 the two, i.e. *dravya yajña* and *jñāna yajña* are important and relevant even today. *Dravya yajña* is the rudimentary form of institutions of production of marerial goods and *jñana yajña* are institutions of acquiring knowledge. *Bhagavadgītā* declares *jñāna yajña* to be superior to *dravya yajña*. IV.33 declares: *śreyān dravyamayād yajñāt jñāna yajñaḥ paraṁtapa/sarvaṁ karma akhilaṁ pārtha jñāne parisamāpyate //* "Superior is wisdom-sacrifice to sacrifice full of material, O Harraser of your foes. All actions, without exception, O son of Pṛthā, is comprehensively completed in wisdom." To comprehensively complete or end an action is to perform it as action originating in *brahma* so that it is as good as *akarma*. This is possible only by wisdom. Hence, institutions of acquiring knowledge are superior to institutions of production of material goods. *Bhagavadgītā*'s ordering of institutions of acquiring knowledge and institutions of production of material goods corresponds to the ordering of political institution (*polis*) and institutions of production of material goods (*oikos*) in Greek civilization of the same period. There institutions of production of material goods (*oikos*) were subordinated to political institution (*polis*).

In *Bhagavadgītā* III.10 it was declared *sahayajñāḥ prajāḥ sṛṣṭvā purovāca prajāpatiḥ/anena prasaviṣyadhvameṣa vo'stviṣṭakāmadhuk* // "Having created mankind together with sacrifices, the *Prajāpati* said of yore, 'By this you shall propagate; let this be to you the desirable bestowing cow'." The mythical setting in the beginning of creation indicates that what is said holds good from time immemorial. The validity of what is said is prescriptive. What is indicated is that mankind is never without *yajña*, i.e. without unity and solidarity or without practice of institutions. Man is man because of his belonging to institution and performing institutional action.

Kṛṣṇa represents the institutional personality. When Arjuna asks in VIII.2: *adhiyajñaḥ kathaṁ ko'tra dehe'smin madhusūdana*— "How and who is *Adhiyajña* (the Entity concerned with Sacrifice) here in this body, O Madhusūdana?" Kṛṣṇa answers in VIII.4: *adhiyajño'hamevātra dehe dehabhṛtāṁvara* / "The *Adhiyajña* (Entity concerned with Sacrifice) is I (*Puruṣottama*), here in the body, O best of the embodied." So, Kṛṣṇa represents the institutional personality in man. Hence, as explained earlier in IV.13 he is actor the way institutions act, and yet he is non-actor just like institutions which really cannot act by themselves. So, though the idea of *yajña*, *yajña puruṣa*, Kṛṣṇa the *Adhiyajña*, who is actor since action can be attributed to this person, yet it really cannot act goes on to highlight *Bhagavadgītā* is trying to conceptualize institution as a person and how to perform institutional act as a member of an institution, so that the action can be attributed to the institution and it does not become a mere personal private action of the individual.

1.3.6. Dr. Ambedkar's Erroneous Standards of Judgement

In this context when injunction is given to perform *yajña karma* it is not injunction for ritual action as Ambedkar claims, but it is injunction to perform institutional action, as institutional action and not as a personal private action. In spite of his knowledge of law which deals with such complex modern arrangement of institutions which is a modern state it is really a poor reflection on his legal knowledge that he could not fathom the distinction of institutional action and personal private action of individual which is being conceptualized in *Bhagavadgītā*. He could not really reach or fathom the *ratio decidendi* of *Bhagavadgītā*'s discourse as he could not move past the *obiter dicta* of *Bhagavadgītā*'s case. The *ratio decidendi* of Ambedkar's judgement of *Bhagavadgītā* rested on latter's *obiter dicta* and as the former neither focused nor fathomed the *ratio decidendi* of the latter. The *ratio decidendi* of Ambedkar's discourse was followed as precedent by Ambedkarites. Since, the *ratio decidendi* of Ambedkar's discourse never really succeeded in fathoming the distinction of institutional action from personal action, or the distinction of *ratio decidendi* from *obiter dicta* of *Bhagavadgītā*, the Ambedkarites following the *ratio decidendi* of Ambedkar's discourse never really succeded in fathoming the distinction of institutional action from personal action or the *ratio decidendi* of *Bhagavadgītā* from its *obiter dicta* when their turn came. They carried over the error of the *ratio decidendi* of Ambedkar's discourse and his judgement on *Bhagavadgītā*. The result is that the *ratio* and the action required by liberal democratic institutional arrangement was abandoned in *dalit* discourse in favour of private action for private group interest confusing the latter (the group interest) with the *ratio* of the former (the liberal democracy).

Conclusion of my evaluation of Ambedkar's discourse on *Bhagavadgītā* is that it set very poor standard of scholarship and judgement. He never, succeeded in understanding or interpreting in context any verse of *Bhagavadgītā*, nor did he succeed in making a unified sense of the text as a whole. It had implication for the kind of hermeneutic capacity he carried into legal hermeneutics where each law is to be interpreted not only in relation to precedents, but also every other law that has a relation to the issue. He did not exhibit such capacity to understand verses from *Bhagavadgītā*. The entire body of law also needs to be understood as a unity to run a unified liberal egalitarian state. He did not exhibit this capacity for synwork at least in interpretation of a text like *Bhagavadgītā*. I venture to conjecture, it is only a conjecture not a verified thesis, that an elaborate constitution like Constitution of India which was drafted by a committee chaired by Ambedkar has required within a short span of sixty years more amendments than the amendments of Constitution of United States of America which is more than two centuries old, because of poor draftsmanship of legal document which was drafted under the chairmanship of a legal mind that hardly understood expressions in its context or ever had a synthetic view of the whole document. The poor standards of scholarship exhibited by Dr. Ambedkar's discourse and judgement on *Bhagavadgītā* is what is not only followed but also imitated and copied by the scholastic *dalit* discourse in universities in particular and by wider *dalit* discourse in general resulting in complete rejection of the legacy he left in the form of institutional arrangement of modern state of India in favour of private group interest.

2. What is the Strength of Savarṇas, Derived from Bhagavadgītā?

2.1. Savarṇas do not Derive Strength from Varṇa or Jati System

After understanding the *dalit* discourse from Ambedkar to the contemporary young *dalit* scholars and its automatically visible poor standards of scholarship and reason, but equally clearly expressive of frustration and anger of the *dalit* group which is deflecting them from the cooperative business of running the modern institutions and propelling them towards yearning for the impossible ideal of pushing out the *savarṇas* from all modern institutions, it is time to draw attention to the strength of *savarṇas*, a strength that they derive from *Bhagavadgītā*, a strength that gives them not only edge, but always keeps them ahead, a strength that is not available to the *bahujana samāja* in spite of their numerical strength requiring their most popular leader to rethink whether to take *savarṇas* as *manuvadi* adversary or co-operative sharer of power without whom she cannot retain her power, because the *bhujana samāja* has turned a blind eye to the secret doctrine of *Bhagavadgītā* to focus only on the superficial, contextual, incidental, accidental reference to *varṇa dharma*. So, let me reveal a bit of that secret doctrine.

The teaching of *Bhagavadgītā* is described as *rahasyam* (IV.3), i.e. mystery. According to Kṛṣṇa the doctrine of *Bhagavadgītā* is *guhyānā jñānam* (X.38), i.e. hidden knowledge. It is *paramaṁ guhyamadhyātmasaṁjñītam* (XI.1), i.e. the most secret song of *adhyātma*, i.e. *Brahman* embodied as self. *Bhagavadgītā* itself is *guhyatamaṁ śāstram* (XV.20), i.e. the most secret text. According to *Bhagavadgītā* (XVIII.63) Arjuna was given *guhyād guhyataraṁ jñānam*, i.e. knowledge more secret than the secret one. The advice of Kṛṣṇa to Arjuna was *sarvaguhyatamam* (XVIII.64), i.e. the greatest of all secret knowledge, *paramaṁ guhyam* (XVIII.68), and *guhyaṁ param* (XVIII.75), i.e. the highest secret. Even though the mystery of action was revealed to Arjuna and the words of Kṛṣṇa were revealing the secrets of action, the words of *Bhagavadgītā* have confounded the *dalit* scholars including Dr. Ambedkar.

In *Bhagavadgītā* the knowledge given to Arjuna by Kṛṣṇa is declared by him to be *rājavidyā rājaguhyam,* i.e. knowledge of administration, secrets of administration in IX.2. One may object that here *rāja*— is not used in the sense of 'of administration' but in the sense of 'best of' as in '*rājadanta*' so, that these expressions mean respectively best of knowledge and best of secrets. This objection is not acceptable, because the *vidyā* (knowledge) and *guhyam* (secret) is known by tradition to the *rājarṣis* according to Kṛṣṇa in IV.2 & IX.33, but it is not known to *maharṣis* in X.2. Here, if we go by the objection then we have to accept that *rājarṣis* are best of *ṛṣis*, which is not the case as *maharṣis* remain still superior and better than *rājarṣis*. What makes *rājarṣi*, a *rājarṣis* is his *rājavidyā, rājaguhyam* (knowledge of administration, secrets of administration). So, when in the introduction to her book, Malinar claims that the "specific knowledge" Kṛṣṇa reveals "is called *rājavidyā*, the 'knowledge of kings' or royal knowledge"[23] she was in the right track. An objection is raised by a reviewer Vishwa Adluri that her's is a grammatically questionable translation on following ground:

"Compounds of the form *rāja*— (e.g., *rājadanta*) are best translated as "best of" or "highest"." *Pāṇini sūtra* 2.2.3 (*rājadantadisu param*) applies here. The usual order is inverted in *rāja*—compounds and the *upasarjana* moves to the end. Accordingly, *rājadanta* is not "the tooth of kings" but "eyetooth". *Rājavidyā* should be translated as "the best of knowledges" rather than as "the knowledge of kings," as Malinar does."[24] This objection is based on misapplication of the rule of *Pāṇini sūtra* 2.2.3. Indiscriminate use of this rule will result in *anartha*. For example, this rule cannot be applied to *rājakoṣa* or *rājabhavana* to mean best of treasury or the best of house respectively, as these compounds were not traditionally understood by grammarians with such meaning. The meanings of these two expressions are respectively "the treasury of the king" and "the house of the king". But where Malinar went wrong was that she claimed that this knowledge is knowledge of new kind of sovereignty, but actually it was not knowledge related to sovereignty rather related to administration of any sovereign institution. This neutralization of sovereignty was done because it was not knowledge of somebody as a *rājan* but as a *ṛṣi*, i.e. *rājarṣi*. It was not *rājaguhya* as a secret regarding sovereignty but as a secret regarding administration of a sovereign institution. To the extent that the reviewer Vishwa Adluri finds "Malinar's equation of *guhyatamam* with *rājavidyā* in the sense of knowledge of kings is textually problematic", he is right but the ground which he gives, i.e. "the words *guhyam* and *guhyatamam* recur in the context that are explicitly not political" is wrong for the *guhya* knowledge here is the secret of administration of any institution. The knowledge of the self which one finds in *Bhagavadgītā*, is actually the conception of personality of institution related to its administration. It is beyond the scope of this chapter to develop this conception further.

But, this secret knowledge required for administration of an institution is not knowledge of *varṇa dharma* or how to maintain the *varṇa* order, as the latter knowledge was neither secret, nor hidden from the public gaze from the time of its inception, for it was a public order out in public maintained in public by publicly visible means, however, harsh those means may be, however unpalatable those means may appear to be now to contemporary sensibilities. There was nothing secret about *varṇa dharma* there was nothing secret about its defence. Nor was there anything secret regarding the order of *jātis* as it was practiced in India. It was as public as the public hatred of *bahujana* regarding *savarṇas* in contemporary public discourse. It was as open as the open advocacy of *bahujana samāja* in public discourse to displace *savarṇas* from modern public institutions. Since, secrecy of administrative knowledge had been emphasized not once, not twice, but at least eight times in *Bhagavadgītā*, it must be something else. It is this *rājavidyā rājaguhyam* (IX.2) that *savarṇas* receive consciously or unconsciously, reading *Bhagavadgītā* directly, or listening to it recited by others, or indirectly *via* chance comment of some *savarṇas* who has read *Bhagavadgītā*, or someone who has read *Bhagavadgītā* passes it on even may be unknowingly to their next generation and it keeps percolating down the generations of *savarṇas*. It is this *rājavidyā rājaguhyam* (IX.2) that gives *savarṇas* an edge and puts them always ahead and it is the ignorance of this *rājavidyā rājaguhyam* (IX.2) that keeps *bahujana samāja* struggling unsuccessfully to cope with *savarṇas* with frustration and anger towards the latter, but not really knowing what is keeping them behind despite all the provisions of law, all the affirmative actions of government and state, and even after sixty years of assertiveness due to assumed numerical superiority etc.

2.2. Savarṇas Derive Strength from Knowledge of Temporality in Bhagavadgītā

With this introduction which must have increased everyone's curiosity, I will merely present one verse like a grain of rice from a cooked pot of rice to use an old simile, or as a tip of iceberg to use a modern analogy. That verse is VIII.26. It says: *śuklakṛṣṇe gatī hyete jagataḥ śāśvate mate/ekayā yāty anāvṛttim-anyayāvartate punaḥ //* "Because these bright and dark movements of the world are conceived as eternal; by the one a thing goes not to return, by the other it returns again."

What does it mean? Let me explain. *Śuklakṛṣṇe gatī* is two kinds of movement of time and things in time. Nothing in the world is permanent, neither time period nor the thing with its time period. Let us assume that this discussion is taking place in the month of *māgha* in *vikramī saṁvat* 2069. The month of *phālguna* of *vikramī saṁvat* 2069 is in the depth of future. When the time comes *phālguna* of *vikramī saṁvat* 2069 will emerge from future and become present. This movement of the month of *phālguna* of *vikramī saṁvat* 2069 will be its *kṛṣṇa gatī*, a dark but ascendant movement of the month. So, long as this dark ascendant movement lasts, i.e. it is in *kṛṣṇa gatī*, that period of the month is *kṛṣṇa pakṣa* 'dark wing'. But this dark ascendant movement of the month will not last for ever, on the *amāvasyā* 'dwelling together [of sun and moon]' the direction of movement will bend and take a u-turn and it will proceed in opposite direction, i.e. the month is moving on its bright descent movement. This is the *śukla gatī* of the month, and so long as the bright descent movement of the month lasts that period is *śukla pakṣa* 'bright wing'. When the month of *phālguna* of *vikrami saṁvat* 2069 enters into its *kṛṣṇa gatī* coming from future to its present it is to return after completion of this movement, the direction of movement as explained bends on *amāvasyā* to take a u-turn in opposite direction, i.e. to return. But once the month of *phālguna* of *vikramī saṁvat* 2069 enters on its bright descent movement, i.e. *śukla gatī* it is moving in a direction from present to past and it will never return from there once it enters the past. The bright descent movement, i.e. *śukla gatī* of the month lasts for the entire *śukla pakṣa* and on the night of *pūrṇimā*, the cycle of the sojourn of the month gets completed (*pūrṇa*) and the month is no more present as it has now entered past.

We have to keep in mind this distinction of movement *kṛṣṇa gatī* and *śukla gatī*, the former being the movement from which thing returns and the latter being the movement from which nothing returns. The verse is telling that everything in the world is characterized by these two movements.

Everything in the world of movement emerges from the unknown depth of future and enters its present time from which it will return, i.e. it is in its *kṛṣṇayāna* 'dark vehicle', but after reaching the peak of its existence in its present time it turns back to return and then enters into movement from its present time to go into past and to remote past from which it never returns, i.e. it is in its *śuklayāna* 'bright vehicle'. From time immemorial these two movements of things in *jagat*, the world of movements, are recognized, as everything has a temporary presence in *jagat*, everything has only a limited cycle of present time in *jagat*. In Indian thought the two ends of the present time, i.e. future and past, to complete the cycle of present time meet. What it means will be indicated in Chapter X, which we are not discussing. Since, present time of a thing is a cycle, as it enters the cycle of present time it is in its that movement in present time which will bend back to return, but once the thing has entered the second half of its present time crossing the peak of the cycle of its present time, it is on its that movement from which it will not return.

These two movements characterize the *jagat* in many ways. Looked at from the point of view of any one thing in the world, its movement for entry into *jagat* (from its future to its present) is from the same door from which it exits from the *jagat* (from its present to its past) completing its cycle of present time in *jagat*, and this door is recognized in Vedic literature as sundoor. Since present time itself is a cycle, moving in a cycle, whether the present time is present *kṛṣṇa*, or present day, present month, present year, present *yuga* etc. the moving present time is characterized simultaneously by two movements with opposite directions, one direction of movement that begins the cycle and the other reverse direction of movement that ends the cycle. In one *kṛṣṇa* of present time both movements with opposite directionalities are present, making it appear as if *kṛṣṇa* of present is static, but actually it is characterized by two distinguishable movements with two opposite directionalities respectively. This becomes much clearer when we think of causality in *sāṁkhya satkāryavāda*. At every moment *kārya* (effect) is moving in one direction, from its future time to its present time, *kṛṣṇa gatī*, as it is entering *jagat*, becoming present, becoming *yukta* with present time and coming into existence. But at the same very moment *samavāyī kāraṇa* (material cause) is loosing its *samavāyī tantu* (material), it is in a movement towards going out of existence, moving from its present time to its past, *śukla gatī*, it is in its movement to exit from the world, it is in a movement to become *viyukta* with its present time and it is in a movement that has direction exactly opposite to the direction of movement of *kārya* (effect).

These two movements with opposite directionalities and from one of which a thing returns and from the other it never returns are recognized from time immemorial. Even in *Ṛgveda* these two movements are recognized in numerous *mantras* of different *sūktas*. I cite just one example. These two real movements of time are represented in *Ṛgveda* VI.9.1: *ahaśca kṛṣṇamahararjunaṁ ca vivartete rajasī vedyābhiḥ / vaiśvānaro jāyamāno na rājā'vātirajjyotiṣāgnistamāṁsi* // "One half of day is dark, and bright the other: both atmospheres move on by sage devices. Agni Vaiśvānara, when born as Sovran, hath with his lustre overcome the darkness."

So, one of the injunctions of administration advocated in *Bhagavadgītā* is to have the knowledge of these two temporal movements of things in *jagat*, the world of movement. What has this distinction got to do with administration of institutions? What advantage the capacity to distinguish these two kinds of movements gives to the person? Let me explain.

2.3. Knowledge of Temporality and Administration of Institutions

These two movements characterize even institutions. Every institution, whether *varṇa* order, caste order, modern constitutional state, church, kingdom, *zamindari*, fiefdom, polis, or empire when they emerge from the depth of future into present they are on the ascending movement, they will last in that movement only for a limited period which may be very large of thousands of years or a few hundred years or a few decades, but after reaching its peak of existence its movement will bend and take a u-turn, and it will enter its descending movement, which may last long or small, but once the institution has entered on its descent it is going out of its present existence to become something of past.

Jagat is world of movement. So, at every moment when one institution is in its descending movement it is giving way to another institution which is on its ascending movement like cause and effect. For example, during the renaissance the Roman church as political institution was on its descending movement, but at the same time due to same movement the modern secular state as a political institution was on its ascending movement.

The injunction of *Bhagavadgītā* is that by discerning the simultaneous movement of two institutions one that is on its ascent and the one on its descent, *be always on the side of ascending institution* never be on the side of descending institution. That is *dharma* which is eternal. Let me tell you when it is time of ascent of emerging institution and descent of outgoing institution nothing can stop it, for time is the propeller of these two movements. Try howsoever hard you may, with whatever presumed numerical strength, with whatever presumed power however great no one can stop these two movements ascent of one institution which is emerging with simultaneous descent of the other institution which is on its way out.

It will be beyond the scope of this essay to explain the details, for which one has to read entire *Bhagavadgītā*. But let me state that it is one and the same movement that has three aspects and hence they go together. The movement of time, movement of thought and movement of institutions is one and the same. Then, corresponding to the two movements (ascent and descent) of time and two movements (ascent and descent) of institutions there are two movements (ascent and descent) of thought. A thought that recognizes the distinction of two movements of time and institutions and corresponds to the ascending movement of the two is calm, happy, self-controlled and legitimate, reasonable and when expressed in words it will be recognized as legitimate and true by others. If the thought fails to make a distinction of two movements of time and institution, which is the same thing as ignorance, it will *necessarily* move with the descending time and institution, will *necessarily* find itself compelled by emotions beyond control like anger and hatred, will be agitated, morbid and devoid of legitimacy and reason and when expressed in public will be recognized as illegitimate, unreasonable and untrue. Well my friends, it is this secret doctrine of administration of institutions that enables the *savarṇas* to be always on the side of ascending time, always on the side of ascending institutions with accompanying thought and knowledge. But *bahujana samāja* due to its neglect of knowledge of *Bhagavadgītā*, unable to distinguish the ascending and descending movement of time and institutions keep arriving at the descending institutions whose peak time is over, inhabiting the descending time, find themselves with dark thoughts compelled by emotions beyond control like anger and hatred, which is agitated, morbid and devoid of legitimacy and reason and as public discourse recognized as illegitimate, unreasonable and untrue whether judgement on it is pronounced or not. To use a metaphor the *savarṇas* because of their knowledge always find themselves swimming with the tide of time, moving easily into the ascending institutions, but *bahujana samāja* because of its ignorance of *Bhagavadgītā*, always finds itself struggling against the current of the descending time trying to preserve and man the descending order whose time is over and is moving into oblivion.

Unless *bahujana samāja* comes out of its self-absorbing ignorance and acquires the strength of *savarṇas* which they derive from knowledge of *Bhagavadgītā*, they will always find *savarṇas* way ahead of them even if they achieve absolute majoritarian political power, with cent-per-cent reservation in all governmental institutions of administration, production and education, for these are institutions which *savarṇas* are vacating voluntarily realizing their own personal strength for alternative institutions which are emerging and ascending which they have started manning.

2.4. A Word of Caution

Let me utter a word of caution once again derived from *Bhagavadgītā*. In X.24 it is time that is speaking in first person: *sarasām asmi sāgaraḥ* "of lakes I am the Ocean".

When the *kālaḥ* (time) is presented as *sarasāṁ sāgaraḥ* "of lakes the Ocean", the time is the future, as in Vedic tradition future is represented as *sāgaraḥ* (ocean) with depth and it has no measurable length like *skambha* or *meru* which represents past and of course present is always a circle whose two ends meet. The *sāgaraḥ* (ocean) with depth is an apt metaphor for future here, because the *lakṣa* (the goal, the end, the target) of action is in the depth of ocean of future. How is the *lakṣa* (the goal, the end, the target) of action found? It is found by churning of the ocean of future. But do not ask me what churning of *sāgaraḥ* (ocean) of future is? It is a thought process that one can learn from *Bhagavadgītā*, which is too complex to be described in the space of present essay. It is significant that in Indian mythology one of the things that come out when ocean (*sāgaraḥ*) is churned is the lethal poison, which has been also depicted as *halāhalam* and *kālakūṭam*. Both the names are very significant. The term *halāhalam* is from *halāhalam* where *halā* (*ha iti līyate ha+lā+ka+tāp*) means water and *halaṁ* (*hal ghañarthe karaṇe ka*) the instrument of plowing and hence together indicates an impossibility, something that appears possible, but actually impossible like plowing the water. Similarly, the term *kālakūṭam* is from *kāla+kūṭam* where *kāla* directly refers to time, here future time represented by the ocean and *kūṭam* is something false, illusory, fraudulent like a gamble full of risk and nothing else or a fraudulent plan etc. Somehow the tradition has missed the equivalence of *yogaja* meaning of both the terms, which refers to something illusory and impossible. This is the lethal poison of illusory and impossible goals we set for ourselves to be achieved in future and hence something illusory and impossible that comes out of the depth of the ocean of future meaning that the aims we set for us are never realized in the future. The goals set by "I will" accompanying "I think" are the lethal poison, because these are illusory and impossible plans. Here, we must not forget the struggle of Kant till the last of his writing with the question: how can the nature discerned by "I think" be hospitable to the law (Categorical Imperative) we set by "I will"? It is a question, he never succeeded in answering and finally, he left this question to be solved by his faith in God, which amounts to recognition and admission of the illusion that the goal is. But if you discern the two movements of time and things in time you do not set goals at all, the goal is already set by time, you merely participate in the ascending time with ascendant institutions. That's all.

Here, I cannot resist the temptation of drawing attention of the readers to the play of *kū* in *kūṭa* of *kālakūṭa* and *kū* of *kuvera*.

Kū means the *kalarava*, a little long drawn *rava*, a slow *rava* of birds till the *ravi* the symbol of a new day emerges like *lakṣa* from future into the present. If you have no patience, you are in a hurry, make the *kū* short to make it *ku*, you make *kū* deficient, hence *kū* means deficient, lacking something, here laking the length of *kū*, and you become *kuvera* with collecting so many deficient *ku*(s), which is his wealth *lakṣmī*, the *ku*(s) which have got attached to him. In such situation the *kālaḥ* which is the future associated with *kū*, i.e. *kalarava*, becomes the past associated with *kuvera*, the potent *kāla* (death) which is there in *kālakūṭa*. We should not forget at every moment (*kṣaṇa*) both directional movements of time are taking place. If we loose patience we loose the movement of time from the future to present and succeed in getting hold of time moving from present to the past. So, churn slowly, *mandara*, like *kū*, the *kalarava*, the *mandara rava* of birds, then only the *amṛta*, the real *lakṣa*, like *Ravi* will appear in the present for you.

2.5. A Modern Objection and the Flaw in Dalit Discourse

Let me end this essay with reply to an anticipated objection. The objection that I anticipate from my *dalit* scholar friends is that I am advocating an antiquarian cyclical conception of time with ascending and descending movements of time and things in time. My *dalit* scholar friends have become too modern, I am sure. Time according to modern mind has linear unidirectional movement from future to present to past and correspondingly relative to this movement of time the movement of things in time is in the opposite direction, exactly like the way station appears to move in opposite direction from a moving train. In this analogy moving train being time, the things in time are like station. So, things in time or states of affair in time appear to come from past into present to enter the empty future. Be it noted that two movements which are in opposite direction were recognized by moderns, but instead of recognizing these two opposite directional movements to be movements of time and things in time, the moderns in their zeal to have neat categories made one directional movement to be movement of time and the other movement, which is opposite directional movement, to be movement of the states of affairs in time. These two movements, even as directional movements opposed to each other in direction, were not united to form a circle as both were straightline movements and hence remained mere independent parallel movements.

No doubt our *dalit* friends, coming from past, having become too modern in the present, find themselves with free will with the power of majority or presumed majority in the present, to freely shape their future by their action in the present, as they enter the empty future to grab it by power displacing the *savarṇas*.

But, why is that not happening making them angry in frustration of their goal? Are *savarṇas* really interfering in the achievement in *dalit* goal as they enter the empty future? Is future really an empty unoccupied territory where the two nomadic tribes, *dalit* and the *savarṇas*, are rushing to settle with respective power of numbers? Let me analyse with my feeble antiquarian mind which had sojourned in the present world to experience the discontent of the sixtieth *śaradṛtu* of discourse with others, which is as manieth as the exilaration of the *kusuṁkara* of *pratyavamarśa* with the self with even more antiquarian, in fact eternal, experience of two movements of time and things in time.

Let me state my conclusion first which I will be establishing: *Persons, with a modern mind, having no faith in the performance of action on the basis of knowledge of duality of temporal movement of time and things in time, return again and again to the course on which the institutions are going to their death never to return again.* The people, with modern mind, who do not understand the duality of temporal movement of things and do not act accordingly, always again and again find themselves swimming against the current of time that is dragging institutions to their destruction from which these institutions will never return. Modern are my *dalit* friends who find themselves defending and trying to preserve institutions which are on their way to extinction in time.

Let me explain how this happens to the people of the modern mind. Since, modern mind does not accept the circularity of present time, it does not accept duality of movement of present time and duality of temporality of things in present time as explained previously. There is only one unidirectional movement of time from future to present to past for the modern mind and correspondingly relative to this movement of time the movement of institutions in time is in the opposite direction from past to present to future. So, institutions in time or state of affairs in time appear to come from past into present to enter the empty future and hence, for the modern mind we are free to shape the institutions in present by our action to carry them into the empty future. As the modern mind thinks of unidirectional movement of state of affairs from past to present to future which movement of things have they succeeded in getting hold of in their mind when looked at from the point of view of *Bhagavadgītā's* dual temporal movements of things?

Let us focus on one thing say the Roman church as an example given before. In the mind of modern man present form of Roman Catholic Church has emerged from its historical past form and as it moves forward into future where its form will change again etc. This is the only temporal or historical movement of Roman Catholic Church conceivable in the modern mind due to modern conception of time which is unidirectional moving from future to present to past. The temporal or historical movement of Roman Catholic Church captured by modern mind represents which of its two temporal movements distinguished in the way *Bhagavadgītā* conceptualizes the duality of temporal movement of things? Let us inquire. Since the idea of something (other than time) emerging from the future into the present is inconceivable in the modern mind due to its conception of unidirectional moving empty time, nothing can emerge from future. Only things emerging from past into the present will enter the future. All things temporal are impermanent. The things like Roman Catholic Church emerging from past into the present moving into future represents the movement of thing from its birth with rudimentary form to its maturity and eventual decline and future demise. This is exactly the directional movement distinguished in *Bhagavadgītā* which moves only in one direction that is towards the extinction of the thing in time never to return. The modern mind has only captured the half of the cycle of movement and has straitened it. This is my conclusion that modern people who have no understanding of time with its dual movement and things in time with their dual movement in time, return again and again to the course on which the institutions are going to their extinction never to return again. Hence, with respect to an instituion existing in modern times like the surviving caste order and modern state my modern *dalit* friends relate exactly the way the popes and Catholic hierarchy related to the curch when it was declining during renaissance, trying to preserve its shape to retain their advantage.

Modern mind simply cannot comprehend the other movement of things and institutions, i.e. things emerging from future into the present and cannot understand the action involved there. The then popes and catholic hierarchy try, however, hard with whatever presumed power of majority of Catholics of Europe of renaissance period, whatever they did to preserve the church and its power actually led more to its decline. But the decline of church through that very movement was also a movement of another institution, which was on the acsendency, whose contours were not visible at that time, whose contours became visible only after the renaissance was over and the beginning of modern period was recognized with Reformation and Counter Reformation. The movement of decline of church was the movement of ascendancy of the yet to be named institution. Only when the ascendant institution had already entered the present from its future and advanced in the present for some time along with the decline of the church that the ascendant movement of that new institution caught the attention of theoreticians and received the name of modern state, which afterwards took the shape of secular state. But recognition of the ascendant movement came too late when the flock had fled from the church to the modern absolutistic state.

Now, my *dalit* friends who have become modern are swimming against the current of downward movement of the caste order which started much earlier with *Bhakti* movement and later *Brahmo Samāja* and *Arya Samāja* movements and which gathered speed under freedom struggle under leadership of Mahatma Gandhi and when it was about to become irrelevant in the post-Independent India, suddenly, the modern *dalit* friends thought of preserving it and using it to their advantage and the struggle by *dalit* to preserve it against the current of its decline began. The *savarṇas* by and large are on their way to exit from it vacating it in favour of the *bahujana samāja* who have started relishing the carcas of once upon alive monster called the caste system. After Independence the modern state was received by India when it had already entered its downward trend in Europe and never really took-roots or ever became strong and once again our *dalit* friends started thinking of using it to their advantage when it had already taken a u-turn world over and in India too and had already vanished from many places like Afganistan, Iraq, Pakistan, and many African nations etc. I am referring to the phenomenon of failed states which is a misnomer as if these states can pass again. These are not failed states but extinct states never will they return again. Here, in India, the *savarṇas* started vacating the state in favour of *dalits*. Where is the flock of *savarṇas* going? They know how to discern the two movements of time and things in time. They are moving away from declining institutions to the ascendant institutions which are yet to achieve its proper shape to receive a name, but now vaguely recognized as private enterprsise, which, my friends, is a real misnomer. Private is only in contrast to public which was always a state institution, since, the new is emerging not side-by-side with the state like market to be called private in contrast to state, the new ascendant institutions are not private, but something else to which *savarṇas* are flocking. The *savarṇas* are surfing with the tide of time of ascendant institutions; they are still far ahead of the *bahujana samāja* which has chosen to swim against the current of time of declining institutions. Even if the *bahujana samāja* succeeds in getting reservation in private enterprise it will make no impact on the emerging institutions which are not really private and hence, it will have no impact on the condition of *savarṇas*. Every step the *bahujana samāja* is taking to strengthen their position in the declining institutions by entrenching them like caste order, state, democracy is really unknown to themselves is hastening the destruction of '*kalpa*' of these institutions propelling the institution further towards its decline with increasing speed. Here, '*kalpa*' is a technical term which means the power and principle of functioning of an institution by which it holds together distinguished from other institutions and enables the institutions to function properly. *Bahujana samāja* in its zeal to use the institutions like caste order, state, democracy and to entrench it against their declining movement is really succeeding in taking steps which are hastening the process of destruction of '*kalpa*' of these institutions which is further increasing the '*kalpa*' of ascending unnamed institutions furthering the advantage of *savarṇas* who have started flocking to them, widening the difference in *bahujana samāja* and *savarṇas* leaving *bahujana samāja* baffled and angry and exasperated.

The fundamental flaw in the thinking in *dalit* discourse is that from the very beginning it is incapable of penetrating the *ratio*, reason or '*kalpa*' of things. The *ratio*, reason or *kalpa* of anything is always connected with and never dissociated from what do not really belong to the *kalpa* of the thing. A thing is always more and beyond its *kalpa*. *Dalit* discourse in understanding a thing always gets hold of that aspect of the thing that does not belong to the *kalpa* of the thing but it presumes it to be *kalpa* of the thing.

2.6. A Hypothetical Example to Explain the Flaw in **Dalit** *Discourse*

Let me construct a very simplified picture of the issue. Consider *kalpa* of a specific scripture. The *kalpa* of a scripture is that it is a specific text with a script so that it can be copied and it can be read, it can be recited, it can be memorized, can be learned by heart, can be re-scripted, can be translated, can be understood etc. But *kalpa* of no scripture can include that it must have a specific number of pages, one copy of the scripture in small handwriting can be of just one hundred pages, but another may be of three hundred pages. Similarly, the *kalpa* of scripture does not include that scripture must be scripted on paper pages. It can be scripted on stone tablets, it can be scripted on wooden plates, birch bark, leaves of *bhoja*, or palm tree, or scripted digitally etc. But, now suppose as it happens in history the script and language of the scripture remains the same, but the spoken language evolves and in time many words of scripture are no more in use in spoken language and many words in spoken language have acquired new meanings and a time comes the difference of the spoken language is so great from the language of scripture that the scripture now hardly makes any sense. Of course, research is done to understand it. But not being able to understand the scripture, to show allegiance to the scripture, rich people started having very smartly bound volumes of scripture and richer people started having scripture with covers decorated with gold plating. Poor people found themselves with only very poorly printed scriptures on poor quality paper. Poorer people found themselves with only old soiled copies of the scripture with torn pages which is shared by many persons. So, the society got divided and poor people revolted. The religious hierarchy could not afford to alienate the poor, as they were numerous and a reformation movement started to standardize the scripture. People started insisting on scripting a scripture with a particular font of the script with a specific size on page of specific size with specific colour made of paper with strict specifications and become so fastidious about these specifications of scriptures that they start developing an expertise in identical reproduction of scripture. This skill was in much demand. Funds were diverted from undertaking research in understanding scripture to research in refinement of skill of reproducing identical copies of the scripture. The emphasis grew on learning of this skill and educational institutions vigorously intrduced programmes to impart this skill and more and more funding was available for research to develop greater skill in more faithful reproduction of the scripture with more and more accuracy with what is taken as the standard scripture. This emphasis on material specification of the scripture led to a situation where they completely forgot the language of the scripture, they forgot how to understand it, they forgot how to pronounce it, in fact the time comes when no one can read it, nor understand it, but they can make a perfect material copy of the specific book which they designated as the scripture and continue to reproduce it and consider it an holy act to have it at home, to visibly carry it in hand on streets on say wednesday on their way to their place of worship and back, to have it reproduced, to fund it etc.

If we follow the train of thought of *Bhagavadgītā* the original *kalpa* of the scripture is now destroyed, along with it the original scripture is dead. But, from the scripture has emerged something with a different *kalpa* which may still be called the scripture, but the scripture which was something that could be read, recited, understood that scripture is dead, but a material thing which is reproduced perfectly which is not something that is read, understood or learnt, but can be possessed, carried in hand, reproduced and funded has replaced the scripture. What was the error of these people that led to destruction of *kalpa* of scripture and scripture was dead? The materiality which did not belong to the *kalpa* of the scripture was taken as the *kalpa* of the scripture. The people were not even aware that they are doing it. They thought that they are preserving the scripture. But, the people could not understand the *kalpa* of the scripture, got hold of the materiality of scripture and were so enamoured by it that they took it to be the *kalpa* of the scripture. The streps they took to preserve the scripture by standardizing it really hastened the process of destruction of *kalpa* of the scripture.

Well my friends, this is the ignorance in which our *dalit* friends are caught unaware as exhibited by my examination of *dalit* discourse. Ambedkar mistook the accidental contextual reference to *varnòa* as the soul of *Bhagavadgītā* missing its essence by miles. It was like making the mistake of taking *obiter dicta* as the *ratio* of judgement and utilizing it as precedent. Of course, our *dalit* friends imitated and copied the great *dalit* leader (as claimed by *Bhagavadgītā* III.26, but criticized by Ambedkar, which was a kind unacknowledged endorsement of *Bhagavadgītā,* III.26 and rejection of criticism of Ambedkar of *Bhagavadgītā,* III.26 if not through explicit contention, but through unacknowledged performance) and started paying attention always to the accidental contingent association of the thing, missing the essence of things, as if as a kind of political strategy. They miss the essentials of the constitutional articles, but harp on the accidental contextual riders on the essential articles to the extent that the rider is taken as the essential article and the essential article is taken as the *mere proviso* to what they have declared as essential. Similarly, knowledge and open discussion as the essential of democratic decision which is realized in a democracy in various ways (for example, operation of legal knowledge in legislative decision by providing power of its review to higher courts whose members are not elected, but selected due to their legal knowledge) one of which being going by majority when there is no consensus to take immediately as knowledge on the ground that there is greater probability of more people being right than wrong. This contingent contextual realization of knowledge through majority decision in democracy is now taken by *dalits* as the essence of democracy so that democracy means pure majoritarianism which is the ground of all legitimacy in *dalit* discourse as shown above. This *vikalpanā* of democracy is making democracy *vikalpita* in both the senses of making democracy devoid of *kalpa* (one sense of *vikalpita*) and letting emerge an alternative to democracy (another sense of *vikalpita*). State and the institutions of states according to any political thought are meant for performing certain functions, even though they differer as to what the functions of state are depending on whether the theory is advocating minimalist nightwatch man state or maximalist welfare state. But, none of the political thought conceives the essence of state and state institutions to be arrangement of distribution of salaries. This is a contingent accidental modern addendum to the modern state, as in classical times the state functions were performed by lot, by rotation, by election, or fear of coercion etc., but there was no payment for it, it was without payment. But, our *dalit* friends have turned state upside down in their discourse true to the *verkehrte Welt* of their discourse. For them essence of state and all public institutions is that it is an arrangement of disbursement of salary and they demand as a matter of social justice that proportionately to the population size the salaries be disbursed to them through the mechanism of caste based reservation. No doubt, my *dalit* friends are taking every step through argument or political action which is leading to the destruction of *kalpa* of these institutions with all its consequences. That is like democracy, the state is also getting *vikalpita*. The legacy of Ambedkar was the constitution, i.e. the public institutional arrangement of welfare liberal egalitarian democratic state which by quirk of time threw up an agenda of replacement of *savarṇas* by non-*savarṇas* in this public institutional arrangement by policy of caste based reservation. But, this contingent agenda has become so primary in *dalit* discourse that it is leading to rejection of the public institutional arrangement of welfare liberal egalitarian democratic state from which that agenda emerged. I wonder, if that public institutional arrangement of welfare liberal egalitarian democratic state is destroyed through the *dalit* action by way of discourse or political mobilization, or participation in institution in the manner they are participating as shown above, what will happen to the agenda of *dalit* discourse and politics which is to displace *savarṇas* from these very institutions whose *kalpa* is destroyed by *dalits*. So, the agenda is self-defeating and hence impossible. The *dalits* have entered, through their discourse in political action and institutional participation, in the eye of ever fast spiralling tornado which is going to blow-up the public institutional arrangement of welfare liberal egalitarian democratic state into non-existence which they intend to man along with it destroying the *dalit* agenda.

2.7. A Historical Example How **Dalits** *Defeat Their Own Agenda*

Let me illustrate my work by one more example. This is not a hypothetical example, but a real historical example. Let us go a little back into history of modern *dalit* movement, which started as *suya mariyadai* (meaning 'self-respect') movement in Tamil Nadu in 1925 under the leadership of E.V. Ramasamy (also known as Periyar) against the brahmins. When the movement gained momentum in thirties, Bharatidasan became the poet laureate of the movement. He wrote a drama entitled *Iranian* in 1934 which was a parody of a received *paurāṇika* mythology of *Hiraṇyakaśipu* and *Prahlāda*. In his parody Prahlāda was presented as a stooge of Brahmins and the demon *Hiraṇyakaśipu* as hero. This most talked about drama of the poet laureate of the self-respect movement bristelled with vulgar profanities against all who were revered by Hindus. Other authors followed suit and wrote parodies of *Rāmāyaṇa*, glorifying *Rāvaṇa* and vulgarizing

Rāma. The troupe of the self-respect movement moved from village to village, town to town, scandalizing everybody, police in tow. Sensation waned as time wore and Brahmins and *savarṇas* had the satisfaction of pride that the so-called movement for self-respect thrived on superficial parody of their literature without ever getting the meaning of any of their text. The movement exhibited not self-respect but lack of self-respect. It exposed that the authors had no sense of shame in indulging in public profanities or defiling religion. Here, too they concentrated on the inessential superficialities of religions which they picked-up for parody without ever getting the *kalpa* of Hindu religion which can never be defiled or vulgarized or vandalized. The Brahmins whom the leaders of the movement wanted to provoke remained calm. The movement turned into political party when Periyar took over as president of Justice party to rename it Dravida Kazhagam which split after Independence to give rise to a dominant faction Dravida Munnetra Kazhagam (DMK) under the leadership of C.N. Annadurai while the parent faction declined. Dravida Munnetra Kazhagam split again giving rise to All India Anna Dravida Munnetra Kazhagam under the leadership of M.G. Ramachandran, which is being led now by his protege a self-confessed Brahmin lady in Tamil Nadu, who is sentenced to be locked up in jail and had a brief spell in jail on corruption charges, and another faction, i.e. DMK is led by a patriarch whose daughter and other party leaders are cooling their heels in jails on charges of mindboggling corruption. I wonder what happened to the self-respect of the *dalit* in either faction. *Dalits* are experts in defeating their own agenda. *Savarṇas* have to do nothing in this regard and they do nothing in this regard. They have to just wait and watch and that is what they do.

2.8. Conclusion Regarding the Modern Dalits

Let me revert back to the earlier claim of mine that our *dalit* friends have become too modern, even more modern than the *savarṇas* who still read some antiquarian texts of antiquarian times. Our *dalit* friends have no time for such frivolities of *savarṇas* as they are too busy with the social task of reforming the society to bring social justice and perfect democracy. They have exercised their free will! Why not! They have set their goal with free will. They are performing action in concert in present time to achieve the goal they have set. They are in majority. They can achieve their goal through political action, provided the *savarṇas* do not obstruct them! But how can the minority of *savarṇas*, who are still reading antiquarian texts, really interfere with the majority of *bahujana samāja*, who are modern and read modern revolutionary discourse of Ambedkar, who have embarked on the political journey to reach their destination which is almost within their reach? But wait, why are they angry? Something is amiss. Is it the presence of the minority of *savarṇas* that is really amiss with India? Let me investigate once again with the theoretical lens.

Since, our modern *dalit* friends have become modern and have no time for antiquarian text like *Bhagavadgītā*, which in their opinion teaches nothing except *varṇa dharma* as it is what they have heard from their great leader they cannot recognize the two movements of time and things in time as it was done by antiquarian people. One who does not discern the two movements of time like a modern man, catches hold of unidirectional time moving from future to present to past, corresponding to *śuklaḥ gati* of present as described in *Bhagavadgītā* and catches hold of the movement of things from past to present to empty future corresponding once again to *śuklaḥ gatī* of things as described in *Bhagavadgītā*, because he has straitened the *śuklaḥ gatī* of time and things in time on the basis of his modern conception of causality with its irreversible movement from earlier time of cause to later time of effect. If that is questioned then, of course, the directionality of time can be irreversively fixed by the law of increasing entropy. His causality is no more *sāṁkhya* causality with its dual movement of *samavāyi kāraṇa* in its *śuklaḥ gatī* and *kārya* in its *kṛṣṇa gatī*. What is lost to the modern mind and *dalit* friends, is the *kṛṣṇa gatī* of time and things in time which is movement from future into present of both time and things in time. As the very name of the two movements suggests one is bright easily visible, but the other is dark invisible and modern man without a sharp penetrative mind, but only a shallow mind catches hold of what is obvious on the surface, but what is slightly deep and in the shadow of light it cannot notice. We must not forget that the thing emerging from future into the present and their movement are hidden in the shadow of the existing things which are in the glare of light of modern historical knowledge and the movement of existing things from present to future which is brightly visible to keep the modern mind busy in social engineering, wholesale like Marx or piecemeal like Popper, in saving them, stopping their movement towards their extinction unaware of what is happening in the shadow which is out of focus. Brightness of movement of science and technology and social engineering so obviously visible to the modern man and our *dalit* friends has dazzled them so much for so long, that they have become incapable of seeing the shadow or what is happening in the shadow. Let me give a word of caution, much has happened in the dark shadow of the brightly visible science and tehnology and socio-political engineering to achieve so-called social justice and it is a matter of time that it is about to emerge from the shadow to make itself visible or may be as I am saying it, it is visible to me, it has already emerged. By the time the modern man and *dalit* friends take their attention off, from science and technology and the socio-political engineering for so-called social justice, or the *dalit* agenda they are indulging in, to notice what is emerging from the shadow of science and technology and their socio-political engineering it will be too late, they will not know what has hit them sweeping them off their humanism and sweeping off their human institutions like state, democracy, and the private enterprise in the market etc. The modern mind pays a heavy price due to this loss and blindness towards the *kṛṣṇa gatī* of time and things in time. *The modern mind now has to perform action in present time by free will setting goal for empty future with free will conceiving time moving in one direction governed by the causal movement of things in time conceived once again in the modern way or by law of increasing entropy.* This is simply a contradiction. The straitening of time to make it move in one direction was achieved by making everything in time governed by irreversible directionality of modern causality where cause is earlier, but invariably giving rise to effect which is later with increasing entropy in time. Nothing in time can escape this causality and directionality of its movement, nothing can excape the law of increasing entropy. So, where is the scope for will in this world, to perform action with free will, where is the scope for setting ends by free will in this world of modern man. Kant noticed the contradiction. He declared the will and activity of will to be outside time. Even after having noticed the contradiction he refused to face the question how the will which is timeless can have effect and in what sense in the temporal world of his modern conception. Will as the denizen of timeless world of noumenon and noumenon as the world where moral law operated by the very nature of free will with nothing to hinder it remained a mere dialectical negation of the causality with strict necessity and phenomenon strictly governed by causality and law of increasing entropy. And how the two worlds, one timeless the other temporal, interacted to allow timeless will to interfere with the necessity of temporal causality was never explained, but papered over by declaring man to be inhabitant of the two worlds which was as good or as bad as earlier claim of Descartes that the mind and body which by their very nature cannot interact, but interact through pineal gland. So, the moral law operating without inhibition by free will in timeless world of noumenon remained a perpetual 'ought' in the phenomenal temporal world of causality. Kant never succeeded in uniting the ideal of moral law set by free will with the nature governed by causality. So, a modern man setting goals for future by free will and using the knowledge of causality to achieve his social goals is an illusion if we go by the train of thought of *Bhagavadgītā*, an illusion born of the refusal or inability or both to recognize the *kṛṣṇa gatī* of time and things in time. So, implication is clear there can be no *dharma* for such a man no performance of action with *dharma* for such a man, as Kant realized to his chagrin trying to overcome till the end of his life the problem of realizing the ideal of moral law in this world.

What are the contours of ascending institutions in the present time? How does the '*kalpa*' of an institution emerge, function, increase, and get destroyed? What are the marks by which ascending movement of institution is distinguished from descending movement of institution? How are the steps taken by my *dalit* friends to use and entrench caste order, state, and democracy going against the current of decline of these institutions are really further hastening the current of decline by hastening destruction of their respective '*kalpa*' will be taken up for further investigation in another paper.

Notes

1. Terry Brighton, 2009, *Masters of Battle: Monty: Patton and Rommel at War*, Penguine Books, New York, p. XV.
2. Hans-Georg Gadamer, 2004, *Truth and Method*, second revised edition, translation revised by Joel Weinsheimer and Donald G. Marshall, Continuum, London, New York, p. 359.
3. Speech in the Virginia Constitutional Convention, December 2, 1829, accessed on 6th December, 2014 at 3.22 p.m. from the web site http://www.constitution.org/jm/18291202_vaconcon.txt
4. Letter to James Monroe, October 5, 1786 (On interest and happiness), accessed on 6th December, 2014 at 3.30 p.m. from the web site http://www.founding.com/founders_library/pageID.2213/default.asp
5. James Madison (1751-1836), U.S. President, Madison to Benjamin Rush, March 7, 1790. W.T. Hutchinson *et al.*, The Papers of James Madison, vol. 13, pp. 93-94, Chicago and Charlottesville, Virginia (1962-1991), accessed on 6th December, 2014 at 3.40 p.m. from the web site http://www.poemhunter.com/quotations/famous.asp?people=james%20madison&p=5
6. B.R. Ambedkar, *Mr. Gandhi and the Emancipation of the Untouchables*, Chapter IX, "Caste and Constitution," Accessed at 3.14 p.m. on 6th December, 2014 from the following website *http://www.ambedkar.org/ambcd/42.%20Mr.%20Gandhi%20and%20The%20Emancipation%20of%20The%20Untouchables.html*
7. Hans-Georg Gadamer, 1976, " Hegel's 'Inverted World' ", in his *Hegel's Dialectic: Five hermeneutic Studies*, tr. P. Christopher Smith, New Haven and London: Yale University Press, p. 35.
8. Nalini Pandit, 1992, "Ambedkar and the *Bhagwat Gita*," *Economic and Political Weekly*, Vol. 27, No. 20/21 (May 16-23, 1992), p. 1063.
9. *Dr. Babasaheb Ambedkar: Writings and Speeches*, Vol. 3, pp. 270-75.
10. *Ibid.*, pp. 376-79.
11. *Ibid.*, p. 361.
12. *Ibid.*, p. 321.
13. *Ibid.*, pp. 362-63.
14. Cf. Jayant Lele, 1988, "On Regaining the Meaning of the "*Bhagavadgītā*", *Journal of South Asian Literature*, Vol. 23, No. 2, *Bhagavadgītā*: On the Bicentennial of its First Translation into English (Summer, Fall, 1988), pp. 150-167; and Romila Thapar, 1984, *From Lineage to State:* social

formations in the mid-first millennium B.C. in the Ganga Valley, Oxford University Press, Bombay.

15. The similar conclusion was reached by Romila Thapar much earlier on historical consideration of Post-Mauryan period. She treats the *Mahābhārata* War as a major time marker. It marks the end of an epoch. Kshatriya rulerships are about to make way for the monarchical states of the middle Gaṅgā valley. "The intensive sorrow of the battle at Kurukshetra is not merely at the death of kinsmen but also at the dying society . . .", Romila Thapar, 1984, *From Lineage to State: Social Formations* in the mid-first millennium B.C. in the Gaṅgā Valley, Oxford University Press, Bombay, p. 141.
16. Ajuna was not standing for the emerging practice. It was Kṛṣṇa who was standing for the emerging social practice. If we follow the narrative of *Māhābhārata* the real conflict was between Duryodhaṇa and Kṛṣṇa to shape the emerging practice.
17. I am following here the general hermeneutic practice as advocated by Hans-Georg Gadamer in his magnum opus *Truth and Method*, Second, Revised Edition, translation revised by Joel Weinsheimer and Donald G. Marshall, Continuum, London and New York, 2004.
18. Cf. Hans-Georg Gadamer, 1983, "What Is Practice?", in Hans-Georg Gadamer, *Reason in the Age of Science*, Tr. Frederick G. Lawrence, The MIT Press, Cambridge, Massachusetts, pp. 74-77.
19. Plato, *Republic*, pp. 334a ff.
20. http://works.bepress.com/cgi/viewcontent.cgi?article=1025&context=kedar_joshi (accessed on 4/10/2012 at 11.55 a.m.)
21. "Social and Economic Aspects of the *Bhagavadgītā*", *Journal of the Economic and Social History of the Orient*, Vol. 4, No. 2 (August 1961), p. 203.
22. *Bhagavadgītā's* reinterpretation of *Karma Saṁnyāsa* through Kṛṣṇa's dialogue is dealt with in another essay of mine entitled, "*Kāma*, *Saṁnyāsa* and *Karma* in *Bhagavadgītā*", unpublished.
23. Angelika Malinar, 2007, *The Bhagavadgītā : Doctrines and Contexts*, Cambridge: Cambridge University Press, p. 12; *cf.* also p. 145.
24. Vishwa Adluri, "Angelika Malinar, The *Bhagavadgītā* : Doctrines and Contexts", *History of Religions*, Vol. 50, No. 1, Religion of the Alien and the Limits of Toleration: Ancient Perspectives, Guest Editor, Philippe Borgeaud (August 2010), p. 104.

Index